D0803277

From Baltimore
to Bohemia

From Baltimore to Bohemia

The Letters of H. L. Mencken and George Sterling

Edited by
S. T. Joshi

Madison • Teaneck
Fairleigh Dickinson University Press
London: Associated University Presses

© 2001 by Associated University Presses, Inc.

All rights reserved. Authorization to photocopy items for internal or personal use, or the internal or personal use of specific clients, is granted by the copyright owner, provided that a base fee of $10.00, plus eight cents per page, per copy is paid directly to the Copyright Clearance Center, 222 Rosewood Drive, Danvers, Massachusetts 01923. [0-8386-3869-4/01 $10.00 + 8¢ pp, pc.]

Associated University Presses
440 Forsgate Drive
Cranbury, NJ 08512

Associated University Presses
16 Barter Street
London WC1A 2AH, England

Associated University Presses
P.O. Box 338, Port Credit
Mississauga, Ontario
Canada L5G 4L8

Permission to print letters and other documents by H. L. Mencken has been granted by the Enoch Pratt Free Library, owners of the literary rights to the writings of H. L. Mencken. Permission to print letters by George Sterling has been granted by the Bancroft Library, University of California at Berkeley, owners of the literary rights to the writings of George Sterling.

The paper used in this publication meets the requirements of the American National Standard for Permanence of Paper for Printed Library Materials Z39.48-1984.

Library of Congress Cataloging-in-Publication Data

Mencken, H. L. (Henry Louis), 1880–1956.
From Baltimore to Bohemia : the letters of H. L. Mencken and George Sterling.
p. cm.
Includes bibliographical references and index.
ISBN 0-8386-3869-4 (alk. paper)
1. Mencken, H. L. (Henry Louis), 1880–1956—Correspondence.
2. Sterling, George, 1869–1926—Correspondence. 3. Authors, American—20th century—Correspondence. I. Sterling, George, 1869–1926. II. Joshi, S. T., 1958– III. Title.
PS3525.E43 Z497   2001
818'.5209—dc21
[B]   00-046629

PRINTED IN THE UNITED STATES OF AMERICA

Contents

Introduction

No ONE NEED BE SURPRISED THAT THE RELATIONSHIP OF H. L. Mencken and George Sterling was one of marked cordiality, even though they met on only a few occasions; for their correspondence—dating back as far as 1914, but especially frequent from 1918 to Sterling's suicide in late 1926—reveals many points of similarity in attitude and temperament. Even though their strongest bond may have been their fondness for alcohol during the early years of Prohibition, they exhibited many other parallels in their understanding of life and literature.

George Sterling (1869–1926) enjoyed considerable celebrity in his time, especially in his adopted state of California, but has lapsed into an unjust obscurity, largely through changes of fashion in the appreciation of American poetry. Born in Sag Harbor, Long Island, Sterling studied briefly at St. Charles College, a Catholic seminary in Ellicott City, Maryland (where he was not far from the boy Henry Mencken growing up in Baltimore) before moving to Oakland in 1890. Shortly thereafter he met two of the leading literary figures in California, the poet Joaquin Miller and the great journalist and short story writer Ambrose Bierce; by 1901 he had become fast friends with the young Jack London. Sterling began writing his first poems in the later 1890s, and under Bierce's astute tutelage he published a scintillating volume, *The Testimony of the Suns and Other Poems* (1903), featuring his great "star poem," *The Testimony of the Suns,* an orgy of cosmic imagery that Bierce rightly believed to be something new in literature. Sterling's poetic influences are clear enough—the early Romantic poets, Swinburne, Bierce himself—and throughout his life he adhered to formal meter and rhyme. He became an especial master of the sonnet.

In 1905 Sterling moved to Carmel, at the instigation of a real estate agent who was seeking to make the place appealing by turning it into an artists' colony. Here Sterling became the "King of Bohemia," persuading numerous other writers to settle there for shorter or longer periods—Mary Austin, Upton Sinclair, Sin-

7

clair Lewis, Nora May French, James Hopper—along with such other figures as Arnold Genthe, later to become a renowned photographer. The publication in 1907 of Sterling's other long poem, *A Wine of Wizardry,* accompanied by a laudatory article by Bierce, created a nine-days' sensation, the poem being alternately lauded as the pinnacle of fantastic imagery and condemned as merely a bag of verbal tricks. It was collected in *A Wine of Wizardry and Other Poems* (1909). Two years later *The House of Orchids and Other Poems* capped Sterling's early reputation: the unofficial "Poet Laureate of San Francisco" appeared on the verge of achieving a national reputation.

That reputation, however, was never realized. Although several other collections of poetry followed, and although Sterling regularly appeared in leading magazines of the day, including the *Atlantic Monthly,* the *Nation,* the *Saturday Review,* and *Harper's,* Sterling had the misfortune to remain consciously behind the times as a poet. He violently repudiated the Modernists and was in turn repudiated by them. Although Harriet Monroe accepted a few of Sterling's poems shortly after founding *Poetry* magazine in 1912, she reviewed his *Beyond the Breakers and Other Poems* (1914) coolly: while admitting grudgingly that "I find in Mr. Sterling a gift, a poetic impulse, which might have carried him much further than it has as yet," she generally concluded, in reference to Sterling's antiquated and rhetorical diction:

> The truth is, this sort of pomposity has died the death. If the imagists have done nothing else, they have punctured the gas bag—English poetry will be henceforth more compact and stern—"as simple as prose," perhaps. . . . When Mr. Sterling learns to avoid the "luscious tongue" and the "honeyed wine," he may become the poet he was meant to be.[1]

But Sterling already was the poet he was meant to be—and Monroe and her ilk simply didn't like him. Sterling did indeed have some supporters—Bierce, Edwin Markham, the Nebraska poet John G. Neihardt, W. S. Braithwaite, William Rose Benét, Theodore Dreiser, and (more guardedly) Louis Untermeyer—but most of these were either themselves antiquated by the 1920s or of no great influence among the Modernists. Sterling's unexpected death created a momentary flurry of interest, especially in San Francisco, but it died down quickly, and Sterling himself was rapidly forgotten outside his adopted state.

One of those who could have perhaps done his bit to aid Sterling's reputation was Henry Louis Mencken (1880–1956). Sterling became associated with Mencken at the very time that the latter was achieving the status of America's leading essayist and critic. In 1919, the publication of *The American Language* and *Prejudices: First Series*—the latter derived largely from his reviews in the *Smart Set*—caused Mencken to be perhaps the most widely respected, and feared, critic of the 1920s. The five other volumes of *Prejudices* that appeared in that decade constitute perhaps the finest American critical writing of their time, and Sterling himself hugely enjoyed the volumes he read. It becomes eminently clear that one of the strongest bonds between the two writers was a mutual dislike of Modernist poetry. But, aside from running Sterling's work frequently in the *Smart Set* and the *American Mercury,* and mentioning him at random in various review articles, Mencken did not in fact "push" Sterling as vigorously as he might have done. But at least he found Sterling a lively correspondent—one with whom he shared a number of mutual associates.

The chief of these was Ambrose Bierce, who remained a vital figure of discussion among the two writers even after his disappearance in Mexico in late 1913. The 150-odd letters that Sterling received from Bierce are among the most substantial letters ever written by the California cynic; and without Bierce's initial assistance Sterling would have had a much harder time establishing himself as a poet, even in California. Mencken, for his part, corresponded only briefly with Bierce in 1913, but, as he relates engagingly in his later memoir-essay, "Ambrose Bierce" (1925; reprinted in *Prejudices: Sixth Series*), he was on one occasion regaled by Bierce's cheerful morbidity as the two of them attended a funeral. Mencken does not specify the occasion, but it was probably the funeral of Percival Pollard, an iconoclastic critic and friend of Bierce who died in 1911 and whose books—notably *Their Day in Court* (1909) and *Masks and Minstrels of New Germany* (1911)—were much admired by Mencken. Mencken is, indeed, in many ways a twentieth-century Bierce: his tartly satiric journalism bears numerous similarities with Bierce's long-running "Prattle" column in the *San Francisco Examiner,* and Mencken's brief collection of satirical definitions, "The Jazz Webster," is nothing more than a compressed *Devil's Dictionary.*

Other mutual colleagues provided many points of discussion for Mencken and Sterling. Willard Huntington Wright (the *Smart Set*'s editor in 1913) had, in 1910, written a piquant article on Sterling's Carmel literary circle for the *Los Angeles Times,* and both writers kept abreast of his subsequent career. Theodore Dreiser was of course one of Mencken's leading associates, and their stormy relationship is chronicled both in Mencken's posthumously published *My Life as Author and Editor* (1993) and in their voluminous correspondence.[2] Sterling came to know Dreiser in 1920, and persuaded him to write a laudatory preface to the third edition of Sterling's scintillating poetic drama, *Lilith* (1926). Other figures such as James Branch Cabell, Anita Loos, Zöe Akins, and Norman Boyer (a former editor of the *Smart Set*) were also fodder for discussion.

With the onset of Prohibition, both Mencken and Sterling developed a kind of siege mentality, each gaining strength from hearing of the other's triumphs in securing liquor. Booze was plentiful both in Mencken's New York and Baltimore and in Sterling's San Francisco; but since beer (Mencken's drink of choice) appeared a bit easier to procure than the hard liquor (notably Scotch) that was Sterling's preference, Sterling had a harder time of it. Sterling's repeated references that the Scotch coming from Canada was "green" and not suitably aged may, as we will see, take on ominous aspects when we consider his suicide.

Both Mencken and Sterling recognized that Prohibition was merely a symptom of a wider outburst of puritanical moralism that swept the country around World War I. Literary censorship was another symptom, and Mencken found in Sterling a fervent ally in such matters as the suppression of Dreiser's *The "Genius"* in 1916, the attempted suppression of James Branch Cabell's *Jurgen* (1919), and, in 1926, the famous "Hatrack" case, growing out of a story published in the *American Mercury*. (At the same time, however, Mencken was compelled to reject a number of Sterling's submissions because he knew that their publication would immediately bring down the censors upon his head.) Sterling, for his part, registered his protest against bourgeois morality by widespread sexual involvements, frequently with married women; and he also took care, when literary dignitaries visited San Francisco, to have both booze and a willing damsel for their use. In early 1926 Sterling summed up two of his chief interests: "I did more screwing and less drinking in 1925 than in 1924. Even at that I had over a thousand drinks."

Mencken was rather more hostile to American culture than was Sterling; in fact, Mencken hesitated to send Sterling a copy of *Prejudices: Third Series* (which contained numerous attacks on American institutions), since he knew that Sterling had written many patriotic poems during the war. But Sterling reassured

Mencken that it was only the landscape of his native land that he appreciated, echoing Bierce's complaint that the problem with America was that " 'tis infested by my countrymen." On the matter of religion there was greater congruity; if anything, Sterling was more atheistic than Mencken. Their articlericalism frequently found vent in the closings of their letters, whether it be the ironic "Yrs in Xt." or the tart "Yours for the reform of God."

In the early years of their relationship, of course, the focal point of discussion was the *Smart Set*. It would be cumbrous to provide a detailed history of this "magazine of cleverness," nor is there any need to do so, for Carl Dolmetsch's comprehensive account,[3] along with the wealth of detail provided by Mencken's own *My Life as Author and Editor,* supplies as much information as anyone is likely to require.

The *Smart Set* was founded in 1900 by Arthur Grissom and the flamboyant publisher Colonel William D'Alton Mann. Grissom died the following year, and the editorship was taken over by Marvin Dana. In its early years the magazine attained celebrity by publishing the early work of O. Henry, James Branch Cabell, Sinclair Lewis, and others. Charles Hanson Towne was the editor for the period 1904–8, and he was succeeded by Fred C. Splint, who became managing editor, and Norman Boyer, a Baltimore newspaper man and friend of Mencken who became assistant editor. Mencken was hired in late 1908 as the "literary editor," and from November 1908 to December 1923 wrote the magazine's review column. It was this vehicle that gained Mencken his initial celebrity as a literary critic, especially when he championed the work of Theodore Dreiser. George Jean Nathan took over the magazine's theatre column in the fall of 1909.

In 1911 Mann sold the magazine to John Adams Thayer. Thayer offered the editorship of the *Smart Set* to Mencken at this time, but the latter declined, as did Nathan when the editorship was offered to him. Norman Boyer became managing editor, but his unadventurous reign ended in early 1913, when Thayer hired Willard Huntington Wright. Wright's guidance of the magazine could hardly be called unadventurous; indeed, Wright's radicalism—he assiduously cultivated iconoclastic contributions from such Europeans as Frank Harris, Max Beerbohm, W. B. Yeats, and August Strindberg—caused advertisers to rebel and readers to be outraged. Wright was pressured to leave in late 1913, and Mark Lee Luther took over. But under Luther's regime the magazine foundered, and Mencken and Nathan considered resigning. Shortly after the outbreak of World War I, Thayer, in a panic over the magazine's drop in circulation, sold the *Smart Set* to Colonel Eugene R. Crowe, the magazine's paper supplier, and his colleague Eltinge Warner. Warner offered the editorship to Nathan, who agreed only on condition that Mencken be named coeditor. Mencken and Nathan also acquired one-third financial interest in the magazine. The issue of November 1914 was the first to be officially edited by Mencken and Nathan, and they retained control until the end of 1923. Under their tenure, the magazine became, in spite of its low pay, a haven for sophisticated work from American, British, and European writers alike, including Dreiser, Cabell, Eugene O'Neill, F. Scott Fitzgerald, the Irish playwright Lord Dunsany, and many others.

Sterling found the magazine particularly to his liking, and—especially after Mencken raised his rates to 50¢ per line for poetry—a choice venue for the publication of his shorter lyrics. While not buying everything Sterling sent him, Mencken accepted far more than he rejected. Thirty-two of Sterling's poems, two short plays, and dozens—perhaps hundreds—of epigrams appeared in the *Smart Set*. In 1921 Mencken even asserted that he wished to have a Sterling poem in every issue of his magazine. It would not be entirely accurate to say that Mencken felt that Sterling was only a "magazine poet"; he took the trouble to censure William Lyon Phelps for not even mentioning the California poet in *The Advance of English Poetry in the Twentieth Century* (1918). Although he found Sterling's flawlessly crafted verse, usually laced with lyrical romance and not infrequently with sexual suggestion, the ideal poetic filler for the *Smart Set* and, perhaps, the ideal foil for the Modernists, he did not—as we shall see presently—regard Sterling as one of the leading literary figures of his day.

Sterling was also intent on steering some of his colleagues to the *Smart Set*. He brought to Mencken's attention the brilliant young poet Clark Ashton Smith (1893–1961), who had achieved celebrity when publishing *The Star-Treader and Other Poems* (1912) at the age of nineteen, and would later become a leading writer of tales of fantasy and the supernatural. Sterling's friend May Greenwood also became an occasional contributor to the *Smart Set*.

Although Sterling spent a year in 1914–15 in New York in a bootless attempt to churn out short stories for popular magazines, he did not know Mencken well enough to meet him during the latter's frequent New York visits. The two writers missed each other again in 1918: Sterling had come to New York for another extended period in the summer, but had to return abruptly to San Francisco upon the suicide of his ex-wife, Carrie.

When Mencken came to San Francisco in the summer of 1920 to cover the Democratic National Convention, he finally had a chance to spend time with his friend. The letters themselves reveal little of their activities, but we receive some amusing sidelights from other correspondence. In response to a comment by Dreiser ("Sterling says he is in doubt whether he will let you live in S. F.—that you're not worthy of its Bohemian resources—that you select impregnable virgins and cling to water as it were your heart's blood. How so? Come through?"),[4] Mencken thundered:

> Sterling is a low libeller. I drank alcohol each and every day I was in San Francisco, whereas he had to go on the water wagon and remained there six days running. It is true that I consorted with a virgin and that she is a virgin still, but that is simply because I was very tired and she was very amiable. Sterling announced months in advance that he had a boudoir companion for me—that all I'd have to do would be to go to her place and hang up my hat. But when I arrived she was non est, and so I had to scratch around on my own hook, seeking both sparring partners and a virgin to soothe me with her talk. I had a hell of a good time. George was superb, but history must record that he went on the water wagon. So much in simple justice to my honor. I would not have any reputable man think that I was actually sober in San Francisco. As a matter of fact, I came down with a severe alcoholic gastritis, and was ill in bed all the way home on the train—a ghastly experience. If you ever hear anyone say that I was sober, please call him a liar. I am touchy on such points.[5]

Clearly Mencken was greatly entertained. Not only did he attend the annual "Jinks" of the Bohemian Club, but he met the actress Jane O'Roarke, whom Sterling had known for some years. Mencken later admitted that he actually "fell in love" with Jane, and he remained sporadically in touch with her for years, even though she eventually married another man. Mencken was also captivated by San Francisco; toward the end of the year he wrote to Sterling: "I must see San Francisco before they put the formaldehyde into my veins. And maybe twice more. You can't imagine what a gorgeous impression I took away." As for Sterling, he celebrated Mencken's visit by an extended drinking bout, writing nearly incoherent telegrams to Mencken for weeks after his departure.

Mencken's return to San Francisco was, however, delayed for six years. In the interim Sterling regaled Mencken with accounts

13

of the notorious Fatty Arbuckle trial in 1921–22, his visit to Hollywood to help Doug Fairbanks on *The Thief of Bagdad* (1924), and the like. The correspondence is suspended for several months in 1922 while Mencken was traveling in Europe.

With the foundation of the *American Mercury* in 1924, Mencken again looked to Sterling for contributions. Poetry did not occupy a large place in the magazine's contents, so Mencken urged Sterling to try some prose. As early as 1918 he had tried to persuade Sterling to write a monograph on Bierce; in 1921 he proposed that Sterling write something—perhaps an entire book—on San Francisco, and for the *Mercury* he sought an article on the effect of Prohibition on the city by the bay; but Sterling declined in each instance. He found prose far more difficult to write than poetry, although what little prose he did produce was as well crafted as his verse. Mencken did, however, manage to get several articles of literary reminiscence—notably on Bierce and Joaquin Miller—out of Sterling, as well as an engaging memoir of the boxer Pete McCoy, whom Sterling had known as a teenager.

Mencken finally made his way back to California in the fall of 1926, in the company of Joseph Hergesheimer. Sterling expressed considerable irritation that Mencken was being delayed in Los Angeles and Hollywood (places that both he and Mencken loathed), for Sterling was impatient to partake of the plentiful stock of liquor he had accumulated for Mencken's visit. Although he seemed largely to blame the delay on Hergesheimer, Sterling at one point noted whimsically but acutely: "Some cinema cat has her claws in you." This was, in fact, the truth; for a chief motive in Mencken's visit to southern California was to pursue his relationship with the actress Aileen Pringle.[6]

What followed thereafter is made clear by various letters by Mencken printed in the appendix. Mencken arrived in San Francisco on 15 November and immediately went to the Bohemian Club to see Sterling. He found Sterling "suffering great pain": evidently Sterling had begun to dip into the stock of accumulated alcohol. In his later years Sterling reacted to alcohol with increasingly severe bouts of some kind of ailment: Sterling himself believed it to be gastritis, but an autopsy conducted after his death found nothing wrong with his stomach. On the evening of the 16th Mencken again went to see Sterling, but received no response when he knocked on Sterling's door; all Mencken could do was to leave a note at the door. The next day it was discovered that Sterling had died, in all likelihood by suicide: the pain caused by his drinking had evidently impelled Sterling to swallow the vial of cyanide that he had kept on his person for years. Mencken believed that Sterling may have already been dead by the time he had come to his room on the 16th.

Mencken was quick to squelch reports that he and Sterling had had an argument or a falling out. On the evening of the 17th, a short memoir by Mencken appeared in the San Francisco *Bulletin;* this was expanded into a touching obituary that appeared in both the *Chronicle* and the *Examiner* on the 18th, later reprinted in the *Overland Monthly* and published as a separate broadside. For the rest of his life, extending as late as 1950, Mencken unfailingly assisted scholars interested in Sterling (notably Henry Dumont, an acquaintance of Sterling who wrote an unpublished biography[7]) by providing information on his relations with the California poet.

I have noted that Mencken perhaps did not do as much to promote Sterling's work as he could have. He never reviewed any of Sterling's books, although he could well have taken note of two later poetry volumes, *Sails and Mirage* (1921) and *Selected Poems* (1923); and he professed great admiration for Sterling's poetic drama *Lilith.* But Mencken perhaps strove to put Sterling on the literary map in a different way. In late 1925, after receiving several fine prose articles from Sterling for the *American Mercury,* he took the initiative of speaking to his publisher, Alfred A. Knopf, about a book of such reminiscences by Sterling. Had Sterling buckled down to write such a volume, he might well have staved off the literary obscurity that rapidly engulfed him after his death. It is particularly unfortunate that Sterling did not write anything about Jack London, whom he rightly claimed to know better than London's own wife did; but considerations for the feelings of London's daughter Joan prevented him. It is clear that Sterling, although a fine poet, is now of greatest interest to literary history as a general man of letters: his wide association with leading authors of his period—Bierce, London, Dreiser, Sinclair Lewis, Upton Sinclair, his many colleagues in Carmel and San Francisco, and of course Mencken himself—would make him a figure of note even if his poetry were entirely forgotten.

Five years after Sterling's death, Mencken received a query from Alfred A. Knopf about a biography of Sterling that was under consideration. Mencken was not encouraging: "I don't think it would be worth while to do a biography of George Sterling. His life, after all, was relatively uneventful, and his writings were scarcely important enough to justify dealing with him at length."[8] The comment has infuriated Sterling's supporters, who assert that such a biography might have helped to perpetuate Sterling's memory. But in all frankness, Sterling perhaps did not deserve a biography all to himself, even in 1931. Several decades later, Franklin Walker wrote the ideal account in *The Seacoast of Bohemia* (1966), a kind of communal biography of Sterling and his entire literary circle at Carmel. It is in just such a work—as a *primus inter pares*—that Sterling takes his proper place as a literary figure.[9]

While George Sterling cannot be said to be one of H. L. Mencken's closest or most important colleagues, their correspondence does provide fascinating glimpses into the day-to-day operations of the *Smart Set* and the *American Mercury*, sidelights on Mencken's and Sterling's literary work, and, more generally, the temper of the Jazz Age, with its booze, its women, and the literary celebrities that made it distinctive. Even if one knew nothing of either Mencken or Sterling, these letters would provide unique glimpses into an era whose glamour persists to this day.

A Note on This Edition

I HAVE PRINTED THE LETTERS IN THIS VOLUME WITHOUT ALTERATION (save for correction of a few obvious typographical errors) except in one detail: I have eliminated printed addresses by Mencken and Sterling on their standard stationery. Hence, all letters by Sterling, unless otherwise indicated, bear the stationery of the "Bohemian Club, San Francisco"; all letters by Mencken, unless otherwise indicated, bear stationery giving his home address (1524 Hollins St., Baltimore). Any words placed in brackets indicate editorial additions or addresses or other printed matter on the letters aside from the above addresses.

My notes focus a bit more on Sterling than they do on Mencken, since the former is less well known. Only the date of publication for most book publications by the two writers is provided; full bibliographical information can be found in the bibliography at the end of the volume. In many cases it was impossible to specify the poems or other works Sterling submitted to Mencken in various letters; in such cases I have not supplied a note. In some instances I have supplied a conjectural attribution of the item.

I am grateful to David E. Schultz, Richard K. Hughey, and Alan Gullette for assistance in the preparation of the text and notes. I am also grateful to the libraries that supplied photocopies of the letters and granted permission to print them: the New York Public Library (Rare Books and Manuscripts Division and Berg Collection); the Enoch Pratt Free Library; the Bancroft Library, University of California; the Henry E. Huntington Library and Art Gallery; the library of Mills College; and the University Research Library, University of California at Los Angeles. Most of my research was done at the New York Public Library, the New York University Library, the San Francisco Public Library, and the Bancroft Library, and I am grateful to the librarians of these and other institutions for their assistance.

17

Abbreviations

ALS	Autograph letter, signed
AM	*American Mercury*
ANS	Autograph note, signed
BAN	Bancroft Library, University of California (Berkeley, CA)
BES	*Baltimore Evening Sun*
CE	George Sterling, *The Caged Eagle* (1916)
EPFL	Enoch Pratt Free Library (Baltimore, MD)
GJN	George Jean Nathan
GS	George Sterling
HLM	Henry Louis Mencken
HUN	Henry E. Huntington Library and Art Gallery (San Marino, CA)
Life	H. L. Mencken, *My Life as Author and Editor* (1993)
NYPL	New York Public Library
SFPL	San Francisco Public Library
SM	George Sterling, *Sails and Mirage* (1921)
SP	George Sterling, *Selected Poems* (1923)
SS	*Smart Set*
TLS	Typed letter, signed
TN	Typed note
UCLA	University of California at Los Angeles

From Baltimore
to Bohemia

The Letters

1914

[1] [GS to HLM] [ALS, NYPL]

43 S. Washington Square,
New York,
Dec. 4th, 1914.

Dear Mr. Menken:

You may think this ballad is a bit too long, but it seems to me that length is no very great objection if a poem *tells a story,* and tells it swiftly and in a forthright way. Anyhow, this is by far the best ballad I've ever written.[1]

Sincerely,
George Sterling.

1916

[2] [GS to HLM] [ALS, NYPL]

Sept. 4, 1916.

Dear Mr. Menken:

Of course! Go on with the articles you mention and stop wasting your time on negligible novels. You should give a few pages to Dreiser, though, as often as he appears.[1]

Sincerely,

George Sterling.

[3] [GS to HLM] [ALS, NYPL]

Sept. 21, 1916.

Dear Mr. Menken:

You couldn't have found anyone in America more willing to sign this than I.[2]

There are no writers of consequence within my reach just now, or I'd get other names. No doubt, though, you've already communicated with H. L. Wilson, Jack London and James Hopper.[3] The address of the last named is "Carmel, Cal."

I've always been a strong admirer of Dreiser, despite his weight and gait.

Sincerely yours,

George Sterling.

P.S.

I've not been sending stuff to Smart Set because I can't afford to write verse for two bits a line—the price you last paid me.[4]

G. S.

[4] [GS to HLM] [ALS, NYPL]

Sept. 30, 1916.

Dear Mr. Mencken:

I've sent on the "protests," as you request, and of course they'll be signed. What a refrigerated ass Matthews[5] is! He should have lived in Salem when the witches were being scorched.

I've just finished "The Man of Promise,"[6] and like it immensely. I'd be glad of Wright's address, any time you have the leisure.

All success to you and the "S. S."

Sincerely,

George Sterling.

1918

[5] [GS to HLM] [ALS, NYPL]

Mch. 14th, 1918.

Dear Mr. Menken:

You wrote something when you wrote your last book, to paraphrase the escaped melodist. I pass myself the floral tribute when I say that I am in full accord with all you say about Conrad, Dreiser and the Puritans. Almost. You underrate Bierce's war-stories, I think. I've not read them for ten years. I'm not enough of the music-master to follow you on Huneker—he seems pedantic to me.[1]

Anyhow, Xt bless you for your light on a most lonesome coast! No one else seems to have the nerve & ability to say what should be said. Always you say it so clearly and wittily—an ink of crystal acid. Go to it! I buy "Smart Set" only to read you and Nathan. (The club takes it, but it's always stolen by some fellow gentleman the day it arrives!)

I used to see Dreiser in Mouquin's—winter of 1914–5.[2] He always had a peach with him. I think the same one. I wanted to go up and tell him he was all right, but never found courage. I think he had done a deal of seducing to get all his dope for his tales. Such experience is mostly wasted on the doer of verse, who has either to make it more vivid than reality or leave it alone.

I was on to Conrad & Dreiser from the first. I read "Almayer's Folly," or else "An Outcast of the Islands,"[3] as soon as it appeared, and was sure of its quality. Did you ever notice that "The Nigger of the Narcissus" is a satire on altruism? I'm sure it is, but no one has so far said so. Jack London and H. L. Wilson think not; but I feel sure I'm right. That ship is too true an allegory of this our earth.

Don't you think you underrate the value of Kipling's "Brushwood Boy," "Wireless" and "They?" Also "The Greatest Story Ever Written?"[4] Away ahead of his other stuff, I think.

Out here all is joy. No one, I think, bothers much about anyone but his neighbor's wife. I just sent home the serious but damned

28

virile Neihardt,[5] and look forward to welcoming John Masefield soon.[6] I hope he packs a thirst with him!

I didn't really expect you to run that "Swineherd" song.[7] I've others that will put a slightly less strain on your distinguished nerves, and shall send you some soon. I don't send out any more poems "for sale," but am doing a lot to please myself. I'd love to have Sumner[8] read them! I've tired on war stuff: it's too much like scolding.

Have you noticed how good a man James Hopper is at his best? He's a disciple of Conrad.

But don't bother to reply to all this!

Yours ever,

George Sterling.

[6] [HLM to GS] [TLS, HUN]

Baltimore, March 18th [1918]

Dear Mr. Sterling:—

"The Roman Wall" is so fine that I am going to take it to New York tomorrow, and try to break down Nathan's papal interdict upon all poems above 20 lines.[9] He has a theory that poetry in the magazines is read only by women above 38 years and 160 pounds. He says that they begin to snuffle at the 10th line, and can't read beyond the 20th. It is impossible to shake him out of this belief. But I hope that your flouting of right-thinking will overcome him. As for me, I like the poem immensely. If you have any short things, let me see them, by all means. Our bins are nearly empty.

Dreiser and I have had a falling out, now six months old. It is not bellicose; we simply can't agree on the things he has written during the past few years. Needless to say, I shall start no offensive against him. I think some of his late stuff (still in ms.) will get a walloping, and that he will eventually admit my sagacity with tears streaming down his front. But maybe I am wrong. In any case he still keeps his manly powers and is first cock in Greenwich Village.

I am delighted that the prefaces interested you. My own weakness is music, and so Huneker has my vote. His musical stuff is the best America has ever seen, and there is very little so good on tap in Germany or Austria. I surely agree with you about Hopper. But the Saturday Evening Post has probably finished him. Why not a public monument to its victims? The list is long. Consider, for example, Rideout.[10] He is as dead as a fish. Wilson and Hergesheimer[11] seem to survive, but most of the rest have lost legs and arms. My next critical book, if ever I do one, will exhibit the corpses, including Irvin Cobb, who was born dead.[12] A good place for the monument would be in front of the Curtis Building in Philadelphia.[13]

Of Kipling, I am most in favor of "Kim". But the stuff he has done during the past six or eight years has been so idiotic that it makes me sick. Even his poetry, re-read, gets a bad flavor. There is a cheap bounder hidden in him. I had never thought of the satire in "The Nigger". You are probably right. The whole of Conrad is a devastating satire. I had a letter from the old boy lately. He is very gloomy, can't work, and talks of doing one or two more books, and then giving up. The war has depressed him a lot; he has a young son at the front.

There is a scheme afoot to print a series of small books on latter-day American authors. Would you care to do Bierce? Say 20,000 or 25,000 words—no more. I have a notion to do George Ade, a better man than most.[14] No one has ever written about him. I suppose satisfactory financial arrangements can be made: several publishers are interested.

Sincerely yours,
H L Mencken

[7] [GS to HLM] [ALS, NYPL]

April 16th, '18.

Dear Mr. Mencken:

I wanted to reply to your kind letter of the 18th ult. the day it arrived, but decided to spare you: your correspondence must be an awful burden.

I'm glad you liked that "Roman Wall." I had no intention of "submitting" it—merely stuck it in the letter to amuse you. I was sure Nathan would not use it: with his views of poetry why should he concede an inch? However, your suggestion as to Mr. Smith was a good one: he gave me $30. for the thing—and I was going to *give* it to Reedy![15] I sent R. this "Moll," but he thought it too old-fashioned, and I let Upton Sinclair have it for his Hell-knows-what.[16]

I'll be glad to send lyrics to "Smart Set," the only magazine I ever *buy,* so long as you're willing to pay fifty cents a line. Damaged goods you may have @ 25¢.[17] I have sent S.S. a few things in the past few months, but they were rather risqué, and I doubt if

they got as far as your favoring eye. I enclose a sample—
"Infidels."[18] I don't blame Nathan for shying from it, at that.
Your first duty is to keep out of jail.

About that Bierce book: I'd like to do it, and think I've the dope
on him, for he was my mentor for many years. But I'm too lazy to
write it, and won't string anyone along with my vain promise.

I've just been reading over my Bierce letters, and find I've 150
of them![19] How the old war-horse used to kick London and Sinclair! I was almost too socialistic for him in those days, myself.

"May the Lord be with you—but inattentive!"[20]

> Yours ever,
>
> Geo. Sterling.

And our "French restaurants" are world-notorious!

Great stuff in "Damn!"[21] By the way, the de Goncourts have a
chapter on kissing. Beware the girl who cares very much for it!

> G. S.

[8] [GS to HLM] [ALS, EPFL]

April 22nd, 1918.

Dear Mr. Mencken:

Read the enclosed clipping, and thank what-
ever gods may be that you weren't born any later.[22] In my opinion, that sort of thing will be the rule in the U.S. within a few
more years. We'll be hag-ridden. As for your beer, get away with
all you can before 1920! I suppose we'll all be able to get a sort of
home-made moonshine, distilled at no small hazard.

Clark Smith, our young poet of the Sierran foot-hills, sends me
a prose-poem of extraordinary beauty.[23] I'm begging him to send
it to "Smart Set." If he doesn't, I shall. He is a precocious, morbid
youth, with a strong savor of Baudelaire.

You needn't return the clipping—scare Nathan with it. And
you need not waste time in replying to my idle letters.

> Sincerely your admirer,
>
> George Sterling.

[9] [HLM to GS] [TLS, BAN]

April 29th [1918]

Dear Mr. Sterling:—

Let me see the Clark Smith stuff, by all means. Have him send it to me as above and I'll give it immediate attention. My very best thanks.

Oregon is behind the East in moral endeavor. Here the public parks are patrolled summer by policewomen armed with pocket flashlights. They sneak upon a young couple in the thrall of love, wait until the youth invades the gal's person, and then flash the light and drag them to the watch-house. As for prohibition it takes noble and elaborate forms. A friend of mine has a charming place on the South river, near Annapolis—ideal for Sunday parties. Now he is threatened with court martial if he brings in so much as a bottle of beer. And why? Because the United States Naval Academy is five miles away. Also, give your eye to the enclosed.

Sincerely yours,
Mencken

[10] [GS to HLM] [ALS, NYPL]

Apr. 30th, 1918.

Dear Mr. Mencken:

I've never heard "Tom and Mollie," and Wilson isn't likely to enlighten me, as he's "sore" at me just now. But if you object only to that line, behold the change![24] I never mind changing lines, so long as it's an improvement, as seems to be the case in this instance. But I fear that Hun, Nathan, will dig up an objection of his own.

I really *should* like to do that booklet on the Shadow-Maker.[25] I've over a hundred of his letters to me, and copies of other ones, and I knew him long and intimately. But it would take me at least a month to write the thing, and I suppose I'd get only royalties for the work, and even those a year afterwards. Macmillan wanted me to write a life of London, whom I knew better than his own wife knew him; but as it was only a royalty matter, I refused. I don't expect *much* money, but I like to get it in a hurry, like all wastrels. By the way, here's a poem I wrote to amuse Jack. It's not my own reaction to the cosmos, at all, but an effort to further objectify (she split!) his "White Logic" stuff in "John Barleycorn."[26]

Harriet Monroe[27] wanted to use it, but I would not let her, as I don't want it thought I've reached that stage yet. I'm old, bad, and hungry for illusions, so long as they're pleasant ones. But— I've my imagination, as you'll note. Show the thing to that brute Nathan, who'll probably think it optimistic!

I feel guilty whenever I make you read my letters. Bear with me yet a little while!

Yours ever,

George Sterling.

Psst! Don't bother to reply to this: I may be writing again to you in a few days.

G. S.

[11] [GS to HLM] [ALS, EPFL]

May 3rd, 1918.

Dear Mr. Mencken:

Here is a magnificent "prose poem" by young Smith, our T.B. of the Sierran foot-hills.[28] I feel sure you'll want it, but if you don't, do not trouble to return it—send it to Jimmy Gibbons,[29] who must revel in that sort of thing.

What number of the "Post" contained your views on poetry? I see they got Brother Wheeler's goat.[30]

It is a cool, bright afternoon. I think I shall go forth and commit adultery.

Yours ever,

George Sterling.

[12] [HLM to GS] [TLS, HUN]

May 6th [1918]

Dear Mr. Sterling:—

My vote is for the sonnet as it stands: a sweet bullet for the righteous. There is very small chance that Nathan will demand a division. He suffers from twelve different diseases, and is emptied of all rectitude. Even spitting into the eyes of the saints now becomes hazardous. The new espionage act gives the Postmaster General almost absolute power to censor American magazines. He may deny the mails to any one that he doesn't like, for any reason or no reason. No crime is defined; no hearing is allowed; no notice is necessary; there is no appeal. I venerate these late triumphs of jurisprudence. You should read the act. The newspaper accounts of it put a soft pedal upon it.

33

"The White Logic" is fine and rolling stuff—in fact, gorgeous. You put the words together magnificently. It's a pity you won't do the Bierce and London books. The market for that sort of thing is very limited—hence the coyness of the publishers—but it ought to be done. I await the Awakening of your Better Nature.

That you are not familiar with "Tom and Molly" distresses me. It is taught in the primary schools here in the East. The author, I suspect, was Mark Twain. Or maybe Lyman Abbott.[31] Here is the authentic text:

> Tom and Mollie on the beach,
> Enjoying their youthful follies;
> The sun is hot on Tommie's back
> And the sand is hot to Mollie's.

Other versions exist, but this is the pure one.

Sincerely yours,
H L Mencken

[13] [HLM to GS] [TLS, BAN]

May 10th [1918]

Dear Mr. Sterling:—

My vote is for the Smith piece and I think Nathan will vote for it too. What is Smith's address? It doesn't appear on the ms. My best thanks.

That adultery is still lawful in California rather surprises me. Down here it is forbidden by sumptuary laws and its practise is as dangerous as going over the top. A few years ago the suffragettes of Maryland proposed a statute providing 10 years imprisonment for the first offense and castration for the second. A sober fact. We had to use a lot of money to kill the bill in committee.

Yours in Xt.,
H L Mencken

[14] [GS to HLM] [ALS, NYPL]

May 15th, 1918.

Dear Mr. Mencken:

The address of Clark Ashton Smith is

Auburn, Cal.

He has lots more of that prose-poetry stuff, some of which you'll find printable, I'm guessing. Anyway, I'm glad you liked what I sent you.

Of course we've laws agin adultery here, but I never heard of

34

them being enforced. Folks around the Bay here are more vital, I think, than elsewhere in these United States—that's on account of the cool climate. Many visitors exclaim at the complexions of our women. Also we inherited from the forty-niners a good deal of sexual lawlessness. This is a great city for drinking, too, with many cabarets. So I'm betting there's more pushing per capita here than elsewhere. Los Angeles doesn't count, for all its movie girls.

Come and find out for yourself. I'd be glad to have you as my guest at the next grove-play of this club, which is on the night of August 3rd.[32] One usually goes to the grove a few days prior to that.

It's a lot of fun. I used to share a three-compartment tent with London and Wilson; but now London's gone and Wilson has bought in with a bunch who use a Jap valet and two refrigerators.

Courage: I'm nearly done. May I submit my stuff to you instead of Nathan, who, I think, doesn't like me—if indeed he ever gives me a thought? However, I don't want to infringe on any of your laws. I sent a lyric to S.S. this morning. Wait till you see my "Lilith!" The Comstockians will jail me, all right.[33]

May God keep you long on the job!

    Sincerely,

        George Sterling.

[15] [GS to HLM] [ALS, EPFL]

        May 28th, 1918.

Dear Mr. Mencken:

        I'll bother you with just one more letter, to accompany this sonnet of young Smith's.[34] It's aloof and classic, like most of his stuff, but poetical, like all of it.

Probably you'll prefer to write to him directly, but I didn't want you to miss this sonnet. His most human work is a few love lyrics he showed me, last winter. Perhaps you can get him to send them on.

He's tubercular, but I've a rich lady here supporting the family, and he may keep for several more years.

Damned interesting, all that about your eastern smut-hounds. Our principal exhibit gave up his ministry to go into movie making.

H. L. Wilson will be in Maine all summer, where he and "Tark" will try a new play.[35]

    Yours ever,

        George Sterling

[16] [GS to HLM] [ALS, EPFL]

June 10, 1918

Dear Mr. Mencken:

Obedient to the prophetic quality of your eye, our local Puritans *have* put on the screws, as you'll note from the enclosed clipping. The act has caused lots of talk here, as our French restaurants have been sacred ground up to now. Well, I'm safe for a while yet. But that cruise of yours sounds tempting.

I'm enclosing a sonnet by young Smith that intrigues me decidedly. Perhaps it's a bit too exotic for you, though. I mean for "S.S."[36]

Heaven knows how that young man is to come out, physically. He's in an ideal country for the cure of T.B., and I have old Sen. Clark's daughter-in-law supporting him and his parents.[37] The trouble is, he has not the will-to-live—not "the guts of a louse," as London used to put it.

I'm glad you like Spanish wine! That and beer for me. Since London's death I'm off Scotch and cocktails.

Yours ever,

George Sterling.

[17] [HLM to GS] [TLS, HUN]

June 15th [1918]

Dear Mr. Sterling:—

I agree with you fully: a very intriguing sonnet. But probably a bit too heathenish for our fat women, who want the direct business of amour—the attentat. I surely hope Smith gets on his legs. A fellow of much the same sort is Orrick Johns. He has done some very fine things (unpublished), but seems to have no steam. Physical incapacity is also at the bottom of it; I hear he has lost a leg. A year or so ago I got him a publisher for a book of verse. At the last moment, without my knowledge, he pulled out a lot of good stuff, and put in a lot of swill. Result: a rotten book.[38]

The Poodle Dog is not the last. I have agents in moral circles, and they tell me big plans are afoot to purge the country of all sin under cover of the war. I am quite serious. The plans to save the soldiers from fornication, already in progress, are astounding— women spies, shot-gun quarantines, badges for boys with the clap, etc. I wrote an article denouncing this Methodist saturnalia three months ago, but no one will print it. Under the new espionage act it is probably downright unlawful—30 years at Leavenworth or Atlanta. This act, strictly constructed, forbids mentioning the fact that any soldier is indisposed sub-equatorially. It is libel on the army.

Meanwhile, the reports of the Public Health Service, issued weekly, show a great deal of venereal disease in the army—the inevitable result of efforts at suppression. Turn now to the enemy. Two German auxiliary cruisers were laid up at Norfolk for nearly two years. Every officer and man, under one pretext or another, got shore leave. And yet during all that time there was NOT ONE case of venereal disease on either ship. Simple medical measures protected the whole crowd; the chief surgeon (a man I happen to know) put them into effect without asking anybody's leave. Well, these identical measures are forbidden in the U.S. Navy by express orders of Josephus Daniels.[39] I have his order. He argues that protecting the boys would encourage them to sin, and that he couldn't look into the eyes of their moral fathers with that on his conscience.

Meanwhile, I gradually pass beyond the age of consent. If you are not merely boasting in saying that you dam nigh got caught in the Poodle Dog I congratulate you.

Sincerely yours,

H L Mencken

[18] [GS to HLM] [ALS, NYPL]

[The Lambs
130 West 44th Street
New York]

July 14th, 1918.

Dear Mr. Mencken:

       I'm here in New York for a few (I hope) months, and trust you'll give me a chance to hoist one with you the next time *you* are here.

I drop in at the Lambs[40] for my mail two or more times a day, so if you left me a message per telephone letting me know when I could call you up, and where, it would give me the opportunity for a chat with one whom I so sincerely admire.

Yours ever,

George Sterling.

[19] [HLM to GS] [TLS, BAN]

July 15th [1918]

Dear Mr. Sterling:—

I am just back from New York, damn the luck! But I'll probably run up again in about three weeks. It will be a great pleasure to look you up. We are approaching the beginning of the end. In six months a glass of beer will bring $2.

Yours sincerely
H L Mencken

[20] [HLM to GS] [TLS, BAN]

August 3rd [1918]

Dear Mr. Sterling:

My apologies for not tracking you down. After one trial, ineffective, I succumbed to alcohol, an affair de coor, and some damnable business that got me into a state of mind and brought me back to Baltimore. I'll return in a couple of weeks, and I surely hope you let me see you. Are you going to visit Washington? If so, why not drop off in Baltimore? The malt is running out, but what remains is excellent.

Yours in Xt.,
H L Mencken

[21] [GS to HLM] [ALS, EPFL]

Sept. 10th, 1918.

Dear Mr. Mencken:

My former wife suicided,[41] and I had to hasten back to God's Country (temporarily). I'm damned sorry our trails didn't cross! I'd have gone to Baltimore to find you, had I remained in N.Y. longer. As it is, I'm unlikely to go east again in a hurry. For one thing, the price is almost prohibitive. And Gotham in the good old summertime—never again!

Well, I met several persons I'd wanted to meet, including Dreiser, who tried to steal my girl (so did Carman),[42] but was (pro tem. at least) unsuccessful. I meant to have some chats with him, but had to light out too soon.

I'm enclosing what I think is a good lyric. Its author is a young man in Madison, Conn.[43] If you can use it, let *him* know. He has no fancy ideas as to prices. If you don't care for it, just give it to the goat; but let *me* know.

Say: I've a one-act play I wrote around an experience that London had. Two men and a woman. Is it any use to send it to you? It's rather dramatic in spots.[44]

It's good to be back in a cool city. I had a call from young Jennings[45] last week—an ingenuous and likeable youth, with more illusions in a minute than we'll have in the years remaining to us—as is right, if he's to poetize.

Strange, that W. H. Wright should have returned to Los Angeles, of all the towns on earth![46] I am wondering why he abandoned N.Y., to which I'd assumed he was incurably addicted. He is wasted on The Pure.

My publisher can't afford to bring out my dramatic poem "Lilith" this year, so I'm sending it on to Macmillan's, who asked for it repeatedly when I was in N.Y. It'll be too late for the fall publications, though.

I wish I could see more of your articles: where do you appear?

> Sincerely ever,
>
> George Sterling.

[22] [HLM to GS] [TLS, BAN]

September 22nd [1918]

Dear Mr. Sterling:—

I was in hopes that you'd still be in New York when I got back. Dreiser, it appears, was on the trail of both of us, and came near finding me, despite the difficulties that I got into. I had intended coming to the Coast this autumn, but the expense was beyond me. Last Sunday I went to Pittsburgh and from there to New York. The cost was staggering.

The Dowd poem interests me a lot; my best thanks for letting me see it. The one objection to it is that I have at least six poems in type on the same general subject. All of the young poets are saying good-bye to their girls and writing about it. But I shall try to get something else from Dowd. He should do good work.[47]

Macmillan should be able to do the book after January 1st. At the moment all the publishers are tied up by bindery difficulties. The binderies have not only lost a great many men to the army and the munitions works; they are also oppressed by astounding union regulations. I hear some queer tales.

I am doing no articles at present save those printed in the Smart Set. I had a contract with the Evening Mail, running to September 11th, but when Rumely was jailed and the bondholders took possession they tried to hornswoggle me, and after a long row I quit work and took $250 cash for my unexpired contract.[48] Stoddard, who is now in charge, seems to be a cheap fellow.[49] I am sick of newspaper work and shall probably do no more. Once the war is over I plan to set up an anti-uplift sheet, and have some fun. Meanwhile, however, I may be drafted and perish.

Sincerely yours,
H L Mencken

[23] [GS to HLM] [ALS, EPFL]

Sept. 30, 1918.

Dear Critic:

Eet ees a cr-r-r-rime, as my dear friend Martinez[50] is wont to say, that we didn't have at least one jag together in New York or Baltimore. And you were thinking of a trip to the Coast! You're dead right about the rates: I figure that the rates have about doubled, for trips involving a Pullman.

When you start the anti-uplift paper, let me in: I'll contribute gratis.

I hope you won't be drafted. *I* am too old—nearly forty-nine now, only a few laps behind God.

"Smart Set's" obstinate opposition to the holy state of matrimony emboldens me to enclose this one-acter, which I wrote last winter, to give a blonde ingenue a chance to show her shape. Perhaps you could use it, with a little carpentering; equally perhaps it isn't subtle enough for you or George Jean.

I've not heard yet from Macmillan's about my scarlet "Lilith," and fear that Brett thinks it immodest.[51]

May God keep off your trail!

Sincerely,
George Sterling.

[24] [HLM to GS] [TLS, BAN]

October 7th [1918]

Dear Mr. Sterling:—

"The Dryad" has the refined, moral touch that I admire, but in our very next number there is a short sketch (not in play form) in which one of the ancient animals tackles Christendom—in brief, the same general ideer, though most different in treatment.[52] I am putting the matter up to the learned

40

Nathan. I send an advance copy of the Smart Set with the other piece.

All these parts are ravaged by the influenza, which seems to be amazingly deadly. An undertaker's wagon gallops past my house every few minutes. The thing is really gruesome. Alcohol, I hear, is a prophylactic. At all events, it is pleasant to think so.

If Brett does the book, and the slightest flavor of indelicacy is in it, I shall complain anonymously to the comstocks and have it put to the torture.

Sincerely yours,
M

[25] [GS to HLM] [ALS, EPFL]

Oct. 30th, 1918.

Dear Mr. Mencken:

It pleased me to find that "The Dryad" was not objectionable enough to "the learned Nathan" to make him reject its mild improprieties. I almost wish I'd given more time to it and so avoided a few or so crudities.

Anyhow, I'll be glad to see it in "Smart Set," which is the only magazine I can read. The others seem to get worse every year. Perhaps it's only I getting old. But have you tried any of their war stories?!!

I'm enclosing a fine lyric by a girl I know.[53] It would please her to see it in print, and I've other things of hers as good if you don't care about this one. That is really her name; and I don't even dare give her middle one!

Influenza reigns here too, and I have to wear a gauze muzzle whene'er I take my walks abroad, which isn't often. It's ten bucks fine if one doesn't. The local Chinese catch the disease, but it never kills one. . . . Those damned Macmillans haven't written yet about my Lady Lilith. Perhaps they're worrying about the part of the *2nd Act* where Tancred and Lilith meet on a moonlit islet, minus their bathing-suits. By the way, I took a swim in the Pacific a few midnights ago, with another fool. We were both a bit tanked. The girls guarded our clothing faithfully, but that wouldn't have helped had a cop come along. I don't mind the notoriety, but object to the fine.

Yours ever,
George Sterling.

[26] [HLM to GS] [TLS, BAN]

November 4th [1918]

Dear Mr. Sterling:—

My vote is surely for the Greenwood poem—a very excellent thing. My best thanks for it. The printers will undoubtedly play hell with it. They have now reached such a state of inflammation that they obey no orders and answer no protests. Take it or leave it. Imagine a printer objecting to being called a lousy son-of-a-_____—I mean affectionately, casually, in the regular course of business. The trade has much changed. Well, let us wait until the war is over, and the munitions plants are all closed, and they go back to setting type.

I have just been reading William Lyon Phelps' new book on poetry—an amazing piece of balderdash.[54] Imagine such swill being solemnly swallowed. He lavishes praises on various college boy poets, bows politely to Ella Wheeler Wilcox, Herman Hagedorn and Cale Young Rice—and forgets you and Lizette Reese altogether.[55] The thing is colossal, almost incredible.

The carnality you described would be quite impossible here in the East. You mention a simple fine. The penalty in Maryland for bathing in the altogether is a 2 years hard. The girls would have been penned in some Y.W.C.A. and exhorted to remember God.

I have much suspicion of Macmillan: the place is full of Pecksniffs. Knopf is to do my next couple of books (one is now going into type),[56] but I have a mind to print privately after the war. A thing I have in mind is a treatise on democracy, with lists of the victims.[57] As for the magazines, I never look at them. It is bad enough to read the sort of fiction mss. that agents send in. Fifty or sixty mss. are equal to having a tooth pulled.

Yours in Xt.,

H L Mencken

Nathan has been laid up by the influenza and is still very wobbly. His brother died of it last week. I hear gabble that a good many cases look like bubonic.

[27] [GS to HLM] [ALS, NYPL]

Nov. 12th, 1918.

Dear Mr. Mencken:

Thanks for another of your interesting letters! I'm glad you liked Miss Greenwood's poem: she'll be a proud girl to see herself in print.

What you say of Phelps is warming to my heart. I read his stuff when it appeared in the venerable "Bookman," and inferred at the start, from his absurd overvaluation of Lindsay,[58] that I wasn't high in the gent's estimation. But I really expected a line or two, along with the small-fry.

Not that such praise matters a whoop: I'd a billion times rather have *your* approval. Somehow, professors of English literature have never fallen for my rhymes. But that he could have overlooked my poetic better, Miss Reese! It is indeed stupefying, and I hope you'll give him a Biercian whack. As for me, I'll prod him anonymously when the chance comes: to assail him openly would give him too much of a show to yell "Sour grapes!"

I've met Ella. She's all right when not committing verse. I know Cale Rice, too: he was my guest at one of our grove-plays—a saintly young man, whose poems would be much more worth while if he'd quite moralizing and sentimentalizing. Charlie Towne,[59] by the way, has a delicious name for him—*Pale* Young Rice!

Harry Leon Wilson writes our 1919 grove-play, and it's to be given in June instead of August, to beat the prohibitions to it. If you can get out here, do come: it may be out last "wet" Jinks, though California went dry.

I'm told that London's widow purposes to bring out in a book his love-letters to her.[60] If she does it'll be the ghastliest happening in our western literature. The mere thought of it is horripilating! As I know her well enough to make my word count, I may be able to avert such a tragedy. My ex-wife turned all my letters to *her* over to one of her surviving sisters, and I see a tough job ahead of me, retrieving them. Damn our youth anyway! Me for the forties and fifties!

Just had to dig up some coin to pay a girl's fare from N.Y. to S.F., and am feeling pensive. Hop Phelps for me, and restore my customary thoughtlessness!

Yours in His Fatherhood,

George Sterling.

[28] [HLM to GS] [TLS, BAN]

November 20th [1918]

Dear Mr. Sterling:—

London's widow I don't know, though I have talked to her by telephone. Her book on their Hawaiian affairs[61] was a silly thing—written like a high-school girl's essay on the subconscious. He and she appear to have carried on love-making in moving-picture terms. I surely hope you manage to kill the love-letters. At the age of 24 I wrote one that brought an indignant husband on to my hands and damn nigh saddled me with his singularly idiotic wife. This lesson soaked in.

What is to be done about Phelps God knows. He is an amiable old boy and I hate to tackle him with all arms. I have written a few paragraphs of kidding. I doubt he does much damage. Even such fellows as Hackett and Bourne gag at him.[62] After all, there must be some ass to write books for women school-teachers, and so mellow their sad lives.

Why don't you do some prose? The war has filled the country with mushy, hypocritical snuffling. Moralizing becomes a universal curse. I think that there will be a reaction, and that a few books will be enough to bring it on.

Yours in Xt.,
H L Mencken

[29] [GS to HLM] [ALS, EPFL]

Nov. 24, 1918.

Dear Mencken:

Is the enclosed squib too raw for "Smart Set?" I rather like its beginning and end, but fear it's too crude.[63]

I've been lit for the last three days, or I'd have written ere now. Young Jennings was here for luncheon with me, last week—a most naive and likeable youth. He sells more poems than anyone I know of (I don't call Brayley's and Guiterman's stuff "poems.")[64]

A chap who has four theatres our here (Earnest Wilkes) wants to produce "Lilith!" As it would set him back about $50000., I am giving him advice to the contrary. But he's an amiable cuss.

Here's hoping some Bolshevik printer doesn't shoot you up!

Yours ever,
George Sterling.

[30] [HLM to GS] [TLS, BAN]

November 29th [1918]

Dear Sterling:—

Alas, a bit over the wavering, impalpable line separating art from Blackwell's Island. The notion that perfectly

44

good girls lean back with a sigh and murmur "Well, then, hurry up and let's get it over"—this doctrine makes progress. But it is still unlawful to argue (a) that the aged are constipated, (b) that aunts are ever Sapphist, and (c) that Tom cats are bawdy. Could you modify these lewdnesses? Change the name of the pamphlet to "Brotherhood of Men and Nations," by John D. Rockefeller, Jr. (It actually exists) Make the Sapphic aunt merely diabetic. Halt the second paragraph at the word "night". Change William Lyon Phelps to Paul Elmer More.[65] So castrated I'll be hot for it, and no doubt Nathan will join me.

I was horribly tight in New York the last time. It was a massive overdose and I have been rocky ever since.

I heard the other day of the death of J. M. Kennedy in London—influenza. An excellent man; his book on the United States told some hard truths.[66] The war, of course, shut him off.

Yours in Xt.,
Mencken

[31] [GS to HLM] [ALS, EPFL]

Dec. 3rd, 1918.

Dear Mencken:
That's all right about Phelps: it has just occurred to me that the old boy thinks I'm immoral, and a bad influence in local rhymesmithing! So I am pleased and unresentful.

Some prose I'd like to do. I *think* a lot of it, but am too lazy to get it into black and white. Here's a blasphemous bit I wrote lately. Likely enough you can't use that sort of thing, and I'll have to give it to the "Liberator."[67]

I'm to have luncheon with Mrs. London tomorrow, and shall pump her about the love-letters. I had nerve enough to write such things to only one woman, and I think they're safe enough. Each letter contained a sonnet, so she has them in a safe-deposit box![68] But husbands have tried a few times to wish wives on me. As I had one then, it never went. Now I'm again exposed to the elements.

Also I shall now go and drink a Martini or two to your peace of mind.

Yours ever, George Sterling

[32] [GS to HLM] [ALS, EPFL]

Dec. 5th, 1918.

Dear Mencken:

I have subjected the enclosed masterpiece to the ruthless eviscerations that you indicate, and hope it'll keep us both out of jail. I hated to give up that "constipation," though.

If you were any tighter in Gotham than I've been in San Francisco, the last two months, you were going some! Only about six more months, you know.

Apple-orchards ought to become valuable—hard cider. It's not so bad after one becomes a bit used to it.

Here's a sonnet that seems in the "S.S." atmosphere.[69] I know I'm causing you to write a lot of letters, but pray forgive me: I don't know anyone else that writes your kind.

I close with a toast I committed last night:

> Happy be all you remember!
> Sad be all you forget!
> I am yours to the end of the trail,
> And may it be long and wet!

Yours ever,

George Sterling.

[33] [HLM to GS] [TLS, BAN]

December 9th [1918]

Dear Sterling:—

I am eager for "The Rabbit-Hutch", and I believe that Nathan will join me. What if it does outrage my religious sentiments? Infidels will enjoy it. We can't all be Presbyterians.

I hope you go with me on the revision of the piece I sent back to you a week ago. It sticks in my mind.

The portrait of the ducks almost makes me ill. During the open season here, now on, there are none to be found: they come after the season closes. As a result, it is hard to get hold of one. I remember when they were as cheap as chicken.

I have just ordered ten bushels of malt and am setting up a small brewery in my cellar. I am taking lessons from a brewmaster who returns to Munich as soon as the war is over. Fear not!

Yours in Xt.,

Mencken

[34] [HLM to GS] [TLS, HUN]

December 11th [1918]

Dear Sterling:—

"One of the Family" still intrigues me, despite the denaturization. I am sending it to Nathan by this mail. The sonnet also has my vote. But isn't the last line in the copy in error? It runs: "Turned to your marbles and consenting mouth." Has the lady marbles? Do you mean marble? I await light.[70]

I have a sound formula for beer-making and a man in Michigan, a former malt dealer, is sending me a large bag of malt. Hops are easy to obtain, and I already have the thirst. I'll report progress. Meanwhile, I am laying in California red wine—the only drink now within my means. The truth is, I like it. I find that a man whose time is worth nothing can make 45 gallons of beer for about $7.

A man in Germany goes to jail for calling the Kaiser a son of a bitch. Final result: war. A man in America goes to jail for having a gallon of red-eye in his house, or (in Indiana) for smoking a ciga rette on the street, or for giving some poor working girl a happy week-end at the seaside. What the answer is, God knows.

Sincerely yours,
H L Mencken

[35] [GS to HLM] [ALS, EPFL]

Dec. 16th, 1918.

Dear Mencken:

I had a notion you were joshing me about the brewing: I'm glad you're not. Go to it! No reason why you shouldn't be a success at the art. But I warn you it'll make you too popular in Baltimore, and end by making you mayor.

I want to thank you for your remarks in the January "S.S."[71] Just what I'd have asked you to say if I'd had the asking! And what you say of Miss Reese is dead right. Well, college professors and homely women usually hate me on sight.

Just what is meant by "héliogabalisme?"[72] I am a poor man, from whom the Lord has withheld much knowledge. But thank God I don't know so much as that man Nathan! No wonder you call him "learned!"

Sorry I can't get some ducks to you! I have them given me about every Monday morning by bloodthirsty friends who've spent the Lord's Day a-potting them. Once in a while I go myself. But it's chilly work to go out on the marshes before daylight, fortified by hooch though one may be. Ducks can't be sold out here, and the common people are roaring that it's a rich man's job. But with market-hunters, there'd be no ducks at all.

It pleased me to find Nathan liking (I infer he's sincere to that extent) "The Rabbit-Hutch." It will grieve the only one of my six married sisters that remains a happy papist, so I'll have to square myself in advance by Christmas presents to her progeny.

Our red-wine here isn't bad, if you get it from a maker who likes you. Usually they dilute it and then bring it back to par-and-pep with brandy. I know a man who has a winery at Rutherford, where young Jennings is, and who is in an eternal rage at the stuff that is sold in the east as California wine. Our best red-wine here is a brand called "La Questa," made by a chap called Rixford.

That "marbles" meant the snowiness of the girl's neck, bosom, and even lower down; though my experience is that they balk at complete nudity on a bed of pine-needles. And pine-needles was all they usually got when I inhabited Carmel. I know it's a trifle obscure, but women will get it, and I suppose it's for them that you run verse.

But I babble, and am now off for an afternoon of refined adultery, for which God bless the rich!

Yours at last,

George Sterling.

[36] [HLM to GS] [TLS, BAN]

December 29th [1918]

Dear Sterling:—

Without any suggestion from me whatsoever Nathan's eagle eye was arrested by the "marbles", and he insists that it will suggest to the intelligentsia that the lady is either a stone-head or has ballocks. Perhaps an insane and pathological notion, but there it is: two pure hearts react in the same way. Remember that, in publishing a magazine, one cannot count upon intellect in the reader: one must assume that she is a little short of idiotic. Hence the advantage of having the advice of a fellow as Nathan, whose instincts are soundly editorial.

I don't suggest mutilating it. But can't we trade it for other goods? Your styles suit our trade, and we want to put out a good Spring line.

Sincerely yours,
Mencken

I spent most of yesterday at a dinner in honor of the historic event in Galilee. Damages: five completely down and out, and one poor colored girl ravished.

1919

[37] [GS to HLM] [ALS, EPFL]

Jan. 7th, 1919.

Dear Mencken:

I've changed that damned word, so if you really want this sonnet of spring, here she is. If not, return without comment, as Bok will be strong for it.[1]

It occurs to me that I'm extracting too much kale from the "S.S." So here's $3.00 back, for a year's subscription. I always have to go out and buy "S.S." anyhow, as some scoundrel always steals it as soon as it goes on our table in the library.

The Cook chap wrote to me twice, requesting details of my past.[2] I modestly refrained from replying to his letters, and am surprised that he mentioned me at all. I've enjoyed being mentioned by you and Bierce, but the rest of the critics are mostly fools. Look at Braithwaite—the stuff he falls for.[3]

I said E. H. Rixford made our *best* claret. His address in the 'phone book is 105 Montgomery St. S.F. The "honest" wine man is my friend Fredk. Ewer, of Rutherford, Cal. If you write to *him*, mention my name. He's a jovial old roughneck.

I'd read many edifying details of Heliogob's career, but wasn't sure of the exact sense of the adjective. To think of him as being infamous and St. Paul revered!

I've tried a coon, somewhat diluted, myself. She was from Jamaica's sunny shore, and may have my imprimatur for masculine lips whenever she wants it.

It was good of you to mention me to John D. Williams. Wish you knew the other John D.! He wrote kindly to me on Dec. 14th, and I've not replied yet! Well, I've only "Lilith," and he'd lose a thousand dollars an hour producing that, as I shall inform him.

My friend James Hopper is back, and brings me a set of dice he found in the cellar of the castle at Chateau Thierry. The Germans had been using them half-an-hour before! I've used them several times already, shaking for drinks, and haven't lost yet. Begin to repent for some of my war-sonnets![4]

I've been entertaining some Russian officers that left on Saturday, en route for langorous Siberia. Was with them for New Year's Eve. They nearly killed me. I dug up a 170 lb. girl for their 200 lb. colonel, and he was so grateful I was afraid he was going to kiss me. He also recommended the girl; but I knew it already.

Again I've been rambling on. "Allah verdi!" as the Russians toast you.

> Yours ever,
>
> George Sterling.

[38] [HLM to GS] [TLS, HUN]

January 13th [1919]

Dear Sterling:—

I never heard of anyone subscribing for the Smart Set before, and so I don't know what the etiquette of the occasion is. I am inclined to keep the money and put you on the exchange list, though this, under the new postal law, is now unlawful.

Thanks for the names of the two wine fellows. I am writing to them. My cellar is growing larger and larger. I begin to believe that diabetes will fetch me long before I drink it dry. I have heavy locks on the door. One sees in Washington what prohibition does. The other day I took a bottle of Moselleblümchen to a friend laid up there. He put it on the sill of his hotel window to cool, and when he went for it two hours later it was gone. Evidently the city fire department had come with extension ladders and stolen it. He was in the room all the while. It was on the fifth floor.

I think the poem is now pure enough for our great family periodical. At all events, I am voting for it. Nathan may detect some other lewdness.

My experience here in the South is that Russians, Frenchmen and other foreigners (particularly Scandinavians) greatly appreciate what we call yellow pine. I once introduced an eminent opera singer (Italian) to a lady of color, and he remained in Baltimore four days—the longest time any foreigner has ever managed to stand the town. Personally I have always avoided the pigmented races. I am the only man South of the Mason and Dixon line who can say as much, and so I stand apart and am regarded as unearthly by the general. A mere vanity.

Johns Hopkins, founder of the university, viewed white women with distaste. He would tramp the streets on scouting expeditions. When his eye was attracted by a Moor scrubbing somebody's front steps, he would offer her 50 cents for her amiability. This is an actual fact. The old boy, worth many millions, made 50 cents his limit, or three for a dollar. This glorious tradition still saves the Johns Hopkins from utter extinction, but it has fallen into the hands of the Methodists and is going fast. Its decay would make a good article. In ten years it will be a mere Yale. The medical school holds up, but the university proper is a mere parody of the original.[5]

Yours in Xt.,
H L Mencken

[39] [GS to HLM] [ALS, NYPL]

Feb. 12th, 1919.

Dear Mencken:

It's over a month since I've persecuted you, and now I write only to urge you to consider the possibility of our attending our Bohemian Jinks, the last week of next June. It may be our last wet Jinks, and should be a memorable affair. The grove-play is by Harry Leon Wilson, and may be very good. These plays are always amazing spectacles, regardless of merit otherwise.

I know the fare is pretty steep. On the other hand, I think you'd find it worth the money. You may have my room here in the club (I have a romance-room in the Latin Quarter that I'd as soon inhabit), and your living-expenses will be no greater than if you were at home. This is true of the Grove also.

Do look ahead and see if you can't fall in with the proposal.

I'm wondering if you got any La Questa. I drank some of it last night, and detected a falling off in its quality. That wine has heretofore been given much time in which to mature; but it may be that the new law has necessitated the dumping of the rawer vintages on the market.

I take the liberty of enclosing another poem by the Greenwood girl. I think well of it, and perhaps you and Nathan may.[6]

Do you know anything about Willard Wright? He is somewhere here in S.F., and contributes three times a week to the "Bulletin" here. I've written to him care of that paper, but have had no response. I'm told he is "utterly down and out." That may be untrue; and yet his articles are lacking in his former snap and wit. I should like to give him some fun, if he care for frivolity any more. It might save him from the Christian Scientists.

In His name,

George Sterling.

[40] [HLM to GS] [TLS, HUN]

February 18th [1919]

Dear Sterling:—

The Greenwood piece bemuses me and I am passing it on to Nathan. My best thanks. I add the formal accusation that you wrote it yourself.

I wish the way were clear for me in the matter of the Bohemian Club revival, but at the moment it seems likely that I'll be tied up. This is because I am going abroad in August, if it be so God's will, and two absences from slavery in one year would be too much. I want to see the sights, transact some literary business in Germany, and at the same time evade hay-fever. Of this, more anon. If there is the chance I'll come to San Francisco invited or not invited.

I have an old affection for Wright, but he has become impossible. Caution: don't lend him any money. He used me roughly in that department, and now tries to dodge the fact by lying about me. What with his financeering, his habitual lying and his imbecile compromising of various friends in New York, I had to remove him from my bright lexicon.

Unable to obtain any La Questa here or in New York, and put into a panic by the rapid depletion of stocks, I loaded up on various other wines. One day, as I stood at the counter, a wine man made cash sales of $3,700. Five niggers sweated in his cellar, smashing bottles, putting on wrong labels, etc. I took a scare, sold my automobile, and laid in what there was. A letter to the La Questa man brought no reply. I now have at least one bottle of every reputable liquor and liqueur, and enough red and white wine to last two years. As for beer, I have secreted 250 bottles.

I note that the anti-tobacco movement has been formally launched in Tennessee. The arch-vice of frigging is now absolutely unlawful in every state east of the Mississippi.

Yours in Xt.,
Mencken

[41] [GS to HLM] [ALS, NYPL]

Mch. 1ˢᵗ, 1919.

Dear Mencken:

Honest to Gawd I didn't write that Greenwood piece! The brat actually lives and writes, and gave herself in wedlock only a week ago, much to my satisfaction.

Here are some lines by a slightly more mature and decidedly

more charming person.[7] I think they are funny, and hope you can use them in spite of their length.

She was with me, Carmen and Dreiser that night at the Brevoort when I wanted you to be there too. She didn't like their mouths, and composed these lines when she got home. You could shorten the thing by making a single line out of those I have put in brackets.

As she is soon to move over here to S.F., you may address her in my care. And some day I'll send you her picture. No—I have a "snap" of her that I'll enclose, tho' it does not flatter her.

I shall be desolated if you can't be with us in June; but of course the European trip is far more important.

I got Wright on the 'phone, to find he was to go to the hospital that day. He said he'd been meaning to get in touch (ominous word!) and would do so in a few days; but so far I haven't heard from him. Thanks for your advice—I had him sized up, though. In Carmel we called him "The man without a conscience!" Well, I knew he was ill, and I was in a position to take him motoring often, and wanted to do him because he was so kind to me in the way of acceptances when he was on "Smart Set." At first he paid me $5. each for epigrams! Them good old days!

Braithwaite asked me, in November, for a poem for his "Victory" page in the "Transcript."[8] I sent him one I could readily have sold, and asked him merely to send me a copy of the issue it appeared in. I heard no more of the matter, so a fortnight ago I wrote him that his courtesy was on a level with his taste in poetry. Natural enough, bleats of surprise. These professors become so used to laying down the law to kids that they're thin-skinned. Well, I've his new anthology,[9] and shall soon write him a letter that will unkink his wool, if he have any.

I'll drop in on La Questa Wine Co. and see if they've any stuff unsold. I should have given you that address instead of Rixford's.

Big "Artists' Ball" here on Mardi Gras. I go as Dante, in the pageant, and afterwards in a leopard-skin! Mrs. Mitchell is going in gauze. I hope to God we don't wind up in the city prison!

Thanks for your patience!

    Yours ever,

          George Sterling.

And he didn't even use the poem in his damned "page!"

[42] [HLM to GS] [TLS, BAN]

[The Smart Set
25 WEST 45th STREET
NEW YORK]

March 7th [1919]

Dear Sterling:—

This Mitchell piece somehow just misses me, probably because it needs some coopering and is made archaic by the reference to Hoover. But it makes me want to see more. What else has she done? Why not get together a small bale of it and let me have a look? It is pretty certain that I'll take some. A sound touch is there.

I am sorry I missed the Brevoort party. The photograph fills me with new regrets for my catastrophe that night. I went down with all hands. Since then, only once—a quiet affair with Nathan and John Williams. We were all put to bed by 9 P.M. Such follies are now beyond my means. I even doubt that I'll be able to lay in any decent amount of La Questa. I have 200 feet of shelf full, my automobile is sold and converted into bottles, and I buy another quart every time I pass a gin-mill.

The Braithwaite coon should be playing with Sam T. Jack.[10] It is amazing how seriously he is taken. Read his critical remarks on new poetry books. They suggest a sophomore imitating Richard Burton. In the May Smart Set, by the way, I am removing the hide of Prof. Dr. Thorstein Veblen, the latest and worst of the campus pests. His books are positively infernal.[11]

Yours in Xt.,
Mencken

[43] [GS to HLM] [ALS, NYPL]

Sunday P.M. 3 / 19 / 19

Dear H. L.

Am busily engaged in driving three real songsters crazy. The R_x is this: first I whistle gaily; that encourages the canary; when he quits the bulbul tunes up, and then the Hindoo thrush gets on to himself. Fact. If you don't believe it, let me divulge that the bulbul has a crest and is sulphur bottomed and the Hindoo thrush has a long twitchy tail and a reddish breast. Even at that I know you'll think I'm seeing things.

Have just sent this to Good Housekeeping:

Things Worth While

To have been a lover of Cath. the Great and bit out her Adam's apple before she spent.

To have been Pilate's coon eunuch, and won back at craps the thirty pieces of silver from Judas.

To be a super-surgeon, and weld Jack Johnson's[12] balls to Willard Wright.

To be Barnum's favorite bastard, and exhibit St. Patrick at the core of an iceberg of creme de menthe.

To be a ninety-foot python, and practice cunnilingus simultaneously on Mary Garden and La Asquith.[13]

To be the Victrola agent with sole rights to the record of Sara Bernhardt[14] being raped by a band of Arizona Apaches.

If Good Housekeeping turns me down, I know I can turn to Smart Set.

Thanking God and you,

G. S.

[44] [GS to HLM] [ALS, EPFL]

Apr. 6th, 1919.

Dear Mencken:

I've spared you for nearly a month, but now feel like breaking out again in a fresh place. First, have you room and tolerance for the two sonnets? I notice you've given Dick Le G. a full page.[15] But maybe Ruth's effect on me will give Nathan the pip, tho I've no idea how he ranks her as an artist: probably not high.[16]

As for my estimate of the younger set in song, you could have it for nothing. But I see no chance of your finding room for it in "S.S.", and enclose it merely for your possible entertainment. Show it to Nathan, if you think he'd like it.[17]

Sorry you didn't care more for the Mitchell thing. She has no more, being a wit and hence addicted to prose.

———

You make me gasp when you speak of only one (1) jag since the Brevoort incident! So that's why you're able to do so much work, including replies to my darn letters. Well, I'll soon be industrious myself, but my regular custom is two prostrations a week, with an occasional extra. No wonder I get so little done!

Did you read H. L. Wilson's jeremiad in this week's "S. E. Post?"[18] He's off in a lot of things, I think. I'm saving it to keep

tab on him. This country is going to be a nation of hard-cider folk,
I think. Not bad for me, as one of my six bros.-in-law has a seven-
hundred acre apple ranch—he being, naturally, a surgeon. It is
near Santa Cruz, and I think of moving there in July and destroy-
ing all insect pests, including the local Penrods.

Can you send me another "Pistols for Two"? Some discerning
scoundrel has pouched my copy.[19]

I've not seen Wright yet: he seems to be steering clear of me: I
wish a few hundred others would.

Yours ever,

George Sterling.

[45] [GS to HLM] [ALS, EPFL]

May 1st, 1919.

My dear Mencken:

I'm wondering if you've received your bomb
yet. If so, remail it to old Phelps.

Thanks sincerely for the "Pistols!" It's a delightful thing. W.
Wright hints mysteriously that *he* was its author.

I note that Nathan is addicted to neuralgia, and wonder if it's
the trifacial kind. Only one man ever discovered a cure for that—
our Albert Abrams.[20] But A. has pupils in New York—other physicians—and if Nathan wants to be cured I'll send him the address
of one. Abrams cured me and several of my friends. It's done by
freezing with a jet of ether.

I'm sorry to say I've no more dramatic stuff to send, except this
one-act affair which I enclose. I doubt if you care for it, and the
situation has probably been used before. But it actually happened
to Jack London, and so I wrote it up.[21]

I'm sorry that you were not able to use the Chatterton sonnets.
She will be out here soon, and I'll give them to some newspaper.
I don't imagine I can steal her from Miller, anyway.[22]

Wright speaks respectfully of you, but doesn't seem to rank Nathan very high. He has given up wine and women, he says; and
yet he's making vain eyes at my Best Ever. No use. But so said
Menelaus.

Geo. Sterling

[46] [HLM to GS] [TLS, HUN]

May 6th [1919]

Dear Sterling:—

With tears and beating of the breast! But imagine how the gal-who-visits-the-lewd-bachelor's-love-gymnasium has been done to death by Greenwich Village dramatists! Every day I receive at least five plays showing the same general scheme—not by George Sterling, alas, but still enough like it to spoil the thing even for Sterling. I have always suspected it. The new technique forbids a self-respecting man to invite the hussies into his house. *They* must provide the couch.

I begin to incline toward the Bolsheviki. A few years more of government by the Burlesons, George Perkinses, Otto Kahns, Josephuses,[23] etc., and I'll raise the black flag and begin shooting out of my window. Life in the East is but one millimetre short of intolerable. In Boston a new law requires every hotel guest to give his home *street* address, and the Polizei send off to find out if he really lives there.

I had lunch with Huneker the other day. He complains that all men have become Jews and that all women attempt his virtue. His picture of the swarms of post-30 wenches coming in from the Middle West was very eloquent. He said: "They are so well educated that they scare a man. Imagine a woman, facing her first sin, saying 'So this is the glans penis!' ". Since then I hear that the old boy is ill. He prints his autobiography in two volumes in the autumn.[24]

Wright makes me sad.

Yours in Xt.,
Mencken

[47] [GS to HLM] [ALS, EPFL]

May 15th, '19.

Dear Mencken:

I was pretty sure you'd not care for my one-acter. But it was all I had to send. I'm now encouraging my best girl to write some one-acters, and you may hear from me some day. She has a pretty wit, which is almost incredible in view of her other merits. Wright is trying hard to steal her, and she reports to me verbatim all he says to her! It's a scream.

I'm glad you like Bronson-Howard's stuff.[25] I've always got a good deal of enjoyment from it. How he did hand it to Mizner in one of his stories! I've been drunk thirty-eight times this year, so far, but have not attempted the use of the needle yet. I hear that dope is going strong in Los Angeles, since that pious town went practically dry.

I'm trying to bend young Jennings to a girl who has lately left her hub. No luck so far—he's a shy woodland thing.

I'm still hoping to see you at our Jinks. A movie of it would vex the Methodists.

Yours ever,

George Sterling.

[48] [HLM to GS] [TLS, HUN]

May 22nd [1919]

Dear Sterling:—

The burst of song intrigues me, and I have no doubt that von Nathan will agree.[26]

I lose the gift for drink. Tom Smith, of the Century, gave a loose party in New York last night and I tried to get as much down as possible. But at 2.30 A.M. I was still so sober that I could eat herring salad off a knife, and so I gave it up. The stuff is watered more and more.

Dreiser was run over by an automobile ten days ago. I saw him night before last. He is not badly hurt, but some stretched muscles hurt a good deal. His "Twelve Men" is doing very well.[27] As he lay in the street an old woman came up and said: "I know that poor old man. He always comes to the Baptist church".

Huneker is floored by some bladder trouble, and his wife is very ill also. I hear that his case is not serious. He will flood many a pissoir before he is taken.

I hope Wright doesn't use a hop-gun on your gal. I met his own ex-next-friend in New York Monday and had a long talk with her, but without discussing W.

Yours in Xt.

H L Mencken

[49] [GS to HLM] [ALS, EPFL]

June 3rd, 1919.

Dear Mencken:

I'm not afraid of Willard doping my gal: he sets *some* value on his balls. By the way, he expects to send for that ex-next of his as soon as his roll is thick enough. Small and red-headed, isn't she? And ultra-devoted?

59

You'll see from the enclosure that this club, at least, is as those without hope. I've bespoken six cases of local port, which is about all I can afford just now. There are no very great bargains on the list, but it's all good stuff that has been in the basement for a decent length of time. I wish I could sidetrack some of that Haig and Haig!

Nathan took the poem: he probably noted its tear-evoking quality. I'll spare S.S. for a while, now.

The Jinks impends. All agree it's to be wetter than the days o' 49. A loathsome proposition has come up, though: to emasculate and censor all cartoons. Great God! I wish I had the fare to Tahiti!

Yours for any old revolution,
George Sterling.

[50] [HLM to GS] [TLS, BAN]
[The Smart Set
25 WEST 45th STREET
NEW YORK]

June 10, 1919

George Sterling, Esq.,
The Bohemian Club,
San Francisco, Calif.

Dear Sterling:

The Wright portrait seems to show a considerable falling off in pulchritude. With the whiskers gone he looks emaciated. I hear that his former friend still regards him with great affection.

The wine committee of the Bohemian Club seems to be doing some profiteering. Some of the prices are considerably above the market here in the East. I have a feeling that toward the end of the present month the rum sellers will get into a panic and throw a lot of prime liquors into the market very cheaply. In that case my agents will not be unwatchful. Meanwhile, I am picking up bargains wherever I find them. Do not be afraid to come East next year. You may not get enough to eat, but you will at least get a couple of drinks a day.

Sincerely yours in Xt.,
Mencken

[51] [GS to HLM] [ALS, EPFL]

July 5ᵗʰ, 1919.

Dear Mencken:

The drought is on the land, though I have so far been little affected, for the chaps (and chapesses) who have laid by are so proud of their stores that they are lavish with them. In a few weeks they'll think better of it, however, and then will come the day of the substitute.

The town is hard hit, though. I was in the ball-room of the Palace Hotel at 11:30 P.M. on the 3ʳᵈ, and found just 67 persons in the rooms. There are usually 600. There were 21 couples dancing, not one of whom was over thirty years of age. And bevo[28] was forty cents a pint! How can the hotel make anything at that rate? Young folks seldom have much to spend—and who can drink much soft stuff?

I find on consulting my calendar that, from Jan. 1ˢᵗ to July 1ˢᵗ, I was "lit" exactly 50 times. On fifty-eight days I drank absolutely nothing; and on the remaining seventy-three days consumed 475 drinks.

When I say "lit" I don't mean reeling drunk: I never get that way. But I'd had anything between 15 and 25 drinks—enough for a headache. Well, I shall be better for five or six a day, and I'll be lucky if I get that many, in a few months.

I enclose some verses by a tramp acquaintance of mine, "Wild Joe" O'Carroll.[29] There's a chance he didn't write them, but I think he **did**, and they're too good not to see print. He's an I.W.W. and God knows what else; but I suppose the S.S. is not ultra-respectable in such matters.

It was a sad occasion when we closed the wine-room here, at 12:55 on the night of the 30th. I saw to it that I had the last drink that went over the bar, and I'm keeping the glass! There were about fifty of us, and a more disgusted bunch you've never seen.

It wasn't till a few minutes before "closing time" that I got back to the club. Enclosed clipping indicates some of my route! It was fast and furious in the big hotels (the Palace and St. Francis), and there was a deal of vomit on the floor, from women unused to the pace.

Wright is still virtuous, and longs for the day when he can have his best girl out here—whoever she is.

Forgive this long and unnecessary letter!

Yours ever,

George Sterling.

[52] [HLM to GS] [TLS, HUN]

July 11th [1919]

Dear Sterling:—

This O'Carroll has the gift, and I am prejudiced in favor of Irishmen and I.W.W.'s, but the steady stream of mortuary verse has rather flabbergasted me. Nine tenths of the stuff I get deals with death in one form or another. Hasn't he anything else? If he has, let me see it.

The Last Night in both New York and Baltimore was tame. The Federal judges in both New York and Maryland decided at the end that 2.75 beer was not intoxicating, and so the news that it would continue to flow took all point out of the celebration. Today the bars in Baltimore are all selling any kind of beer they can get, and most of them are also selling hard liquor, though not straight. I have had four beer evenings dring the past week, with excellent malt in large seidels. As you say, all the hoarders are now giving parties. But in a few weeks they will begin to ponder.

I have enough in my bins to last me a couple of years, but it is hard to protect it. A week ago I took an inventory and found that some one, probably my nigger cook, had made off with 4 quarts of rye, 4 quarts of sherry, some rum and some fine brandy. The enforcement act provides that there shall be no property right in alcohol. Thus it will be impossible to jail thieves hereafter. I have put on a new Yale lock, and go over my stock every Sunday morning. I am planting a bottle loaded with ipecac[30] for the cook, and shall probably add a bichloride tablet to make the effect last longer.

Aleister Crowley[31] lately proposed a fine scheme—to charter a ship, call it the Mayflower, and announce a grand immigration to "some land of liberty". But where is the land? My eyes continue to turn toward Zurich. I'll probably end there.

Yours in Xt.,
Mencken

[53] [GS to HLM] [ALS, EPFL]

July 17, 1919.

Dear Brer in Xt.:

This is a rough deal I get in the August "S.S." A blue moon is not appreciably better than one of green cheese.[32] I noticed several other bad mistakes in the same number. Who's your proof-reader?

O'Carroll seems to have no more poems up his sleeve. He's sailing for Valparaiso, as common seaman, in a few days, and promises to write some if the mates let him. But what are mates for?

Perhaps the Argentine is as near to being a land of liberty as any of them. Good climate, too. One of my sisters (married) in Honolulu wants me to live there. She has a "vacation shack" on the cool side of the island. That I'm welcome to—and may distill my own okolehau.[33] Well, we'll see. Tahiti would be *great* if it weren't for the climate. Most of the islands are steam-baths, though.

You have that "Great Hunger" book sized up correctly, I think. By the way, that Sampter girl of yours is a wonder.[34] I hope she won't marry and quit writing. But maybe she writes to support a husband.

This is getting to be a hell of a country! I'm peeved at my ancestors for helping to start it. They were Puritans, but heavy drinkers—why didn't they stay home? I believe old Harris has the thing sized up about right. Read the enclosed clipping as a sample of liberality. If they attempt such things in California, what won't they try to put over in Kansas or Vermont? O Hell!

Richard Barry is here now. I may take him down to Carmel tomorrow. Owen Wister is here too.[35]

Take a shot at your proof-reader and mention my name to the coroner.

> Yours ever,
>
> George Sterling.

[54] [HLM to GS] [TLS, HUN]

July 22nd [1919]

Dear Sterling:—

You may rest assured that the proofreader will not be sassed and that he will go on doing as he dam pleases. The printers in New York have now reached such a state of democratic freedom that it is utterly impossible to approach them. They make a mess of the magazine every month, and if a complaint is entered they simply demand more money. All of the boss printers are on the verge of suicide. A boy who oils a proof press now gets more than a foreman got two years ago, and is more impertinent. We are actually considering printing somewhere else. But every other big city in the East is suffering almost as much. My one refuge is damning the Blessed Trinity.

Frau von Samter-Winslow is already married—to an advertising man. She is a curious creature, and was once on the stage. I wish I could get more stuff out of her. She writes very laboriously. The other day we bought an excellent story from her—the story of a yokel who comes to New York, is invited home again to a much better job, but refuses it on the ground that he couldn't stand living in a town where it is impossible to see William G. McAdoo and Billie Burke on the streets.[36] A subtle fling at American Kultur.[37]

I was lately invited to join the Authors' Club in New York, and shall be glad to give Binner[38] my invitation card. It is a moral organization and should improve him. I probably astounded the syndics by refusing on the ground that I hoped to leave the United States as soon as possible and to stay out permanently.

New York is in a horrible state. The Beaux Arts, after trying to exist on watery beer for three days, closed its doors. All the bars are deserted, and it is very difficult to get a drink. Between the old Hofbräuhaus at 29th street and the Pabst dump in 125th, not a decent glass of malt is to be had. Here in Baltimore it is much better. One local brewer has about 30,000 bbls. of excellent beer. My nigger cook lately stole nearly all my whiskey and rum, but she left me a lot of good wine and about 350 bottles of Piel's beer. I spent yesterday on the place of a friend who has set out 300 grape-vines and 50 apple trees, beside some hops. He is going into the thing on a large scale. His place is in Southern Maryland, on a peninsula jutting into a lonely river, and ten men with a machine gun could defend it against all the prohibitionists of the county.

As I write news comes in that the whites and niggers in Washington are fighting in the streets.[39] At last my dream comes true! No matter what the result—the extermination of the coons or the murder of all the Southern whites—I shall give thanks.

Yours in Xt.,
H L Mencken

[55] [GS to HLM] [ALS, EPFL]

Aug. 28th, 1919.

Dear Mencken:

It will be a sour month for me when you cease writing for "Smart Set." But to leave this miserable country seems to me the only recourse for one who has the fare.

Meanwhile, the local stocks of hooch hold out well, and I am about to brew a drink popular in Mexico. It's called "tepache," and is made of ripe pineapples and sugar. Sadakichi Hartmann[40] and I indulged in some of it ten days ago, and he hasn't appeared since.

I was in Carmel for a few days last week, and saved a chorus-girl from drowning! You'll ask why, as I do now, for the ungrateful little cat wouldn't "come through," afterwards. It seems she went there to reform. The village is gradually losing the erotic reputation I gave it.

All the Italian restaurants here are violently blind-pigging, and most of the saloons are at it too. Only soldiers and sailors show signs of intoxication, however. My abortion-doctor says that business is better than ever; so maybe there's less drinking.

The coon-killing in the east seems to have been a fizzle, though I daresay it was sufficiently exciting while it lasted. I hope they got the Chicago Kaffir who stole my silk umbrella about this time last year.

It's hell about your printers! I sha'n't kick again: make my moons purple if you have to.

> Yours ever,
>
> George Sterling.

[56] [HLM to GS] [TLS, HUN]

September 3rd. [1919]

Dear Sterling:—

The gal put one over on you, and no doubt she and her stage-hand are cackling over it. The sound technique is to make your bargain before you wade in after her. I shall keep your shame quiet.

Let me have the formula of that pineapple toddy. It sounds very good. I have discovered a man who makes excellent gin—a good deal better than most bar gin. He also produces a capital Creme de Cacao and is at work on vermouth. Last week I got down some of the best pale ale I have ever drunk, made by a man here at a cost of 35 cents a case. The alcohol runs to 4.5%. Smuggled liquors have begun to appear on the local market. Altogether, the Blessed Saints seem to be at the bat.

So far the race riots have been very feeble, but I have hope. Once they are on in earnest I believe the coons will kill man for man. This will make the thing doubly stimulating. I'd be glad to go to work in the nigger munitions factory if they promised to massacre every adult male south of Richmond.

I think we'll take the poem.[41] I am very hay-feverish and can scarcely read.

Yours,
Mencken

[57] [GS to HLM] [ALS, EPFL]

Sept. 9th, 1919.

Dear Mencken:

Nay—the sweet blond beast put nothing over on me, other than ingratitude. I didn't plunge in for her: found her with a sprained ankle, at the base of a cliff she couldn't ascend, and with a surf rising. The ankle was really sprained: I examined it myself, and am now sorry I didn't forcibly go further. It was hard work, getting her out, and I had to go into the sea up to my waist, with all my clothes *on*. I now repent me of my modesty.

I sha'n't inflict the recipe for that pineapple stuff on you till it promises to be more of a success. I've had some fermenting (?) in my bath-room for two days, and so far it hasn't developed enough alcohol. Should it do so, I'll let you know.

This is the day when the fatuous Californian celebrates the admission to the Union.[42] What a country it could have been (especially now-a-days) if it had kept out! We'd have licked and annexed Mexico by this time, too.

The stocks of booze in this club seem to be holding out well, and I refuse twenty drinks a day.

Willard has started a fool discussion in his paper, and I'm playing up to it. See enclosure. I've sent your "seven dollar girl" circular to Sinclair, whose simple heart it will harrow. He may even entrain for Cleveland!

I trust you are still in His care.

Yours ever,
George Sterling.

[58] [HLM to GS] [TLS, HUN]

September 15th [1919]

Dear Sterling:—

The accusation that the American husband is faithful to his wife always enrages women. I used to make it periodically in the old Baltimore Sun and it always stirred up the animals. I publicly ascribed it to poltroonry, and argued that women

66

were more courageous.[43] Introduce this last idea into the discussion and you will have the town all agog.

Your explanation of the Steve Brodie[44] episode is rather heavy. I suspect that you attempted the gal and that she fought you off. Or that she attempted you, and you ran. This last is the more likely. I am writing to the Carnegie Hero Fund.

I am horribly sick today. Either it is a sequel to hay-fever or my old malaria has lighted up. This morning I had a pathologist take a blood specimen. He will hunt it for malaria parasites. I can scarcely sit up and have no taste for alcohol. Maybe it is senility.

Yours in Xt.,
Mencken

[59] [GS to HLM] [ALS, NYPL]

San Francisco,
Oct. 10th, 1919.

Dear Mencken:

A pity 't is about our poor boys! I see hundreds of them on Pacific ("Terrific") St. whenever I'm down there o' mornings—which is often, as it's in the Latin Quarter. They seem to stampede to the vicinity as soon as the lorries dump them at the Presidio. I hope they've the price; but that's doubtful in most cases.

Maybe you've heard of Pacific St. It's famous in deep-water annals, and was the first thing that Masefield asked to be shown, when I began to take him around S.F. But the glory had departed, and he was visibly disappointed.

The "Bulletin" had to call off that purposed discussion, to Wright's disappointment. Male and female members of the bourgeoisie sent in protests at once too numerous and too emphatic.

Here's hoping your sick spell is long over with. I wish you'd send me a specimen of your blood, the next time your barber cuts you—a mere drop on a bit of paper will suffice. We've a doctor here (Albert Abrams, a friend of Osler) who is, in my opinion, a great genius. He'll give you full and disgusting details if you care for them. And if you wish, you may try to fool him and send on a specimen from an Ethiopian or anyone else. I took him with me to my dentist's lately, where he shot a current of electricity through my nut for five minutes. The dentist then prepared for filling four cavities in my lower front teeth, all exquisitely sensitive. He used his buzzer as roughly as he chose to, and did nearly two hours work in a few minutes. I should say that 95% of the pain was eliminated. The dentist was astounded, and I was so tickled that I went on a boom that evening.

Wright telephones me that he has to go to Arizona. T.B., of course. I'm afraid he's done for. Doubtlessly this news should go no farther.

Proof sheets of my "Lilith" come and go. I'm hoping you'll like the lovely slut.

Alcoholic reserves are holding out marvellously. San Francisco knew it was coming.

Yours ever, Sterling.

[60] [HLM to GS] [TLS, HUN]

October 17th [1919]

Dear Sterling:—

I like "To One Asleep",[45] but it would be useless to try it on de Nathan. He has been removed from his nut by the mortuary tone of current poetry. Every day we receive 20 pieces about deceased loves. He yells every time I vote for one. Haven't you anything else? I hope so.

The Boyer piece is dignified and eloquent.[46] I often noticed that look in his eyes. In the office he would sit looking out of the window, deaf to what was going on. I knew him for years; he and I were reporters in Baltimore in 1899. When Nathan and I seized the office via the paper man and other creditors, he at first thought we had performed an atrocity upon him, but later on he found out that we hadn't, and before he died we were all friends again. A curious man. Did you know that his notion of a good time was to put on a dress suit and go to some potted-palm dance on the West Side? Once, when he was telling about such an affair, Nathan said "But is the tail actually good? Wouldn't a clean stenographer be better than any of those wenches?" Whereupon he assured us on his word that he never fooled with the gals—they were quite respectable, etc. On the side of male society, he preferred the crowd at his fraternity house! Chiefly undergraduates.

I doubt that Wright is actually tuberculous. He has been announcing his exile to the mountains for at least four years past. Beware of a touch.

I have had my blood examined by the Johns Hopkins band of dirty brothers. No malaria. No spirochaetae. No nothing. I now feel tip-top. Hay-fever was very mild—chiefly, I think, because I took heavy exercise every day—not golfing or anything of that sort, but laying concrete, lifting bricks, etc. The product is a fine brick and concrete wall, worth $500 in the market.

The supply of liquors down here keeps up very well. I drink more than formerly, if anything. This very week I bought half a dozen cases of Scotch, gin, vermouth, etc., behind the door. I have 400 bottles of 6% beer laid away for my death-bed. It keeps perfectly if laid like wine. It is now over a year old.

God save the Republic!

Yours in Xt.,
Mencken

Dreiser is on his way to Los Angeles and S.F.

[61] [GS to HLM] [ALS, NYPL]

Nov. 8th, 1919.

Dear Mencken:

I don't blame Nathan for not caring to print "mortuary verse," though as poetry it usually ranks higher than the efforts of the Cheerful Muse. As you may have surmised, I take out my solemnities in my verse. That's all the easier now a days, with most of the folk in town determined to use up their stocks of hooch before the treacherous drys put another one over. The Italian restaurants seem to be running "regardless," probably under secret agreement with the police; and I know of one where they've a very fair sauterne @ $1.50 a quart. Fair enough!

Glad you didn't dislike the Boyer verses. Your dope on him is interesting to me, for I really know little about him. Perhaps his distaste for even society tail contributed to his willingness to quit the mortal stage.

Wright is in a town called Sierra Madre, under the mountains. A postal says "Am living on milk and scenery—what a life! But I've put on weight and feel better. Will be back in week or so." But he quit the "Bulletin" here, and I'm not so sure he'll come north again.

Congratulations on that brick wall! When I was a kid myself, I used to saw and chop pitch-pine trees, and if ever I take to the woods again will break in once more. But this city is pretty seductive.

A vast amount of booze-stealing seems to be going on out here. They're lifting hooch just as they used to lift jewelry, etc. I know an old-maid who has over 5000 bottles of old-style beer in her basement. Don't even have to push her to be welcome. So that's all right.

I'm immensely interested in the news that Dreiser is to come to California. Can you let me know when, and if he's under the management of any lecture-bureau? I'd like to show him the sights, and maybe dig up a girl for him if he's amorously inclined. He was, that night at the Brevoort, when he tried hard to get my girl's phone number. She is here in S.F. now, by the way.

I've had Yone Noguchi[47] with me a bit—he's here for the Pond Lyceum. But he's as sad as Masefield was. Why don't poets save their melancholy for their poems, like commendable me? Cale ("Pale") Young Rice is another instance.

Here's hoping you'll pardon this longish letter!

Yours ever,

George Sterling.

[62] [HLM to GS] [TLS, UCLA]
[The Smart Set
25 West 45th Street
New York]

November 14, 1919

George Sterling, Esq.
The Bohemian Club,
San Francisco, Calif.

Dear Sterling:

What Dreiser is doing on the coast I don't know. He is very mysterious about his trip and the one letter I received from him contained a lot of bosh about the injury to his reputation done by a Frenchman who put him down as one of the directors of a psychoanalysis society. He doesn't even tell me his address but asks that his letters be sent to General Delivery, Los Angeles. I have sent only one, denouncing him politely.

The burglary of stimulants in this part of the country goes on at a tremendous rate. I have myself lost a great deal of hard liquor. And it has cost me something to reinforce my store-room. Thieves have begun to make headlong attacks upon country distilleries at night. Down in Maryland every distillery is now guarded by artillery. My own brother, I believe, belongs to one of the roving band of bandits.

Huneker has just written his first novel, and I hope to get a whack at it within the week. I hear confidentially that it is rather high in flavor. He is also soon to print his autobiography in two fat volumes. It was originally written for the Philadelphia Public Ledger and hence had to be made suitable for reading at the domestic hearth, but I hear that he has since added a number of surprising and often regrettable episodes.[48]

If Dreiser comes to San Francisco, you will find him hot on the trail of a couple of fat women. Though rapidly approaching the age of seventy-five, he is a soft and sentimental fellow. Don't bring him to see the old maid with the five thousand bottles of beer. He has no taste for alcoholic refinements.

I wish you would send the Saturday Evening Post piece to Reedy. It is too good to blush unseen. If it were not so infernally long I'd be tempted to use it myself.

Yours,
Mencken

[63] [GS to HLM] [ALS, NYPL]

Nov. 30th, 1919.

My dear Mencken:

For the fortieth time I'm indebted to you for a letter worth reading. How in hell do you do it? Bierce always did. I've 153 of his letters, each one a joy, and think I'll sell them, despite his anathema.[49] If I don't, some one may burn the fine things. I can see that he wrote even his letters-to-men with a view to their final publication, for all of them are etched with the North Star.

Listen (as my favorite stenographer says—and she's a noisy lover): I've just read your Cabell's book, "Beyond Life,"[50] and am variously enraptured and exasperated. I think, though, that he assays as high as anyone but you on his notions; but he makes me mad when he runs into Chesterton's smart-alecky stuff,[51] as he does on a few pages; and when he starts in believing in the Bible. I know he doesn't; but why say so? It's too damn cheap.

I think I'll risk sending "Lilith" to him.[52] I'm going to send you the first or second or etc. copy I get. I've hinted at the book so often that probably you're thinking I'm regarding myself as a second Goethe—and it's an echo of the Faust legend. Well, "marf karo," as Kipling's Afghans once whispered.[53] Heaven knows how it'll affect anyone living, aside from the Comstockery. And they have really no kick.

Still, I'd like to explain to *you* in advance. Thus.

In the last act I've an argument on between Lilith and the

"hero." My fellow Americans will think that the hero has the better of the dispute: I'd like to say that I tried to make it a stand-off, though my negligible sympathies are with Lilith, for whom I didn't say a tithe that might be said. Reason: I'm saving it up for further and final blasphemies.

I must go down to Taits' now. Probably you, as an Easterner, have never heard of that restaurant. But I've just obtained for a young Hawaiian nymph an excellent position in the cabaret as Lulaiste, and want to watch her premiere. If she performs as well in costume as she does in puris, it should make a hit. Besides, she is slim, creamy and twenty.

Had dinner with the "Duncan dancers" last night. Lovely children, but too much risk. Still, one of them was actually familiar with my very unfamiliar Works!

Yours ever,

George Sterling.

[64] [HLM to GS] [TLS, HUN]

December 6th [1919]

Dear Sterling:—

I shall fall upon "Lilith" with the greatest joy. When is the book due? Everything seems to be tied up by the printers' strike. Don't forget to add an elegant inscription. I am trying to make a fat auction sale of my books for my heirs and assigns.

You are quite right about "Beyond Life". A good part of it, to me at least, is heavy going. But don't miss "Jurgen"! It is, in the main, magnificent stuff—the very best that Cabell ever did. Why the Comstocks have let it go I can't imagine. The first half is full of frigging, some of it very agreeable.[54] I am trying to get it done into French and German.

The rigors of Prohibition are ghastly in New York, but I manage to get my share. Night before last I had a capital dinner for $1.25, with an excellent bottle of Capri Tiberius for $1.25 more. A cocktail, of course, is unobtainable, that is, in a public kaif. At L'Aiglon they serve them, but they are made of synthetic gin and cost $1.50. However, Nathan and I have a bar of our own. The other day we invited in John Williams and a couple of others, and surprised them by spreading a table in the office, with dill pickles, pretzels—and very juicy absinthe cocktails. Time: 4.30 P.M. The guests kicked out at 6. Here in Baltimore the bowl flows. I am next to an unlimited supply of ale made *a cappella*—in the manner of the medieval monks. An excellent drink, running to about 6%. Very fair wine is still on sale at $2.50 a gallon. I have a great deal in stock.

Why don't you print some selections from the Bierce letters? Holliday, of the Bookman, would probably fall upon them.[55] Shall I sound him? I'd like very much to read them. I knew the old boy only very slightly, and have no more than a dozen or so letters from him.

Hugh Walpole[56] is lecturing in these parts, and telling the grovelling Anglomaniacs (greatly to their astonishment) that I am a meritorious fellow. He will visit the Coast after January 1st. I trust you to warn him off the wood alcohol, and to introduce him in society.

Yours in Xt.,
Mencken

[65] [HLM to GS] [TLS, BAN]

December 17th [1919]

Dear Sterling:—
Lilith comes just as I am leaving for New York. I'll get acquainted with her on the train. My best thanks. I look for an uplifting and inspiring visit.

The birth of the late Redeemer will be celebrated here in a superb manner. We have a whole cask of grape.

Yours in Xt.,
Mencken

[66] [HLM to GS] [TLS, HUN]

December 26th [1919]

Dear Sterling:—
I have just finished "Lilith"—a very excellent piece of work. Some of the blank verse is gorgeous, particularly Lil's speech of temptation on page 67. And I like the lyrics very much. What happened to the arrangement with Macmillan? The Robertson book is a fearful piece of printing, but in six months it will be selling for $10 as a bibelot. I have a feeling that all of us, within a few years, will be printing privately. The new sedition act, if it passes, will make publishers afraid of my own books. George Moore is a sagacious fellow, probably Jewish.[57] By print-

ing privately he gets extraordinary notices—and more money. Lately I wrote a play with Nathan—"Heliogabalus", a piece of low comedy at the expense of Christianity. Knopf is printing it in a limited edition that is practically private: it will be sold out a week after publication. I'll send you a copy.[58]

That the boys should all fall for Lilith does not surprise me. I picture her as a slim, dark and irresistible wench, full of dark talents. It would be a great pleasure to meet her, though probably somewhat exhausting.

I emerge from Christmas with a dry laryngitis, probably caused by wood alcohol. But the grand fiesta is reserved for Sunday.

Yours in Xt.,
Mencken

[67] [GS to HLM] [ALS, NYPL]

Dec. 31st, 1919.

My dear Mencken:

I'm damned glad that you liked "Lilith!" After sending it to you, I was a bit disturbed, fearing I'd led you to expect too much of the book. And here's one apology (to you only): I could have had Lilith put up a much better argument for her side; but as I'd said for Tancred all (and a bit more) than can be handed the optimist, I had to curb her somewhat, to make the matter more of a contest—a closer artistic balance, in short.

The book is indeed a vile piece of work, and serves me right for having it done inexpensively. Macmillan turned the book down, fearing it wouldn't pay (but it *would* have!). Boni and Liveright wanted it; but I didn't like the part of their contract in regard to foreign rights. And Robertson wanted to publish it; but I can't get statements from him! So I financed it myself, using his name.[59] I gave away 150 books, and the rest were sold in a week, as I expected. Perhaps I'll have a second (and decent) edition in a few weeks. I don't really care: it's off my mind now, and I'm not fame-hungry, though I *do* crave the good opinion of you and a few others. I've just sent "Lilith" to Cabell, by the way, though God knows what an Episcopalian will think of it. He actually professes himself that, in "Who's Who." Well, I used to admit being a Socialist in the same publication, so I've nothing on him.

I've just read the December "Smart Set" from cover to cover, as usual, and was glad to find another story by Thyra Samter. I like L. M. Hussy's stuff too. He's the real thing.[60]

I've been on the wagon since Christmas, getting ready for to-

night. I've taken the whole Bologna restaurant, our only Bohemian (?) one, and allotted the tables to my own friends! Of course
it's a Dutch treat. I purpose to drink only port—don't vomit, now:
it's imported, and has been forty years in wood. I'll have a headache tomorrow afternoon; but of course it's worth it. A lot of the
girls there will be old sweethearts of mine. I shall feel rather Me-
phistophelian.

It will be good to make Walpole's acquaintance. I think I can
give him a good time. The chances are, though, that the University crowd will grab and monopolize him: they always do that to
respectable celebrities when they can, and did so even with the
fiery Rupert Brooke.[61] Well, they'll at least leave Dreiser alone. I
wonder when he's to appear. I've begun to save hooch for him.

Be sure to send me "Heliogabalus." It sounds horribly promising.

I'll get around to Bierce's letters before long. Guess I'll have
them copied, so you may glance at some of them.

Here's Hell to the Prohibitionists and a Happy New Year to
you!

Geo. Sterling.

1920

[68] [HLM to GS] [TLS, HUN]

January 19th [1920]

Dear Sterling:—

Have you heard that the Comstocks in New York have raided "Jurgen"? They announce that it is a fearful work, certain to corrupt the plain people. I heard some time ago that the Society was again in funds, and eager to get back into action. This is first blood. I haven't heard from Cabell. It is, of course, not his funeral. McBride, the publisher, will have to fight.

I was ill with bronchitis over the holidays, and thus had a poor time of it. The annual Christmas dinner of our old dinner club (in continuous existence for ten years) was very tame. Only two members got tight enough to need help. One grew very mellow, wept because of the wrongs he has done his gal, and swore that he would marry her if he hadn't promised his first wife to be faithful. An affecting scene.

When Walpole comes in rescue him in God's name. He is getting a fearful overdose of pawing by society amateurs. Give him my best regards, and tell him I am holding 400 bottles for him.

Yours in Xt.,
Mencken

[69] [GS to HLM] [ALS, NYPL]

Jan. 26th, 1920.

Dear Mencken:

This is probably the last letter you'll care to receive from me when you learn the awful news: I've been made a member of the Institute of Arts and Letters!

Old R. U. Johnson[1] asked me, two years ago, if he could propose my name, and I replied that I was too tough a citizen for his crowd. I meant it, too, but he thought, evidently, I was joshing. Now, without warning, he and the Rev. Van Dyke[2] jam me through, the news comes out on the front page of the newspapers here, and I'm afraid to look sinners in the face. Well, I've written to Johnson and given him an inkling of what he has done.

I will take care of Walpole when he arrives, provided none of the University gang grabs him first. They always try that on celebrities, and often succeed. But I fooled them with Masefield, and am laying for Dreiser. Walpole may have all the hooch and motoring he wants, and a girl too if he be so inclined; not an easy subject to broach to a Briton.

That's too bad about "Jurgen." As soon as I had read the book I began to wonder at its immunity. Anyhow, it will be a good advertisement for Cabell. Probably he doesn't want that kind, though.

I sent him "Lilith," and to my great pleasure got a very kind letter in response. I suppose it'll be all right if I quote a little from it.

"It was very fine and unexpected and generally delightful to have you remember me with an inscribed Lilith. It is a beautiful and noble poem, upon which I make you my very sincerest compliments. All other merits apart, the irony of that final scene is the sort of thing that rouses despairing envy."

Damned generous of him, I'll say! It's a letter like that that somewhat compensates for the general futility of verse-making. Thank God I get my fun in other ways! Also, that I know a girl with twenty-five cases of King William!

> Yours ever,
>
> George Sterling.

[70] [GS to HLM] [ALS, NYPL]

Jan. 28th, 1920.

Dear Mencken:

I've just realized that I've not only forgotten to thank you for "Heliogabalus," but to tell you how thoroughly I enjoyed it. The adjective in its advt. in "Smart Set" characterizes it well for me—"uproarious." It would be almost boyish, were it not for its general sophistication and multiplicity of delicate situations. And it is likely to keep you from joining me in the Institute.

I'm almost of a mind to write a letter to Reedy on the book—a letter purporting to come from the professor of Latin over in the University of California—complimenting you on this rehabilitation of the character of Heliogabalus, heretofore ranked as the worst of perverts! Behold him now as not even a Sodomite, but as a much harassed Mormon! It might fool the Middle West.

Enemies of Nathan and you must have sighed with joy when they saw your pictures on the cover of the current "Smart Set." *You* look too like Ad. Wolgast to be unprepossessing; but N. looks like the former race-track tout in the old days of the Oakland track. I had an interest in a book then (it lost money) and was accustomed to the type.

Sometimes I wonder just how seriously you take "Smart Set." Whatever do you think of it, to me it's the only readable magazine in America. Somehow you manage to print a lot of good stuff, considering the Comstockian censorship. This "Last Love" by Cavendish—I call it a good story. And "The Hope Chest" and "Benediction" are good, too. I've not yet got around to the Hussy novelette.[3] It will not be a bright day for me when you and N. sell "Smart Set."

I ought to be downstairs in a poker-game, so here's good luck to us both! This is a letter requiring no reply. As it is, I blush to recall my drain on your time.

> Yours ever,
>
> George Sterling.

[71] [GS to HLM] [ALS, NYPL]

Jan. 31st, 1920.

Dear Mencken:

Please don't groan: this is only a business letter.

Woke up this morning with a headache, from too much port; so naturally I emitted the enclosed poem, which says a great deal in nine lines, and says it not badly.[4]

Dr. Nathan is authorized to crowd $5. on me for it; though it's worth six.

I'm laying for Walp. He arrives on Monday, I think.

And now in the Name, etc.

> Sincerely,
>
> George Sterling.

[72] [HLM to GS] [TLS, HUN]

February 2nd [1920]

Dear Sterling:—

I take it that you have accepted, and so put on the black cap and pronounce a curse upon you in due form of law.

May you come down with lumbago, hemmorrhoids, measles and the bloody flux. May your best gal deceive you with an actor. May you get a Christmas card from Henry van Dyke. May you be invited to lecture at Tufts and Dartmouth. May you fall on the ice and crack your godless arse. May you die for democracy, and lie in the potter's field. Ten thousand damns and a million hells. Et tu, Rudolph? God help the Republic!

I am warning Walpole to shoot you at sight, and Dreiser to have you poisoned. O mon Doo, mon Doo!

Yours,
Mencken

[73] [HLM to GS] [TLS, HUN]

February 3rd [1920]

Dear Sterling:—

Your scheme for a letter from Prof. Balderdash, of the Latin Department, is excellent, but I doubt that Reedy will print it. His paper is the favorite stamping ground of my onemies. Reedy himself I don't know.

The Smart Set pictures were prepared by Knopf. When the proof came to us we yelled, but finally decided to let it pass. He sold out the whole edition of Heliogabalus a week before the date of publication, including even 50 signed copies for the boobery at $10 a piece. We have since sold the German and Hungarian rights. We have received two offers for the American rights, but have refused them on the ground that the country is uncivilized.

The day you are installed as a member of the Institute, along with Robert W. Chambers and Chimmie Fadden Townsend,[5] I shall solemnly burn "Lilith" and begin writing an article against you. Such blows shake up all the vital parts. Next even Dreiser will be succumbing.

Yours in Xt.,
Mencken

over

The Smart Set is a pleasant recreation. It barely pays for itself. Both Nathan and I have to live by other devices. The chief fun consists in giving promising youngsters a chance. We dig up a good many of them and exhibit them to the nobility and gentry. Then they are offered 5 cents a word by Lorimer, or Hearst,[6] or McCall's Magazine—and go away denouncing us for not paying them 10 cents. It is hard to keep out the Greenwich Village frauds—vers libre, etc. Now and then one of them sneaks in. I read probably 99% of all the stuff produced in the Village. In five years I haven't seen two printable short stories. In poetry, as you may note, we run to sweet stuff—simple lyrics mainly. This is what sells the magazine—this and an occasional hack novelette full of boudoir adultery. We printed a chapter of Cabell's Jurgen.[7] The boobs failed to rise to it. We printed Dunsany for nearly two years before any other American magazine noticed him. Then he was embraced, not as a writer, but as a noble lord and guardsman.[8]

Holt is to be tried on the Jurgen charge this week.

[74] [HLM to GS] [TLS, HUN]

February 6th [1920]

Dear Sterling:—

This sort of thing is absolutely forbidden by the *Polizei*. Imagine it: they yearn, they go up the hill, they lie in the grass, they come down tired. We'd be barred off the stands in Illinois, Ohio, Arkansas, the Gulf States and all of New England. The National Institute of Arts and Letters would issue a bull against us.

Can't you get it to do something for Cabell? Here is a good test. Will it permit a serious artist to be harassed and jailed by a gang of Methodist swine? The Authors' League is hopeless. It confines itself to safeguarding moving-picture rights. The job is for the Institute. The French Institute, in the same situation, would make the welkin ring.

Give Walpole my best regards. He, too, might be able to help Cabell. Tell him to give out a couple of hot interviews.

Yours in Xt.,
Mencken

[75] [GS to HLM] [ALS, NYPL]

Feb. 7th, 1920.

My dear Mencken:

Your anathema maranatha is with me this warm sunny morning, and would dim the daylight had I not already informed the secretary of the Institute that, having found on its roster "the names of Bob Chambers, Ned Townsend and Phelps of Yale," I felt obliged to decline membership in the organization. It seems to me that the drinks are on you, so if there's a soft spot in your cellar that may lend itself to interment, you are qualified to bury there two bottles of whatever among your beverages contains the largest percentage of alcohol. We may not be able to consume them this year, but you'll know that their quality is always improving.

Walpole is a good chap, but, so far as I can see, a very temperate drinker. Three drinks is the most I've been able to get him to enfold at a time, so far. He motored to Carmel yesterday, with my friend Dick Tobin, and will be there till Monday. I was to have gone too, but my mother is ill, suddenly. I've instructed Tobin to show him Harry Leon Wilson, James Hopper and Point Lobos. They should suffice.

I had a letter from Cabell to-day, requesting me to write a letter to M'Bride's man in defense of "Jurgen." Of course I shall do so, and also see that Hopper does the same. And there are others.

I now have Dreiser's Los Angeles address, and am about to address him. I hear he has been presented with a demijohn of gin by the local Epworth League, and has begun a new novel. He sends word to us in the north that he'll visit us. This is, no doubt, a warning for us to collect stocks of gin. Imagine Dreiser, of all men, in Los Angeles! And yet W. Wright lives and thrives there.

I hear the weather's cold in the east. Never mind: it'll be warm enough next summer.

My blasphemous regards!

George Sterling.

[76] [HLM to GS] [TLS, HUN]

February 12th [1920]

Dear Sterling:—

Not only are the drinks on me: I also flop to my knees and bawl my thanks to the Lord God Jehovah, Maker of Heaven and Earth! You are the first man, so far as I know, ever to decline that intolerable honor. May you be the first of a long procession. I think Dreiser is properly primed. If they ever offer him the purple ribbon, he will have at them with a blast running to 30,000 words. Cabell, too.

Cabell's publisher, Guy Holt, was here last night. He turns out to be a very young fellow, and apparently not very cunning. I told him what I knew about the inner workings of Comstockery. He says that his boss, McBride, is a moralist. The net result, I daresay, will be that McBride will make an arrangement with Sumner a la J. Jefferson Jones, [9] and so ditch Cabell. But the episode, in the long run, will do Cabell a lot of good.

More of this anon. I have written a letter to Holt and put others at work. The Vir Publishing Company was founded by my old pastor, the Rev. Sylvanus Stall. He is mentioned in "Prejudices", in the chapter on sex hygiene. A slick fellow, now gone to glory.[10]

I surely hope your mother is better. My sister-in-law is here, undergoing surgery, and her small daughter, aged 4½, is in the house, raising hell. This afternoon a very flashy looking woman came in, trying to sell me some mss. The kid wandered in, observed the visitor speechlessly, and has been imitating her flirtings of the skirt ever since. They begin early.

Yours in Xt.,
Mencken

[77] [GS to HLM] [ALS, NYPL]

Mch. 9th, 1920.

Dear Mencken:

Holy Ghost! Come on out! I've not much booze left, but shall begin adding to it at once, and by the time you're here there should be enough to last through the convention. I wish it were to be in July: our Bohemian Jinks are from the 10th to the 26th of that month.

Do you want me to see about a room for you? Command me in any way.

I got an indignant letter from old R. U. Johnson, in regard to my refusal to belong to his "Institute." He accuses me of using "unwarrantable language" in my letter to the Institute, and says the whole affair is one of the most painful and shocking in his literary career. I've replied with a letter telling what I think of the Institute.[11] Wait till he gets it! By the way, did you ever see a list of the "department of literature" of the Institute? I'll lend you mine if you care to see it. A gang of respectable mediocrities, including Chambers, E. W. Townsend, Will Payne, Henry S. Harrison, Lefevre, Chalfield-Taylor, J. B. Connolly, Chester B. Fernald, Ham. Garland, Wm Gilette, Clayton Hamilton, Oliver Herford, Brian Hooker, Owen Johnson, Geo. Kennan, Ernest Poole, Augustine Thomas and Jesse Lynch Williams! Dozens of others I've never even heard of. I told R. U. that *I* was the insulted one, and that his Institute was a joke. I hope they'll not demand their button back: I put it on the club cat and the outraged animal has lost it.

I wrote to Dreiser at Los Angeles, and had a reply, but he won't *promise* to come up here. Someone told me the old hippo had been presented with a demijohn of gin, and had started on a new novel.

It was something of a shock to have you turn down "The Iris-Hills." I'll bet I can sell that poem to a "respectable" magazine! I'll begin with the Ladies' Home Journal, I think.

Here's another, though, that I'm sure you'll like. You've printed as long; and it'll all go on one page.[12]

Can I get an "American Language" without paying more than $5. for it? I've a notion that I can't.

Yours ever,

George Sterling.

[78] [HLM to GS] [TLS, HUN]

March 15th [1920]

Dear Sterling:—

I have a copy of the Institute stud-book—a fearful and wonderful list. I have a mind to reprint the whole damned thing in Prejudices II. Why the fact of your refusal to join has not been published I don't know. I have told it (in the strictest confidence) to various babblers. The whole episode is rich and stimulating. At one stroke you have accomplished something permanently valuable. Old Johnson is an ass.

The poem you send tickles me vastly. I shove it to Nathan at once. I wish I could send you a copy of The American Language, but it is impossible. I have only two copies, one in sheets, and I need them for the revised edition.[13] Knopf is cleaned out utterly. The book is selling for $10. But there is always a chance that I may get hold of a copy through my Baltimore book-dealer. If so, you get it.

A letter from Dreiser says that he will be in San Francisco in June. I am warning him against the hotels. My quarters are already engaged by the Baltimore Sun. I shall travel, in fact, like a high-class kept woman—no bills to pay and no worries. If Dreiser has any gin, try to get it away from him. He is a tea-drinker. I once wasted a fine absinthe cocktail on him. He thought it was Rhine wine. I shall bring some jugs with me, but they'll probably be empty by the time I pull in. If you can reserve a flagon or two of California grape I'll be in your debt forever.

What is the news I get from Jennings of your mother's death and your own illness?[14] Is he crazy? You say nothing of these things, and your letter was mailed two or three days after his. I hope he lies.

Sincerely yours,

Mencken

[79] [GS to HLM] [ALS, NYPL]

Mch. 23, 1920.

Dear Mencken:

It *is* rather odd that I've had no free advertising in re the Institute. Perhaps they're hushing it up. I have had from Johnson no reply to my pretty harsh letter to him. Dignified silence will be his pose, I imagine—and I'm a barbarian and ingrate.

I hope Dreiser will be in S.F. while you are. You may be sure his gin is gone by this time. I'll have some for *you*, however, and all the white and red wine you want. Mostly Californian; but they're not so bad when you get them *here*.

Yes—my mother died last month, while I was in the hospital. I don't share *all* my troubles with my friends! Shall tell you about my own illness, though, when I see you. Well now.

I'm glad your quarters here are arranged for. I could probably have got you a room here in the club, but a hotel is preferable. I hear it's rather risky to have hooch on the train with one. So be careful.

I've finished the first draft of my dramatic poem, "Rosamund." It's a fatal affair to almost all involved; so you'll note that Shakespeare's influence still survives.

Jennings is a gushing young thing.

Yours ever,

George Sterling.

I introduced Maeterlinck,[15] but don't fall for his soul stuff.

[80] [HLM to GS] [TLS, HUN]
[The Smart Set
25 WEST 45th STREET
NEW YORK]

March 31, 1920

George Sterling, Esq.,
The Bohemian Club,
San Francisco, Calif.

Dear Sterling:

I hope Maeterlinck did not pull his encomium on Dr. Frank Crane.[16] Here in New York he had the literati all agog. Everyone thought he would speak up for Hamlin Garland and Dr.

Henry Van Dyke; instead, he let it be known that Dr. Crane was his favorite author. Crane now wears a plug hat and praises God.

The fact that news of your outrageous act has not come out indicates that it is too painful to be passed on. I have babbled it in all directions but so far no public print has printed the least reference to it. If this conspiracy of silence continues, I shall probably have the fact emblazoned on a sandwich and carry it up and down Broadway. Nathan has lately declined membership to the Elks, the Lambs' Club and Society of Arts and Letters of which Guido Bruno[17] is President. Thus, you have society in hell.

If anything interferes with my trip to San Francisco, I shall certainly take to drink.

If your operation was too indecent to be described in English, let me have news of it in French, with illustrations in full color.

Sincerely yours,
Mencken

[81] [GS to HLM] [ALS, NYPL]

Apr. 15th, 1920.

My dear Mencken:

I dare say Maeterlinck is "variously impossible" (as Bierce used to say) when it comes to trying to think; but I wish I'd written his "Pelleas and Mélisande," by Heck![18] The last one to cop a little Frisco coin was Yeats.[19] I had luncheon with him and thoroly enjoyed his gossip about his English (and Irish) contemporaries, especially Masefield, whom he has it in for, apparently. But Masefield is a bigger poet than Yeats.

I think that the reason my "Institute" scandal is still sub rosa is because poets are considered unimportant folk, as indeed most of us are. If Rex Beach had done such a thing it would have lacked no publicity.[20] You may refer to it in "S.S." some time, for all I care. Here's a clipping on the subject, from a local newspaper.

Don't worry about lack of the grape while you're here. Our dry wines are sadly inferior to the French, but I really like them, as I do anything with alcohol in it. Hold on! I've not tried perfumery yet! I was actually offered a drink of it last night—good quality, for the small bottle of it cost $27.! But there were rum cocktails in sight, and I stuck to them.

Our Jinks begins on July 10th, with the beautiful and interesting ceremony of the Cremation of Care. Can't you remain here long enough to be present at the grove that night, if indeed you can't stay for the play on the 26th? The grove won't be dry.

I've finished my dramatic poem, "Rosamund." It contains one rape and four murders—quite Shakespearean. I think I'll have 300 printed, as with "Lilith." Am going to show it to Margaret Anglin soon, though I'm almost certain she won't fall for it.[21]

"The House of Many Bottles" is a good yarn, and attracted more or less attention locally, it being a Californian tale. I've not met the author, but should like to.[22]

Yours ever,

George Sterling.

[82] [HLM to GS] [TLS, HUN]

April 23rd [1920]

Dear Sterling:—

The Jinks, alas, seem impossible. I'll be back in New York by that time, being jinked by the paper men. Newsprint sold for 15 cents yesterday. Man and boy, I remember when it was 2.80. Nathan and I trailed a paper man to Atlantic City, took along our own ammunition, got him loaded, and still got nothing out of him save his watch and a few cigars.

Don't tell me about California wine. No matter what frauds may say, I insist that it is very good, and hope, by God's mercy, to get down a few seidels of it in June. Here we run to ales. The local ale poteen is capital—rich, creamy, and running to about 8%. We are getting it in 5-gallon kegs—enough for a party of pall-bearers.

Your contumacy to the Institute is too horrible to be noted by the Eastern press. I have given out the news at least 35 times. But though prostitute journalism is silent, everybody knows it, and all the gabble is in your praise. I think you made a killing.

I have just got news that a high school professor in Detroit has been canned for reading from my Book of Burlesques[23] to his virgin pupils. I don't blame the school-board.

In Xt.,

Mencken

[83] [GS to HLM] [ALS, NYPL]

Apr. 29th, 1920.

My dear Mencken:

No—our Californian claret isn't so good as the imported: it hasn't that velvety taste. But as you say, it's not bad. I'm putting by booze for you steadily, and now have port, sherry,

86

burgundy and sauterne. Also Jack Newbegin, our leading book-seller, says you may have (with him) any kind of booze you want, including even absinthe. I know another person who guarantees plenty of gin, claret and sauterne. The great drawback is that we can't drink it openly in the more expensive restaurants, but only in one "Bohemian" joint that I fear you may not care for. I like to do my boozing in a crowd, as a rule.

Do you care for bourbon? Of course that's really the easiest stuff to get. I suppose I'm impossible, for I like *anything* with al-cohol in it! My preference is wine, though. Rhine wine is the best stuff I ever tasted. London could afford to buy it freely, and we used to drink quarts of it at a sitting.

Here are some josh verses, of course unprintable. Do not bother to return them.

> Yours ever,
>
> George Sterling.

[84] [HLM to GS] [TLS, BAN]

May 4th [1920]

Dear Sterling:—

The murder of poor Louis is really far too cruel. He has his place, and I think he fills it very well. But the piece has a seductive eloquence—a very fine job, indeed. What a sensa-tion you could make with a book of such onslaughts. And how much it is needed!

The booze news fills me with the most agreeable sentiments. I am, like you, ombibulous; I drink anything alcoholic. Beer is my favorite for late in the evening, simply because one can hold more of it than anything else. But I delight in all wines wherever grown. Down here the ale is flowing like Niagara. I know at least ten men who have learned how to make it. One of them has just made six kegs. I have a large supply myself, and am adding to it at the rate of a keg a week. I have had to enlarge my wine-room. It is now solid concrete, and bears this sign:

> This vault is protected by electrical switches releasing chlorine gas under 100 pounds pressure. Enter it at your own risk.

I'd give $7 to see Margaret as Joan. What does she weigh?

> Yours in Xt.,
>
> Mencken

[85] [GS to HLM] [ALS, NYPL]

May 13th, 1920.

Dear Mencken:

The editor of the revered "Bookman"[24] is in town, and told my equally revered publisher that Reedy is to be here for the convention. Do you know if that's so? And do you like him? If you don't, I sha'n't go out of my way to have him with us.

My ex-bestgirl has designs on you, and is saving hooch against your advent! She cares only for the famous, and is a big-hearted, handsome creature, but, I fear, a bit too tall for you. Let me know if you prefer a pony—sans hooch. "Our aim is to please."

Since you call my skit on Louis "murder," I'll not try to print it. Having been brought up by Bierce, I thought it mild enough. And the little wart-hog is always hopping on *some* unfortunate.

Dreiser lent his "Lilith" to a movie-actor, and, naturally, finds he's out of a book. He roars so, that I'll have to give my last copy to him. Complimentary but depressing. Just got it back from a fair young thing who offered to trade even (act for act), but I'm over-dated, and prefer for a time to keep the book.

It fills me with awe to think I'm to see Bryan.[25]

Yours,
The Pandar.
(According to "Town Topics.")[26]

[86] [HLM to GS] [TLS, HUN]

May 19th [1920]

Dear Sterling:—

"Mirage" is very beautiful stuff—a debauch of music.[27] It is somewhat long for us, but I am sorely tempted. Just when is your book to be published? Our August number is closing, but September is still open.

The Sun now tries to hedge on the San Francisco trip. It appears that there are not enough wires over the Rockies to carry half the stuff that will be sent out. But the chances are still 10 to 1 that I'll come.

I have no prejudices regarding height, bulk or complexion. All I ask for is a refined and humane manner. I like a gal who is polite. My experience is that little girls are more loving, but that big ones wear better. I am somewhat heavy, and it takes muscle to get me into bed when I am in liquor.

Dreiser is full of his usual mysteriousness. His address to me

remains a postoffice box. I suppose he is in the toils of some fat
movie vampire.

Yours in Xt.,

Mencken

[87] [GS to HLM] [ALS, NYPL]

May 26th, 1920.

Dear Mencken:

If the "Sun" falls down on you I'll have their
plant dynamited!

As to "Mirage," I'm unlikely to have it in a book before Sept.
1st, so go ahead if you care to. I wonder what "the average reader"
will make of such moonshine. But some of your readers can't be
that.

I've been much interested in de Casseres' "The Last Satire of
a Famous Titan."[28] Tell him for me, when next you see him, that
Bierce's hair was white, not gray. His eyebrows, which jutted out
an inch, were white too, his mustache was a sort of yellowish
white, and his face an even pink all over. He was an astonishing
and handsome sight, to me. Oh—and his eyes were blue and very
piercing, without any "malicious sparkle."

And he wrote a damned sight better story than you think he
did.

I'm enclosing for you a Beautiful Poem. As to the other clipping
(from Brisbane),[29] wouldn't that last paragraph be the funniest
thing ever written if only the old devil really meant it. But plenty
of Methodists will mean it.

You don't let me know whether you're friendly with Reedy or
not, nor whether or not you know of his likelihood to be at the
convention. I'd not mind knowing.

Thanks for your kindly comment on my "Lilith" in this
"S.S."[30] And I must get Scheffauer's poem.[31] He and I used to be
"pupils" of Bierce, before Bierce quarreled with him.

Your elder brother in God,

George Sterling

P S

Do you know Holliday, of "The Bookman?" I met him a day or
two ago, and he was to have had luncheon with me here to-day.
Well, he showed up so helplessly soused that there was nothing
for me to do but get into a taxi with him, take him back to his

hotel, and lay him on his bed. He was still peacefully slumbering there at six P.M.

G. S.

[88] [GS to HLM] [ALS, NYPL]

June 11th, 1920.

Dear Brother in Christ:

You have time, before leaving, to drop me a line telling me what hotel you're to go to. Also, if you care to wire me, the day before you arrive, and let me know what train you're on, I'll await you with a motor and a flagon. You'll be able to pick me out of the crowd by my aristocratic nose and the superior fruitiness of my breath.

We're having marvellous weather, cool but sunny, and all San Francisco is saying, one way or another: "O Hell! Wait till the convention begins; every day foggy, with a forty knot gale!" A climate is like a baby: it will never show off.

Your girl waits you with impatient hips.

In His name,

Sterling.

Corks are trembling in their sockets, too.

[89] [HLM to GS] [TLS, HUN]

Sunday [July 11, 1920]

Dear George:—

I wired to Jane[32] this morning, vowing my affection and reporting my arrival. She was instructed to call you up and report the latter. It turns out that the thing that seized me was acute bronchitis. The infection spread from my air pipes to my victual chutes. Results: a stomach so sensitive that nothing would stay in it, and great agony in the guts. Since leaving Oakland Wednesday morning I have lived on three eggs and three plates of ice-cream. But my doctor tells me he will have me on my legs by tomorrow, and fit for New York and my domestic responsibilities by Wednesday. He is a good doctor, and a bitter critic of God. It was capital luck that Owens[33] was with me. He looked after me very decently. Without him, marooned in a berth, I'd have been fit for the embalmer by the time we got to Ogden. The trip was cool and otherwise uneventful. I reached Baltimore in four days, less 42 minutes—extraordinary speed. I have no doubt that that damned all-night session set me off. I had a slight rawness in the throat when it began; by the time it was over I was full of chills. A good night's rest would have headed off the whole thing. Well, we must all suffer that democracy may survive. However, I have now done my share. If they call on me again, I shall begin negotiations with the Japs at once.

I could pump up eloquence on the theme of your welcome to a poor wayfarer, but refrain. I shall not forget it. Low heathen that you are, you yet obey the Rule of St. Benedict:[34] to treat the guest on the theory that he may be the immortal J.C. Himself in disguise. And if not J.C., then at least John the Baptist, or Noah, or Gog and Magog, or Pontius Pilate. Such a man you are! I can think of but one appropriate counterblast, and that is to shove you headlong into a drunkard's grave the instant you get to New York. Or, better still, Baltimore. Here is every drink known to Christendom. Can I tempt you with a beer evening—one keg to every man? Absinthe cocktails to begin, then red and white vins—and then the slow, triumphant struggle with the malt, gurgle, gurgle, gurgle!

I am sending you Helio for La Millier,[35] with Pistols for yourself. Also, a few extra copies of the latter for such cognoscenti as you may favor. I'd like to send a souvenir to Mrs. Travis.[36] What is her name? And her address? And what book should I send. I'll send you the bibliography anon. And a list of your own books that I lack.

I found a washbasket full of mail, about 1/8 of 1% interesting.

In Xt.,
Mencken

[90] [HLM to GS] [TLS, HUN]

July 14th [1920]

Dear George:—

I find that I have the following books of yours:

> Lilith
> A Wine of Wizardry
> The Testimony of the Suns
> Beyond the Breakers

Further, nothing. It goes without saying that I'll be glad to have any missing ones that you have in hand. But if your stock is low don't send them. There is a book dealer here who can get them for me, given time enough. He already owes me money.

I am slowly recovering health and spirits. It appears that the four days on the train, sweating and badly fed, were to blame. When I left Oakland I had only a slight cold. By the time I got to Chicago I was down with bronchitis and gastritis, unable to eat and feeling like hell. I am now able to get about, and shall go to New York this afternoon.

As soon as the list of my books is ready I'll send you a copy, and any volumes that you may lack. The bibliography looks formidable. It was made so for trade purposes.

On returning, I found that a love affair here had got into a volcanic stage, with accusations of gross immorality in the west. I nominate you as a witness that my conduct was chemically pure—that, in fact, I never so much as spoke to a woman. It is astounding how suspicious women are.

The weather here is positively infernal. I sit in my work-room in my undershirt, with an electric fan playing on me, and yet sweat like a June bride. The train trip to New York this afternoon will be a lulu.

I sent you the Helio for La Millier yesterday, along with some copies of Pistols for Two, and one of an old book, Men vs. the Man.[37]

Yours,
Mencken

[91] [HLM to GS] [TLS, HUN]

July 18th [1920]

Dear George:—

I am delighted to be able to inform you that after two all night sessions you have been unanimously elected a Knight of the Imperial and Royal Order of the Holy Ghost of Spain, first class. It was a hard struggle. Nathan held out on theological and patriotic grounds, alleging that you were a freethinker and in communication with the Japs. In the end it turned out that he was amenable to alcohol, and I flushed out his objections with 8% ale. He is sick today, but says he is glad to welcome you.

The ribbon is worn in the left lapel, like the red ribbon of the Legion of Honor. The one obligation lying upon every knight is to lie every time he is asked what the ribbon stands for. I enclose 5 cents worth. The members are:

1. G. J. Nathan, of Fort Wayne, Ind.
2. Baron von Mencken.
3. R. J. Leupold, Argentine consul in Baltimore.
4. E. A. Boyd, of Dublin, Ireland.[38]
5. George Sterling, of Bigin's, Calif.
                    Praise God!

[92] [GS to HLM] [TN, NYPL]

                              1920 JUL 20 AM 7 08
          MS SANFRANCISCO CALIF 19
H I MENCHEN [*sic*]
          1524 HOLLINS ST BALTIMORE MD
HAPPY BE ALL YOU REMEMBER SAD BE ALL YOU FOR-
GET I AM YOURS TO THE END OF THE TRAIL AND MAY IT
BE LONG AND WET IN MY COOL GREY CITY OF LOVE[39] BY
THE RIM OF THE WESTERN SEA I PRAY TO HIM WHO
SQUATTETH ABOVE THAT HE PANDER TO YOU AND ME
GO TO PHILADELPHIA I DID NOTHING FOR YOU IN THE
WAY OF HOSPITALITY I HAD LARGE DREAMS BUT THAT
ACCURSED CHENEY CHILD[40] DUMPED ME SO I SAY THAT
I DID NOTHING AND DESPITE THE ADDITIONAL COST I
REPEAT ASSEVERATE DECLARE AFFIRM AND CLAIM
THAT I DID NOTHING BUT IF YOULL COME OUT IN SEP-
TEMBER ILL SHOW YOU A REAL TIME HEN I LOVE YOU
                    STERLING.

[93] [HLM to GS] [TLS, HUN]

                              July 20th [1920]
Dear George:—
          I assume from your eloquent telegram that you
are stewed again, and hence happy, and full of the spirit of God.
The Cheney intrigues me. If you don't look out, I'll hop a train
and come out to view her. Will you please tell her that I crave a
glimpse of her?
     I am now firmly on my legs again, and cleaning up all my de-
layed work. Nathan, the scoundrel, left me at least a ton of Ms. to
read. All the while I was away he devoted himself to pleasure. His
flat is full of hairpins, garters and stray drawers. When I saw my
desk I dam nigh fainted: it was stacked mountain high.
     I have gone through the Greenwood stuff very carefully.[41] It is
full of the highest merit. The girl gets a tremendous glow of color

into her verse, and I'd like to print a lot of it. Will you please try to stir her up? All of the stuff she gave me seemed to be incomplete, including even that which was typed. Urge her to finish a half dozen pieces and send them to me direct. She has a wonderful flow of brilliant words. I am returning all her notes to you, not knowing her address.

The Jane episode turns out to be sweet and sentimental. God knows why a man should be an idiot at my age, but I genuinely fell for her, and she was lovely to me those six days, despite our two rows. I send her a love letter every day.

But to business! As soon as I get rid of my editorial work I shall begin "On Democracy", the damndest book ever written. Hitherto I have been polite, and even suave. Now for the meat axe, blood on the moon, and three cheers for Pontius Pilate. Well, we shall see. What if it turns out to be flabby and feeble stuff? I'll go into a monastery!

I gave a beer party Saturday night to celebrate my safe return from heathen lands. The illuminati drank gallons of it, and then washed it down with Barbera and liqueurs. Three of them got so tight that they couldn't remember where they lived. They made a hell of a hole in my absinthe.

God help us all.

Yours,
M

[94] [GS to HLM] [ANS, NYPL]

[Postmarked Montrio, Cal.,
July 23, 1920.]

Dear Hen: I'm that splash in the left forewater.[42] Thanks for your letter! I'll reply soon. Headache this morning.

George Sterling.

[95] [GS to HLM] [TN, NYPL]

CS SANFRANCISCO CALIF AUG 2–20
H L MENCKEN
1524 HOLLINS ST BALTO
COURAGE AND PATIENCE OLD DEAR HAVE FINALLY SO-
BERED UP AND SHALL SOON INFLICT A LETTER ON YOU
THE JINKS NEARLY KILLED ME WE HAD A FIFTY GALLON

KEG OF RED WINE YOU WERE GOOD TO WRITE ME SO
OFTEN AND MAKE ME A HOLY GHOSTER I HOPE TO
PROVE WORTHY

                            STERLING

[96] [HLM to GS] [TLS, HUN]

                                    August 3rd [1920]

Dear George:—
            Your telegram relieves me. My agents had re-
ported that you were down with the palsy at the Grove, and bawling for a priest. I am glad to hear that you are on your legs again.

I wish you would stir up May Greenwood in the matter of her
lyrics. And send me some of your own. Have you done any writing? Give my regards to Prof. Lal when you see him.[43] What is his
address? Also, have you ever heard of a Dr. Bohm in San Francisco? A chirurgeon of that (or some similar) name patched me up
in the hall one night. A youngish fellow, with a small moustache.
If you can locate him, send me his address, and I'll send him a
book. He was very nice.

My Christian Register circular has made a profound sensation
among the anointed of God.[44] Every pious louse in Baltimore has
received a copy. They are much rattled, and begin to hedge on the
doctrine that I am Antichrist.

Nathan has been ill, and I have been working a double shift. He
eats too little and drinks too much. Five beefsteaks would cure
him.

Jane's love begins to grow cold, I fear. Ah, what a sad world!

                            Yours in Xt.,
                                    M

[97] [GS to HLM] [TN, NYPL]
Cs Sanfrancisco Calif 9 aug 1920
    H L Mencken
        1524 Hollins St Baltimore Md
God save us all i am still too drunk to write a real letter Jane is
in Losangeles she wrote me a letter but i wont answer it your letters are all wonderful please forgive me because i can't reply to
them you know i love you old scout Prosit

                            Sterling

[98] [HLM to GS] [TLS, BAN]

August 10th [1920]

Dear George:—

Your telegram has just reached me. I envy you, old top! What could be more charming? Keep your nose to the bung-hole until not a drop is left. I had a fine bout last night with 7% ale—very tasty stuff. Night before last: smuggled brandy and some old lager, four years in the cellar. Saturday night: some German cherry brandy, some brown stout, and some kümmel. My guts are delighted. Since my return I have actually had a champagne evening—excellent Moet & Chandon smuggled ashore from a ship in from Buenos Ayres, where it is cheap. With the American market cut off, the French champagne folk are offering bargains elsewhere. Ah, the life of a great seaport!

Jane, I suspect, has fallen in love with another fellow. Sic transit gloria mundi! She kept me sober for six days, and so served God. Hay fever will hit me in a week. It gets me into very bad humor, and I always quarrel with the gals.

May the Holy Saints keep you!

Yours in Xt.,
M.

[99] [GS to HLM] [ALS, NYPL]

Aug. 18th, 1920.

Dear "Hen:"

This worm o' the earth apologizes, tail in air, for this delay in replying to all your good letters. But Eve and J. Barleycorn were too much with him. The Jinks half killed me. Right after them I migrated to Carmel on the trail of a skirt, wife of an Eastern railway official. I partially avenged the travelling public, but she was a wildcat, and I came out of the fracas with "shingles."

That sounds like a comic ailment, like measles or mumps, but 'tis an hellish affliction, and I'm not well yet, tho' Abrams doses me with his current every day. However, the pain has mostly let up, and ten days on the wagon have done me considerable good. I hate to be ill: it interferes so with joy. I sympathize greatly with you in the hay-fever attack. Don't bother to write until you're yourself again. I wish you were back here: I think Abrams would make short work of the damned thing, as he does of most ailments.

The Jinks were enjoyable, as usual. Not so much drinking at the bar; but the various "camps" were all very wet.

It makes me sad to have you speak or write as if I've done any-thing for you when you were here. On account of your work, your addiction to Jane and the Cheney tragedy, I was able to do little indeed of what I'd been planning. Also I had to give some of my time to my brother-in-law, to whom I'm under obligations for his great kindness to my mother when she was in Honolulu.

I write "tragedy" with intent: the girl was here in the city all the time, wild to get you between sheets. Why she didn't visit "Bigin's" at least one night not even she can explain. When I told her of the lie the switch-board girl at her employers' had passed me, she had a cat-fight with said girl, threw up her job, and found employment elsewhere!

Well, she has a new apartment now, with lots of booze, and I wish that you were here—or that my list were not so full.

Thanks awfully for getting me into the Holy Ghosts! That's a real honor. I know Boyd, whom I used to see at Padraic Colum's[45] during the winter of 1914–15. I'll try to be worthy of your worst traditions.

Jane landed some sort of job with Morosco, in Los Angeles, and is working there now. Before leaving, she took me motoring and brought me about ten bucks worth of food and drink. I think her object in so doing was to tell me how much she loved and admired you, expecting me to pass the news along—which I hereby do, with the needless warning that she's a dear little grafter. But one can't help being fond of her. I always allow her to think that I believe she's practically a demi-vierge.

I'm glad you found something to like in my fledgling books. Wait till I get started, however! I'm now going to write mostly for the Society of the Holy G. I sha'n't reprint any of the war rot, except maybe "The Little Farm."[46] The aftermath of the war has made all the rest absurd. Houghton-Mifflin has been asking me for a book of selected poems, for over a year. I'm shy of the notion, for I'm not eager to be made a fool of by their blurbs, as Cale Rice has *willing*ly been.[47]

La Millier got the book, I'm sure, as I left it at Bigin's for her, and I've seen her there, dancing, several times. I'm fighting shy of her.

If you'll be so kind as to send Mrs. Travis a book, I think your Defense of Women[48] will enrage her as much as any of them.

Mrs. W. E. Travis,
  2615 Larkin St.

As for me, I don't want to raid any stock that actually *sells*. Send me, for the time being, "Damn" and the first "Prejudices." I've had them before, but have given them away. I read the "Men etc." with pleasure. You had it all over the bird, though it's no use to argue with a Socialist. I know, for I was one myself, once, "befo' de wah."

As soon as I feel a bit livelier, I'm going to go over Greenwood's stuff and touch it up. Then she can type it and send it to you herself. Much of it should be available. She's a good kid, and I wish she'd get *me* out of her system.

All I've been told about grappa is, that it's a distillation of grape stems and skins.

I've given Bigin this plan of selling it. They keep only ten gallons, in a tin can out in the kitchen, where the cook can *kick it over* if he hears a whistle; and he'll hear Bigin or a waiter if there *is* a raid. The stuff is served in "small black" cups, and has to be drunk at once. As for me, I can't work up any enthusiasm for the stuff. I wish to God I had some of your ale!

George.

[100] [HLM to GS] [TLS, BAN]

August 21st [1920]

Dear George:—

Are you still stewed? If so, God be praised: it is the noblest load I have heard of in months.

I am caressed a bit by hay-fever, and feel heavy and sad. A good time to write political articles. The right bitterness will get into them.

If you encounter any gents who are genuinely hot against Prohibition and want to join in the only sound movement against it, hand them the enclosed. This verein promises to do something. It is not run by idiotic brewers. You will note that the subscription is very low.

Yours in Xt.,
Mencken

[101] [HLM to GS] [TLS, HUN]

August 25th [1920]

Dear George:—

Shingles, is it? Then you have my prayers and sympathy. I believe that hay-fever is a sort of shingles of the mucosa. I am sore from my nose to my anus, and even my gospel-pipe shows a certain feverishness. Such things are the penalties we pay for being happy. Our nerves go, and then we break out like babies with the chicken-pox. Without question, God is a Methodist.

I am sending you Prejudices I and the Damn book by this mail. Prejudices II is now on the press; a copy should reach you by October 15th.[49] I think I'll send Burlesques to Mrs. Travis instead of the Woman book. The latter is rather rough stuff for so innocent a looking gal. It filled Jane with indignation. I still hear from her, by the way. She is going in for intellectual improvement. I fear she suspects that I am untrue to her. Her friend, Coral, took my eye. Let it be recorded on her dossier to her credit that she never tried no graft on me. But God help any poor working girl who did! Tell La Millier that she has the politeness of a fishwife. I gave her a book worth $10 in any second-hand store, and she does not even send me a scented note.

I can't understand the proceedings of La Cheney. Tell her I left town full of suppressed desires, and was ill all the way home in consequence. My suspicion is that she was lying up all the while with some bullish Democrat. But I'll be back! Once more, at least, I must see San Francisco before they put the formaldehyde into my veins. And maybe twice more. You can't imagine what a gorgeous impression I took away. New York seemed an outhouse and Baltimore a dump. Only a thorough bath in ale revived me.

The Order of the Holy Ghost will hold its annual beer-drink and outdoor revival on September 12th, my birthday. God knows, we all wish you were here. We'll have 8 cases of prime ale, beside enough absinthe cocktails to work up an appetite. Kümmel with the coffee. My last brew turned out badly, but I still have about 200 bottles from former brews, some running to 8% alcohol. I hope to have 500 bottles of a new brew by September 15th. Great is Allah! A bottle in each hand, and a coon opening two more! In New York last week I got a case of gin and two of vermouth from a boot-legger—smuggled stuff. The cost is high, but not prohibitory.

More anon.

Yours,
M

Later

I find that I am out of Prejudices and that a copy of the Damn book doesn't exist. I'll get one of the former and send it to you; as for the latter I'll do my damndest. Have you my translation of The Antichrist?[50]

M.

[102] [GS to HLM] [ALS, NYPL]

Aug. 26th, 1920.

Dear "Hen:"

The cards are here, and none of them will be wasted. How can I get a lot more?

As I wrote, the damned "shingles" put me on the wagon, where I've been for over two weeks. Abrams has cured me, however, and I intend to fall off with an exceeding loud sound, at a dinner here this Saturday. Have already laid in a supply of aspirin. Too bad Upton Sinclair isn't here! I've not heard from the Sinclairs since writing him that I didn't think a submitted MS. of Mrs. Sinclair's poems deserved the dignity of book publication. The near-poet is a beast o' thin skin.

I've decided not to correspond with Jane. I resent her virginal attitude. If ever I'm to fall, in old age, for a pure young thing, she must have at least a maidenhead.

I've not felt like writing verse yet, aside from some love-poems I'm sending to that R.R. president's wife in N.Y. They might almost bring her back here, which Heaven prevent!

Yours for the Holy Ghost and aspirin,

George Sterling.

[103] [HLM to GS] [TLS, HUN]

August 31st [1920]

Dear George:—

I enclose some more of the anti-Methodist cards. You can get all you want by writing to the Association. I think it is well planned and that it may accomplish something eventually. But it will take years. It is free from saloon-keepers, Elks, politicians and other such vermin. The aim is to get a large number of decent members, and so avoid taking money from the distillers. To this end the dues are made low. I assume that women are admitted. I shall nominate a few highly respectable retired whore-madams.

Hay-fever has me by the arse, and I am very uncomfortable. But it won't last long. I have six quarts of 6½ ale on the ice for tonight. At all events I'll sleep soundly. The Autumn ale is colossal. Don't let the shingles worry you. They are easily curable. The seat of the disease lies in the nerves. No doubt that red wine gave your nerves a hell of a wrench. How is grappo made? By simply distilling the wine debris? I want to make some.

As a penance for your patriotism—the last resort, etc., etc.—you ought to send a postcard to Scheffauer. He was badly used during the war, and his sole offense was that he differed from Woodrow, the world's greatest horse's ass. He is doing a lot for Bierce and Dreiser in Germany. His address is Cunostrasse 48 / III, Berlin-Grunewald. He married Ethel Talbot, the English poetess (she is very good at the lyric), and they have a kid. I have sent it some milk in cans; the supply is still short in Berlin.

In this week's issue of the New Republic (or next week's) I'll have a preliminary statement of my politics.[51] Give it your eye. They invited me to lay on. Later on, if they stand pat, I hope to stir up the animals.

The Jane affair is on its last legs. I am astonished that you should question the physical integrity of a fair creature who assured me with her own lips that she shrank from the rough stuff. My thought was "Thank God! Here is where I get some sleep". In the East they reach for the gospel-pipe before one can yell for the police. Nathan was actually raped last week. It laid him up for three days.

Gott mit uns!

> Yours,
> Mencken

[104] [GS to HLM] [ALS, NYPL]

Sept. 2nd, '20.

Dear "Hen":

Shingles are a thing of the past, and I've returned to a life of shame. I hope your hay-fever has gone, too. It belongs to Dr. Frank Crane, or La Millier. I'll pass on your pontifical curse to that young Bolshevik.

I wish to Gawd I could attend your birthday party! I and one other will observe it at this end of the line, anyway. That railroad president's wife is offering me $500. a month to come on to N.Y. and attend to her wants. But "an archaic sense of shame" prevents.

La Cheney wasn't holding out on you. She has a fine new apartment now, with lots of sherry and port, and, I hope, sound-proof walls.

"Day long the diamond weather," and I'm to meet a girl out at the beach this afternoon. Pray *do* get back this way! Synagogue wine is selling for $7.50 a gallon, and isn't half bad.

Don't bother any more about "Damn." I've a notion I can get a copy here. But I'd be glad for "Antichrist."

You may have the verses enclosed for nothing, if printed without my name.[52] Use Crane's or Marsden's. Or Paul Elmer More's. No! Use Sinclair's! Put it "U. Sinclair." That'll give him no right to kick, and his wife won't mind.

But maybe you'll think the verses too Wilcoxish.[53]

Yours in the Resurrection and the Life,

Sterling.

P.S.

Use them with Sinclair's name! Go on!

G.

[105] [HLM to GS] [ALS, BAN]
[The Smart Set
25 WEST 45th STREET
NEW YORK.]

[September 10, 1920]

Dear George:

The Wilcox piece is very juicy. But if I used Upton's name he would roast me in the *Appeal to Reason*,[54] and ruin me among the Bavarian Socialists, whom I am trying to line up for Gamaliel Harding, the Ohio moron.[55]

Give me a fine romantic *nom de plume* for it, or I'll sign your own name, and add a dedication to Millier. Do this at once, or be forever damned.

I took **400 c.c.** of horse serum yesterday for hay-fever, & it damn nigh cured me.

God will help us all!

Ys

M

[106] [HLM to GS] [TLS] [HUN]

September 11th
[1920]

Dear George:—

Thanks very much for Mrs. Travis' settings of
your songs. Will you please convey my thanks to her also? They
are very interesting, and I want to show them to some musicians
here, chiefly enemy aliens.

It is whispered on all sides here that the Kingdom of God is at
hand. As you know, I am not ordinarily interested in theological
gossip, but in the present case it seems to be so well supported
that I pass it on. The general belief is that the Redeemer will re-
appear in New York, heralded by 400 angels and surrounded by a
pillar of fire. Is there any news of it on the Coast.

I am down with hay-fever, and having a rocky time of it. But
the thing doesn't last long.

Yours,
Mencken

[107] [GS to HLM] [ALS, NYPL]

Sept. 15th, 1920.

Homo nobilissime!

Please send me the pamphlet expository of
you.[56] Mrs. T. has one, and I've been dipping into it. Don't mind
what that bird says as to your judgment of poetry. I think you
nod but seldom; and poetry is all I've even a vague knowledge of.
You are right in estimating so highly the beautiful "Tears."[57]

For a name of that poemopassion, use "R. Langtry Partington."[58] He's a portrait-painter, and will be secretly delighted.
Only his wife will disapprove, and she can't get at us.

I enclose verses you may like well enough to pay for—a sort of
composite of my Carmel love-affairs. But this brush-fucking was
a poor thing, at its best. Even a silk undervest arrays too much.

About writing to Scheff. I like him, and shouldn't mind corresponding if he'd keep off the war. But I balk at the prospect of an
interminable argument (and he argues with tireless ferocity) that
could be concluded only by my admission that that meek and
blameless nation, Germany, was enticed to war by the perfidious
(here follow seventeen of Scheff's adjectives) England, and driven
to it by ferocious France and Russia. I should have to subscribe
to the further conviction that she treated Belgium in a sweet, big-
sisterly way, and had recourse to her various horrors out of sheer

mercy, with a view to shortening the strife. If I didn't "come through" on all that, I'd have less peace than the Bolsheviki.

No—the prospect does not allure. But I'll ask for no more interesting correspondent if he'd only pass the war up. I doubt if he has seen my sonnets on the subject, and can imagine the fireworks if ever he does. As for them, I don't regret them as being untruthful: I'm merely sore at myself for entertaining so much moral indignation about this pismire planet. It's a slow job un-Yanking oneself. I hope to atone, some day, by a peculiarly pessimistic and blasphemous dramatic poem.

Poor Bigin incurred a Federal raid at last. He took it badly, being timid and very sensitive, despite his size. I was sent for at once (it was only 11 P.M.) but it was impossible, at that hour, to raise the cash bail demanded—$4500.—and he had to pass a sleepless night in the cooler. He told me he had over $10000. in the bank; but checks aren't taken. The raid was conducted in a variously brutal manner, dissolving Mrs. Bigin in tears. Eight of the animals, and the biggest struck Bigin's lawyer in the face, because he wouldn't "go off an' sit down!" Sweet land of liberty, of thee I sing!

By way of a little light whoring, I've composed a "popular" (I hope) song, words *and* music. Title, "I'd Like to, but I'm Scared to!" If some Gothamite Jew takes a fancy to it, and will be 2.75% honest, I may get to Baltimore yet. One of my sisters, as a babe, called it "Bobolo."

Well, you've endured more than enough.

His child,

George Sterling.

Bigin, on my advice, is still selling it (grappa).

[108] [GS to HLM] [ALS, NYPL]

Sept. 15th, 1920.

Dear Brother in Christ:

Don't faint! This is a letter requiring no reply: I wrote to you this morning. But I've just put in part of the afternoon going through "Prejudices" for the second time and a bottle of sound port for the first time, and I find the book a joy-wallow.

What gets me is the fact that I remember most of it so well, feeling as though I'd read it not once but ten times previously. It may be because I agree so thoroughly with about 90% of what you say. And you may not have meant that much of it.

I liked your pen-jabs at that bubble, Amy Lowell. She is a she-pope, and her last book, "Can Grande's Castle," was a big disappointment to me.[59] Just think: she had every opportunity to turn absolutely loose, in imagination and technique. There were no chains. And yet the performance is a flat one.

I'm off to Lafler's[60] for a new-wine orgy. Heaven help my head o' the morn!

> In His name,
>
> G. S.

[109] [HLM to GS] [TLS, HUN]

September 21st [1920]

Dear George:—

You are right about Scheffauer. The poor fellow has been very badly used, and in the main I think he is nearer right than you are, but it is a fact that tho war still obsesses him and that if you got into correspondence with him you would quarrel. Wait a bit. What makes a man vicious is the sense of impotence. As soon as Schef can deliver a few solid licks at American Kultur he will feel better. My own serenity is due to the fact that I always manage to do a great deal more damage than is done to me. In war, of course, a man must expect to get hurt now and then, but it is only when he is strapped to a board and can't hit back that the hurts really hurt. Even at the height of the war frenzy, I always managed to outrage a few patriots so vastly that I had a good time. Since then I have driven some of them half crazy, and thus have satisfied the malice that is in all of us. What we need in America is a concerted movement against patriotism, carried on with deliberate offensiveness—no academic pussyfooting, but a headlong attack. I hope you join. What the movement needs is men like yourself, who can point with pride to their records. My own record is so bad that it is alone sufficient to break the heart of the world. I suppose I am the only man in the East who absolutely refused to buy a Liberty bond or to give a cent to the Red Cross. My sole war activity consisted in damning the Department of Justice for its dirty treatment of German prisoners. My conscience is clear. I'll probably have to go to hell for all this, but the crime was worth the punishment.

Never in the world will I use Partington's name on that poem.

105

I am a burnt child, and dread the fire. Some time ago Hussey used the real names of his friends in a novelette, and now one of them has quarrelled with him and threatens us with a libel suit. By the way, I seem to have mislaid the poem, damn it all. Have you another copy? Leave the nom de plume to me.

The enclosed, for some reason or other, I don't like. What ails it, I believe, is simple, to wit, the fact that poems about lost loves are turned out in Greenwich Village at the rate of 200 kilometres a day. You do the thing eloquently, but after all I don't think you get very far away from the standard model. Take a look, and see whether I am right or an ass. But for God's sake send me something. Also, where is La Greenwood's stuff?

The Bigin raid doesn't surprise me. One by one all such places will be closed. Down here we have given up all hope of reviving the old beer-houses. We have simply transferred our presence to private houses, and built up a circuit. I am now sure of an elaborate Bierabend every Saturday evening, and of a very wet dinner every Sunday evening. Add a casual session or two in the interval, and life becomes possible.

Your idea for the song is excellent. I rather think you'd do better selling it direct to Ziegfeld instead of sending it to a music publisher, all of whom are thieves. If it were sung in the Follies, all the publishers would fight for it.

I am over hay-fever, but the antitoxin still shows itself. For three or four days I was covered with huge hives. I am glad that the shingles are over. I hear at the Hopkins that they are caused by trying to frig two girls at once.

Yours,
Mencken

Jane writes that she is coming to New York. O mon doo!

[110] [HLM to GS] [TLS, HUN]

September 22nd [1920]

Dear George:—

The stuff seems familiar because you probably read a good part of it in The Smart Set. Prejudices II is also old stuff, but with some jazz added. I'll send you a copy anon. It is not yet out.

The Second Coming of Christ is at hand, hurrah, hurrah!

Yours,
M

[111] [GS to HLM] [ALS, NYPL]

Sept. 30ᵗʰ, 1920.

Dear "H. L."

Have had a hard week of it, but my thirst is unimpaired. A letter from Dreiser announces he's to be here for a week, about Oct. 20ᵗʰ. He asks that I steer him around, and I've accepted. Shall begin to save hooch and interview La Cheney, who, fortunately, cares for distinction in men rather than pulchritude.

Thanks for the Antichrist, which I've not yet had time to read. Cabell sends me his "The Cords of Vanity."⁶¹ I suspect you of putting in a good word for me. And Le Gallienne has noticed me at last and sends his last book.⁶² I'm somewhat dilated.

Herewith find badge admitting you to all lodges of the Chinese Y.M.C.A. I've joined the organization, attracted, naturally, by the brothel, hop and assassination privileges, of which I hope to take frequent advantage. You might put Nathan wise to it, and, of course, Boyd.

Bigin's trial hasn't come off yet. He has gone on selling the stuff, but only to folks he knows well.

Yours in the Peace Beyond All Understanding,
George Sterling.

P.S. Nor can *I* find that poem. I think it's well lost. You're right about the longer one. I wrote it only for its musical qualities.

I've another popular song, words and music mine. "Is It as Nice as They Say it Is." But I've no notion how to get such things to Ziegfeld. No hurry at that.

The Hopkins gave you the right dope as to the cause of shingles!

America Forever!

G. S.

[112] [HLM to GS] [TLS, BAN]

October 2nd [1920]

Dear George:—

What of the enclosed? You told me to sign some pseudonym to it, and yet your name is at the end of it. Didn't I write to protest? I'd like to use it with your name. Let me have it back if that is all right. Put your price on it.

All forward-looking men down here believe that Gamaliel the

Moron will carry the country by 3,000,000 majority. It will be a fine jolt for the Presbyterian Jesus. God help the Republic!

Wine-making is in full swing here. Last Saturday I tried some of last year's vintage. It turned out to be excellent. I had to be lifted out of the taxi-cab.

Yours in Xt.,
Mencken

Have you seen the deluxe edition of the *St. Francis Lobbyist?*[63]

[113] [HLM to GS] [TLS, BAN]

October 5th [1920]

Dear George:—

There is some mixup about the poem. Do you refer to the one I sent back to you the other day? If so, sign some name to it and return it. I'll be very glad to print it.

I surely hope Bigin escapes with his hide. The news that grappo has degenerated fills me with dismay. Down here the ale grows better and better. Also, there is a new supply of excellent gin. The other night I drank some of last autumn's Maryland wine. It turned out to be superb—a very fine white wine, not unlike good Moselle. Alcohol content: about 8%. I got fearfully stewed.

It is a shame to waste Cheney on Dreiser. He takes them as they run. If there are any poor old women in sight who haven't the money to pay a man, try him on them.

Yours,
M

[114] [HLM to GS] [TLS, HUN]

October 22nd [1920]

Dear George:—

Thanks very much for the book just received.[64] I shall read it at once. I have a sneaking fear that there is some carnality in it. If so, God will punish you.

I have just got in from New York, where I managed to get four bellyfulls in five days. Tonight I am as sleepy as a bridegroom. The booze is fast running out up there. Decent cocktails now cost $1, and the lowest price for highballs is 65 cents. They have no malt liquor. Wine is 60 cents a goblet—very fair stuff.

A telegram from Jane says that she will arrive Wednesday. I have reserved a room for her at the Algonquin, but I won't be able to meet her at the train. However, I'll see her in a couple of weeks.

Yours,
M

[115] [HLM to GS] [TLS, HUN]

November 1st [1920]

Dear George:—

W. L. George, a poor, lonely Englishman, is heading for the Coast on a lecture tour.[65] If he bobs up in San Francisco, please introduce him to Bigin and see that he is allowed to buy some red wine. His lecture is very moral.

What has become of that poem I sent back to you for signature? And why hasn't La Belle May sent me any of her stuff? I fear the two of you are spending all your time in social relaxation.

I am in a black mood and can't work. Tomorrow the solemn referendum.

Yours,
M.

[116] [GS to HLM] [ALS, NYPL]

S.F. Nov. 1 / 20.

Dear H. L.

Steel your soul for one of my long scrawls!

I've been hitting it up strenuously for several weeks, first with Dreiser, then with Nina Wilcox Putnam and her husband, and finally with Maugham, the "Moon and Sixpence" man.[66]

I got on very well with Dreiser, and like him. His weak point is that four good slugs of Scotch get him pretty full, whereupon he clutches at every woman in sight. It was a shame to have to waste Scotch and Plymouth gin on him; but he told me they were his favorite drinks—and this is San Francisco. He is crazy about the town, by the way, curses Los Angeles, and declares he's coming here to live. He'll be quite the local Joss if he do, and will have some great times. I didn't have to use La Cheney—he brought his own.

I've been re-reading his work, and find it even better than I thought. I had him autograph nine of his books for me. His style is pretty bad; but he has the guts, and most American novels seem rather flimsy and artificial, after his.

The Putnams had been on the wagon for over six weeks, and

109

went on a real tear as soon as they hit town. *He* spent most of his time in bed—an economical move, as he presses $20. bills on anyone he meets, when twenty drinks to the good.

Maugham is a good chap, though hard to become acquainted with on short notice. He affects bourbon, which he carries well. He has retired to Carmel for six weeks, to write a play. I wish he'd write another "Of Human Bondage." That book is much in Dreiser's vein, and Maugham seems much interested in D. Thinks he has been treated shamefully by his countrymen, which is true enough.

I return the verses, to which you may append any name that occurs to you. I suggest Gam. Harding's. I vote for him to-morrow, in default of a better man. I can't use *my* name on the verses, as that would imply a questionnaire for me in S.F. So you may have them gratis.

The drys are treating this town more roughly than any other place in the country, and raids are of daily occurrence. Also we have a big Federal scandal, the Brolaski one.[67] But Bigin's and the other joints go on selling whiskey, and the price is still 60¢ a highball. Good whiskey at the drug stores is about $2. for a full pint. My friend Lafler, at whose home on Telegraph Hill I put in most of my Sundays, has just made 90 gallons of claret, at a cost of about $1.00 per gal.

So it goes. Dry nights are a long way off. I doubt if *we* live to see them. Meanwhile, a copper-bottomed belly to all drinkers of grappo!

Commending you to God's inattention, I remain

Yours ever,

George Sterling.

Cabell sent me his "Cords of Vanity."

[117] [HLM to GS] [TLS, HUN]
[The Smart Set
25 WEST 45TH STREET
NEW YORK]

November 6th [1920]

Dear George:—

It is a pity you wasted that good liquor on Dreiser. His stomach and palate were ruined by eating saleratus[68] as a boy in Indiana, and he is quite anaesthetic to the higher alcohols. His favorite used to be an American brandy that he bought for $1.25 a quart. I always puked after drinking it.

Wine here is growing scarce, but the supply of malt liquor is enormous. Despite a couple of rough parties, I now have 250 bottles in stock, with more on the way. It runs to 6%, and has a very fine taste. My dinner club—9 men who dine together—owns 1,200 bottles, and has bespoken 2,500. Ah, the wisdom and majesty of God!

The poem is here, and the mazuma will follow. What is the matter with May? I expected to receive her stuff long ago. Jane is in New York; I'll see her tomorrow. What she is doing I don't know—some movie enterprise.

Woodrow! Ach, du heiliger Herr Jesus!

Yours,
M

[118] [GS to HLM] [ALS, NYPL]

Nov. 18th, 1920.

Dear H. L.

The check came as a surprise, as I'd said you might have the verses gratis, since I couldn't sign them. Well, the eight bucks are none the less welcome, and you have my thanks.[69]

I wish you were here, that I might have a long talk with you in re "Prejudices," the second crop. It's a book of a thousand felicities and a deck-load of ruth. You make every sentence count, and "The National Letters" is absolutely deracinating! You are Bierce's legitimate successor, and in a broader and more cultured sense. He was less a critic than a wit—but what a wit! It's a pity you two couldn't have seen more of each other.

"The Divine Afflatus" was highly interesting.[70] I think you've hit on a truth there, though, as I'm never constipated nor in poor health (I might be a genius if I were!), I can't say so by personal experience. In my own case, I begin to write, and without conscious effort, as soon as I stop dissipating long enough for the storing of surplus vitality.

I suppose you've seen Jane by this time; and may you have landed her on her plump back! Wish I was in Gotham too. If I could show Ziegfeld my two risqué songs, I bet he'd fall hard for them, if only for the tunes.

I've been at Bigin's a good deal, lately. His ginger-ale highballs are very decent, and half a dozen of them impart a fine glow. But if there's even one stranger in the place, he's afraid to serve us.

I enclose my last poem, which served its purpose.[71] Wish it wasn't too long for your w. k. organ of ideality: that "naked breast" would please Mr. Sumner. Well, stick it among your literary relics.

Christ! This letter is an orgy of I's! Let me state that it's been raining for a solid week.

His child,

Geo. Sterling.

[119] [HLM to GS] [TLS, HUN]

November 23rd [1920]

Dear George:—

"To a Girl Dancing" is eloquent and gaudy stuff; it doesn't surprise me to hear that you are never constipated. I only wish I had never solemnly agreed with Nathan to buy no long poems. It was a sound bargain, editorially speaking, but now and then it stings me.

The flow of alcohol down here continues to be heavy. Last week they tried half a dozen Prohibition agents for taking bribes. Though the Italians who had given the bribes had confessed and pleaded guilty, the jury acquitted the agents, and they are now in business again. Saturday night I got such an overdose of 6% ale that I was quite unfit for the worship of God Sunday morning. I have laid in enough malt and hops to last me five years. My two beers, light and dark, now verge upon perfection. As for gin, we get plenty of it. Only whiskey is scarce. Next year we'll all have plenty of wine.

I saw Jane and her ma in New York last week. She called me up yesterday to say that she had at last found an apartment. They are hard to get in New York. Jane is going out in vaudeville, so she says. As you know, my relations to her are brotherly. I have two girls in New York, God help me.

I have been unable to work on account of pains around the heart. This has been going on for a long while. The faculty finds, however, that the heart itself is sound; the trouble is in the digestive tract. I shall buckle down to serious treatment for this in a few weeks. It is curable.

Bigin will die in jail. The Presbyterians are determined to get us all. I begin to believe that the only remedy is armed force. The day the first Methodist church is burned down, with the congregation in it, there will be better times. I long for the Japs! The moment they land, the niggers will rise in the South and massacre the Confederates, and the Irish will fall upon the Jews in New York. Give the matter your prayers.

Yours in Xt.,
Mencken

[120] [GS to HLM] [ALS, NYPL]

Dec. 12th, 1920.

Dear H. L.

I was down at Bigin's, last night, with the widow of a rich Chinaman. She is a Yank. Much may be expected from that quarter, as she lives over in "Chinatown." I dare say that China gin is fairly palatable.

Anyhow, I was fixed good and plenty last night, for several friends came in, each with a flask of real whiskey on the hip. Dancing was all that saved me from the morning headache. I find four new telephone numbers in my pocket. A "delusion of sexual grandeur" is all right, if one can keep the bluff from being called.

No doubt you've read of our rape-gang, of the lynching, and of subsequent developments. I have written the enclosed verses as a partial palliative.[72]

I don't know where all the hooch comes from, but I encounter it always and everywhere, and it's always old and good stuff. I contemplate taking to the high Sierras, to save the remnants of my vitality. But there are 86 inches of snow at Summit.

Yours for Soviet Russia,
George Sterling.

[121] [HLM to GS] [TLS, HUN]

December 17th [1920]

Dear George:—

Your lines to San Francisco make me homesick. There never was no such town nowhere. I'll be back, if God permits.

I went to see Jane in her new flat last week, and was scandalized to find her bemused by New York, despite the rotten climate. She had a fearful bronchitis, and yet gabbled about the joys of the metropolis. I fear she has lost her mind. I would gladly trade ten New Yorks, with all their Jews on the hoof, for one of San Francisco's hills—or gals.

113

Nathan has been very ill, and I have been working a double shift. Worse, my own stomach has begun to give out, probably on account of too much drinking under Prohibition. Every time that I have immersed myself lately I have puked all over the place. In former times I held everything down, including corks and labels. That San Francisco gastritis is a sample of what I am up against. But the faculty promises a cure.

Hergesheimer let those swine elect him to the National Institute. I sent him a hot letter, and now he is very apologetic. Cabell is laughing. Let them elect *him*, and there will be an explosion.

I read of the lynching, and marvelled. Can it be that there are any girls in California who have to be raped? Down here the art has gone out of existence.

I have got a holiday from the faculty for Christmas. But after that I'll have to go on the cure. Tomorrow the Dinner Club gives a Christmas dinner for 20 men. The first cocktail will be served at 4 P.M. We have champagne, smuggled in from Buenos Ayres.

Yours,
M

[122] [HLM to GS] [TLS, BAN]

December 24th [1920]

Dear George:—

If you are trying to shove that New York gal off upon me, then a pox upon you. I am already in a state of collapse. The winter's trade was never heavier. With Nathan laid up I have had to do all the office practise. Many of them are old and tough.

I got in some Waldmeister from Munich today. Mixed with Moselle wine it makes the king of punches. I have the Moselle and shall presently fall upon it. In New York this week I got two cases of gin and four of vermouth. This, with what I had here, makes me solid for a year. God be praised.

My stomach, which floored me on the way home from S.F., is cutting up, but I have a good doctor, and he says he can cure me.

Three cheers for John the Baptist!

Yours,
Mencken

1921

[123] [GS to HLM] [ALS, NYPL]

Jan. 7th, 1921.

Humble Servant of God!

(You so signed yourself, once.) Behold the free advertising! The newspapers have it mostly correct. However, I wasn't "evicted," nor did I bring any charge against him, though I'd cause to: the big brute soaked me when I was *seated!* Heaven knows he could have licked me with no great difficulty had I been standing up, for I had a skin-full.[1]

He knocked the poor little woman down twice. I did not see that. Now he says he had no just cause to be jealous, and wants to make up with me. He may go to Hell. As for her, she started divorce proceedings yesterday.

My eye's all right, now. His blow cut my eyebrow, and I bled profusely. I got my toad-sticker out, but the women took it away from me.

Ah well! It's nothing to worry over.

We had a hot New Year's eve at the Bologna. I know about half the folks there, and we kept it up all night. Many of the girls were falling down, or dancing on the tables, or going around with their tits hanging out. Great is grappa! I brought my own poison—*port,* of all febrifuges!

Too bad that the Instiloot got Hergesheimer! Can't you make him resign? Or is he too great an admirer of Chambers? Dreiser writes, asking if I can get some hooch for him. I can get some, but can't get it *to* him. Am arranging for a friend there to introduce him to a bootlegger. He seems to be a helpless sort of cuss. He was much intrigued, by the way, by my "Testimony of the Suns." I thought it might get him. Shall pique his curiosity by writing that I've gone far beyond it, since. Perhaps I have.

Honest to Gawd I wasn't trying to work that N.Y. girl off on you! She's now in Bermuda for the winter. For a Christmas gift she sent me a dressing gown that must have set her back about $200. I never wear such things, and am giving it to my dentist.

Your stomach-troubles worry me: you'll be starting a cancer, first thing you know. If you do, remember that Abrams can cure them in ten days. He has done so twice within four months for friends of mine, one of them Mrs. Travis' mother. He is besieged by other doctors, and is wearing himself to a frazzle. Great is fame! To Hell with it!

I'm receiving delightful letters from a girl who is spending the winter up in the high Sierras, where her dad has charge of a big mine. I met and pushed her here, but she's really a country mouse. Her letters are the quaintest & most charming ones I've ever read. She returns in February.[2] I shall go on the wagon till then.

The Federal gang is doing a lot of raiding here, but mostly in the Latin Quarter. All they get is raw red-wine and grappa.

May we meet in Paris!

The redeemed

G. S.

[124] [HLM to GS] [TLS, HUN]

January 12th [1921]

Dear George:—

I am a prejudiced judge in such matters; I am always against the husband. In this case I daresay you gave the poor fellow ample cause to carry on as he did. Nevertheless, my only hope is that a pox descends upon him. Be careful that you do not find yourself dragged to the altar of God.

The quacks are exploring my stomach. Apparently there is nothing very serious wrong. I suspect that chewing tobacco is to blame. I simply can't let off the old Assyrian vice. I am a Southern gentleman to that extent. It is a fine device for getting rid of literary women. Simply reach out for your pantaloons, draw out your plug, and gnaw off a large chew. They leap out of bed and never come back.

Hergy is hopeless. He is actually delighted that those cads elected him. I formally wash my hands of him. At the same election they chose Herman Hagendorn! A fit punishment for Hergy.

I shall do no work until the stomach birds finish. Tell Abrams to save me a bed at his morgue.

Yours,

M

[125] [GS to HLM] [ALS, NYPL]

Jan. 24th, 1921.

Dear H. L.

I've bespoken for you a bed at Abrams' columbarium. Remember that "the dead in Christ rise first," and wait a bit when Gabriel sounds the Saxophone.

Anyone that chews tobacco deserves a worse death than mere ulcer of the stomach. Can't you taper off a betelnut, 3 or something of that sort? Snuff-dipping might help.

"Hergy" is a Jew, I'm inferring from his picture in the Ladies' Home Journal. And the Yid is eager to break into 'most any kind of Gentile organization. Save your heavy artillery for such folk as Tarkington and H. L. Wilson.

I've seen your libel (of course you write *all* of "Conversations") as to my wasting wood-alcohol on you, and have had several interviews with my attorney. He seems to think I've no recourse—indeed, to listen to the chap, who'll drink *anything,* one would infer I'd been complimented. All I can do is to sharpen my bowie and wait till railway fares go down. But "Conversations" is great stuff. I wish you had begun it years ago.4

Here's an old sonnet of mine that you may use if you happen to care to. But I refuse absolutely to take any pay for it. You shouldn't have paid me for that last lyric.

Macmillans write and ask to bring out "my next." Is that some of your work? I know you are addicted to helping the helpless poet. I've written that I've a MS. of lyrics ready, but fear it wouldn't prove especially profitable to them, but that I'd like to see another edition of "Lilith" out. Your prediction that it would bring $10. as a bibelot has come true: Newbegin tells me he can't get one even at that price! Why did I give 190 of them away?

Have been pretty much on the wagon since the 1st, and alcoholic gifts begin to accumulate. I now have gin, Nelly-Prat vermouth,5 Scotch, bourbon, and a bottle each of absinthe and champagne. It will be just my luck for Dreiser to appear. I'd better drink it up with a young model here, late a dancer on Pantages' circuit, who thinks I'm going to write a poem about her shape, which the same is flawless. What do you recommend? One must not forget the spiritual consolation one derives from the discourses of Dr. Dreiser.

Yours for an infamous old-age,

George.

[126] [GS to HLM] [ALS, NYPL]

Feb. 7th, 1921.

Dear H. L.

We'll be glad to get Jane back. The innocence in that girl's face as she tells her biggest lies has always been charming to me. I hope it *is* bronchitis, and not syphilitic sore-throat.

Too bad New York's drying up! The worse the Federal officers treat this poor town, the wetter it seems to become. Good white wine is now sold openly over the bar @ $1.⁵⁰ per bottle, and decent claret @ $3.⁰⁰ a gallon. But a little hooch seems to hurt one as much as a lot of it used to.

I've written several poems lately, but they're all too solemn and *long* for S.S. This one enclosed seems hardly suitable to your sophisticated pages, and I venture to send it only because I note it has greatly tickled the grownups who have read it. I write it to please a little girl. Perhaps St. Nicholas would like it.

My "model" girl is returning from the Sierras soon, so I'm to spend the coming week in "retreat" at the Dominican monastery here. Pray for me!

I see I've been elected one of the three vice-presidents (that word "vice" is ominous) of The Poetry Society. I must begin to take myself, and life, more seriously. I might begin by applying for re-admission to the Institute of Arts and Letters. Hergy is in too reverend company.

What a delightful book "Miss Lulu Bett" is![6] But the Cather woman can write around all of them. The length of "Main St."[7] scares me. 'Guess I'll not tackle it.

No more news of Dreiser. Perhaps he is collaborating with Upton Sinclair.

Yours ever,

G. Sterling.

[Enclosure?]
P.S.

O Hell! You whitened sepulchre![8] You were afraid to run my "Iris Hills," and now you print that sentence about Rodin's young lovers tongue-sucking and stark naked! Your courage must be intermittent.

G. S.

[127] [GS to HLM] [ALS, NYPL]

Feb. 10th, 1921.

Dear H. L.

Here's something I just wrote. I suppose you don't care much for obituary verse; but this has a simplicity and directness that may commend it.[9]

'Was at the wedding anniversary of my youngest sister last night, and had beaucoup de beaucoup of sparkling Burgundy—a deadly drink sometimes.

A friend of mine bottled some sort of home-brew a while ago. One night, the bottles began to go off, one by one. The family (husband, wife, sister and brother-in-law) tried to save it all by drinking it, and were absolutely plastered by morning. 'Wish I'd been "among those present!"

In His name,

George S.

[128] [HLM to GS] [TLS, HUN]

February 18th [1921]

Dear George:—

The obituary poem tickles me much, and I am trying it on von Nathan. You are a talented youth. They will be electing you to the Poetry Society some day.

Nathan tells me that Jim Huneker's funeral was extraordinarily dignified.[10] Not a clerical gurgle was heard. The three speeches were short, and even the actor, Francis Wilson, did not make an ass of himself. The crowd was huge. Mary Garden sat in front, weeping into a towel.[11]

I have been in New York five days, and we had five gaudy parties. Monday was Nathan's birthday, and Tom Smith celebrated it by knocking in the door of his secret chamber and letting out a fine flow of champagne. The next day Zoë Akins staged a very noble social.[12] The third day an eminent lady of the town dined the two of us in state, with a chow dog peeing on my leg. And so on.

God help us all.

Yours,

M

[129] [HLM to GS] [TLS, HUN]

February 22nd [1921]

Dear George:—

Once in a great while Nathan and I disagree. I like "The Three Gifts" very much, but he doesn't; so there you are. But if you put us under the ban for this, then he will take to drink and my work will be doubled.

A note from Jane this morning continues the tale of her troubles. Her nephew is in hospital with a mastoid abcess, a serious business. Some quack had been treating him for a disordered stomach! Such swine ought to be unfrocked and hanged. Her present doctor is my hay-fever man, a very good fellow. He has operated on the kid.

I am up to my arse in "The American Language," and making very fair progress. The book will be a foot thick when I finish it. My stenographer is going crazy.

Yours,
M

[130] [GS to HLM] [ALS, NYPL]

Feb. 23rd, 1921.

Dear H. L.

Hoch everything! 'Don't care much if Nathan doesn't fall for the graveyard verse, so long as you did. I wish I had something decent, or rather indecent, to send you; but everything I'm moved to "let" is so damned long—and solemn. I take out my gloom that way, though God forbid that I take my verses seriously!

All the same, I sent a MS. for a book of lyrics to Macmillans' last week, they requesting such an exhibit. If they take it, which isn't at all sure, they'll probably request me to cut out several poems of impropriety; and I'll concede.

Say—I belong to The Poetry Society already! 'Was a charter member (Bierce jeered me about it) and am now one of its vice-presidents, elected without prior notification. 'Let it go: I like the title. Its secretary has just written, asking me to be one of the judges in its next "prize contest" for the best book of poems submitted. I've declined, saying I'd vote for a girl, and the best-looker at that—though none of them will be good-looking, I suppose. Still, I've known a few, if you call vers libre poetry—I don't.

Moon and Sixpence Maugham called on me yesterday. I had

plenty of Scotch, the Lord be praised! 'Says he dined with Dreiser in Los Angeles, and found him extraordinarily *shy;* and Maugham is no ballyhoo man himself.

Gawd! 'Wish I could have been with you, those five evenings! I used to see quite a bit of Zoë, the year I was in New York—1914–15. 'Never fell for her (she looked too Ethiopian), so she dropped me, finally. A damned bright girl! She lived not far from me in Greenwich Village. 'Suppose she puts up at the Ritz now.

San Francisco seems to be making hooch faster than the Federal officers can pour it into the gutters. Here's a piccer of my model in the Sierras. God hasten her return and strengthen my back!

Yours for His reform,

George Sterling.

[131] [HLM to GS] [TLS, HUN]

April 11th [1921]

Dear George:—

What has become of you? I hear indirectly that you are in jail, but it seems impossible. If you are, put yourself in God's hands. He will liberate you eventually.

Two days ago Christopher Morley printed a line in the N.Y. Evening Post announcing my marriage.[13] Ever since then I have been hard at work trying to put down the libel. All the gals that I have promised to be true to are indignant.

My sister-in-law is very ill here, and my hands are full. To add to my miseries I sprained my right arm two weeks ago, and could scarcely hold a pen for ten days. Imagine how work has accumulated.

Yours,
M

[132] [GS to HLM] [ALS, NYPL]

Apr. 15th, 1921.

Du lieber "Hen!"

I've been too lazy to write with nothing to kick about but the activities of the Federal agents. So you've been spared.

I'm still out of jail, but the Good are hopeful. If you were but here! Can't you come out for the Jinks (Grove Play)? July 16th to

30th. I know it is horribly expensive; but you'd be free of that at the grove.

I read with great interest your ideas on poetry in the last S.S.[14] You seem to me mostly right, and of course may be entirely so. 'Wish I'd enough ambition to discuss the whole thing with you. Well, you're just as well off.

You'll note from the enclosed clippings that the old town is doing its best to keep things moving. 'Never even heard of that "vice den," but met a model last night who'd been there. She says they were a tough bunch—brush-hunters mostly. So the bright lights go out, one by one. We'll yet have to join the Y.M.C.A. for excitement.

Macmillans offered to bring out a book of "selected poems" for me; but I let their proposition slide, not greatly liking it.

I just saw Harry Leon Wilson down-stairs. He has taken up golf, and looks 73 years old. These young wives! The one I marry is going to be at least forty.

I suppose Scheffauer sends you his pamphlets.[15] It seems to me he'd make more impression by being less violent. After a few pages of expletives, everything begins to get frothing. God knows *I* don't like Wilson; but not for Scheff's reasons.

S.F. just showed up with the biggest in-door audience ever to hear grand opera. They used the civic auditorium! Now if we could get Demp. and Carp. here![16]

I've not written a line since January, and d—— few letters. The venerable "Nation" accepted "Mirage." I nearly dropped dead. 'Wish I'd some love stuff for S.S., but am drying up on sich.

Dreiser is still amid the damned.

  Good luck!

       G. S.

[133] [GS to HLM] [ALS, NYPL]

          May 11th, 1921.

Dear [picture of Mencken]:

       Here's a pome you may like. You may have it for twelve bucks, and it should all go on one page if italicized.[17]

Dreiser is here with his movie-queen, and book-collectors are crowding bottles of gin and champagne on him. Of course I get my cut in. The queen is a peach, and seems entirely devoted to him.

I've had a gallon of okolehao sent me from Honolulu, and another friend brings a lot of mescal from Mexico. To such straits do the Sons of the American Revolution begin to be driven. I wonder if Finger[18] is having anything from Patagonia. I had the Dreisers at the Bologna, but he was wised up to grappa, and stuck to ohen.[19]

Was amused by Harris' comments on your knowledge of poetry.[20] I do think you approach it almost entirely with the intellect, but he is led farther astray in the other direction, and sometimes rates as "great poetry" stuff that's not poetry at all, merely what I call "vital verse." And you are dead right as to the Reese sonnet, which is a wonder. I dare say Harris would call "Gunga Din" poetry.

I'm going motoring with a girl aviatrix who has a high-powered car, and shall doubtlessly be dead when this reaches you.

Yours ever,

George Sterling.

[134] [HLM to GS] [TLS, BAN]

May 16th [1921]

Dear George:—

The long piece lifts me; my vote is for it. But why is "Everest" for my archives?[21] I'd like to embalm it in print. May I? Or has it been printed?

Dreiser talks of returning to New York. He will plunge headfirst into domestic difficulties. At least three of his old gals are waiting for him, longing for his embrace. The fellow promises more than he can deliver. He would need eight gospel pipes to work up to his advance notices.

I have so many troubles that I seriously consider escaping the country and seeking refuge in foreign parts. But I doubt I'll ever do it.

The booze supply down here continues to be large. Yesterday I bought a case of Fernet-Branca, 39% alcohol. The wops get it in by the simple device of sticking on a label prescribing a tablespoonful for cramps. I shall get a case of gin and some Rhine wine in New York next week. My cellar now contains 700 bottles of prime ale.

Yours in Xt.,
M

[135] [HLM to GS] [TLS, BAN]

May 18th [1921]

Dear George:—

On experiment it turns out that this will not go into one page, and Nathan stands on our old agreement, only once violated, to keep with one page. Can't I use the other one? Or send me another lyric. God will reward you.

The news of Dreiser's adulterous doings has reached New York and two women there threaten to shoot him at sight.

Yours,

M

[136] [GS to HLM] [ALS, NYPL]

May 20th, 1921.

Dear H. L.

I never think of you as having troubles: they seem incompatible with bachelorhood and seven hundred bottles of ale! Whatever they be, may they be brief!

I too am apprehensive of D's return to N.Y., for from a remark of his L.A. girl, I infer he has promised to take her with him, which seems indiscreet. Abrams found she has cancer of the stomach (this between us), and she's now taking his treatment, at the hands of an L.A. physician.

I trust Dr. Nathan will join you in falling for "A Secret Garden." Otherwise it's unlikely to find magazine publication. I'm enclosing some verses you may have gratis, if you care to run them. The reason I didn't send you "Everest" for possible publication was, that it seems too cold and solemn a poem for the "S.S." Just now, it's with the revered "Nation." But I think I can send you things much more acceptable than that, as I've written much and various stuff this month.

I'll enclose some other nonsense. In the case of the program booklet, look at the advt. of the Columbia Theatre! I found Wm Lyon Phelps' picture in "Vanity Fair," and have pinned it on the door of my room, surrounded by photographs of the Mack Sennet bathing-girls. They don't seem to mind.

Sinclair Lewis, who used to depend for exhilaration, when a resident of Carmel, almost entirely on my demijohn of muscatel, writes me airily now of a purposed visit to Europe, lasting a year.[22] I used to be the giddy swan there, and he the ugly duckling. O tempora! O Hell!

Anyhow, I've Frisco and my health.

Yours ever,

George Sterling.

[137] [GS to HLM] [ALS, NYPL]

May 23rd, 1921.

Dear H. L.

I'm sorry that the "Secret Garden" proved too long, for no other magazine has the guts to run it. I'm enclosing the only two poems I have "at hand." "Everest" is with "The Nation," which will probably take it. I'm surprised that you'd let anything so highbrow into the "S.S." The mildly amatory (and imbecilic) is what your feminine readers crave.

If Dreiser wants to hide from the female of the species, there's no safer refuge from him than the top floor of this club. I am too far, *as yet,* from perfection, to crave the life of a recluse; but danger is another matter, and I'll cast a life-line toward the city of the angels. Dreiser must be saved to us, if only for further details of how Yerkes landed 'em on their velvety backs.

And now in the Name, etc.

George Sterling.

[138] [HLM to GS] [TLS, BAN]

May 29th [1921]

Dear George:—

I think we'll take the other poem. My best thanks. Let us have another when the Muses grab you by the ear.

My house is in a turmoil. My sister-in-law arrived from hospital today after 11½ weeks of it. I think she will recover completely. Simultaneously our old dog, Tessie, a member of the family for 16 years, was called by God. Her funeral this afternoon in the garden was very impressive. I dug the grave myself.

New York, I hear, is to go wet again on June 1st. It has been bone dry for ten weeks—that is, publicly. In private there has been constant and lamentable boozing. I went to a party last Tuesday night on Riverside drive, and was puking all over the place by 10 P.M.

Yours in Xt.,
M

[139] [GS to HLM] [ALS, NYPL]

June 3rd, 1921.

Dear H. L.

I fell thuddily from the W.W. last night, and my head feels like the left hand of the unrepentant thief.

'Wish I could have seen you digging that grave: I bet one of your eyes, at least, was wet. Despite Bierce's anathema, I am for the dog.[23] Have lately written a poem (?) comparing man unfavorably with the canine—an old idea, but not till now put to metre, I think.

Enclosed is a poem you may not think too old-fashioned. Also another, entirely unsaleable, for your private perusal.[24]

I wish I could have seen that article of yours in the Baltimore newspaper in which you reviewed Phelps' book on the drama. If you've a copy handy, lend it to me.[25]

I've been presented with four bottles of "Nelly's prat" vermouth, but lacking gin, scarcely know what to do with them. 'Wish I could express them to *you*.

I note a hopeful article on you in the New Rep.[26] Am glad to learn you're so emotional.

Has Dr. Robertson sent you his psychopathic "study" of Poe? It's good.[27]

In nomine Patris, etc.

G. S.

[140] [HLM to GS] [TLS, BAN]

June 8th [1921]

Dear George:—

The two poems are excellent, and I think we'll do the "Love and Time". You seem to be hard at work again. I am sweating along, chiefly on "The American Language." Never again![28] Hereafter, I'll leave pedantry to the professors.

Unluckily, I have no copy of the Phelps review, and can't get one at the Sun office; no back numbers are kept there, save for the files. It was poor stuff—simply an effort to be nice to the fellow.

Dreiser talks of coming East, but I suppose his movie wench will hold him. He is an easy mark for women.

Hold that vermouth until I come to the Coast again. I'll bring the gin.

Yours,
M

[141] [GS to HLM] [ALS, NYPL]

S.F.
June 13th, 1921.

Dear H. L.

Here's that "Everest" poem, which I'd rather see in "S.S." than in the venerable "Atlantic," anyhow. I trust George Jean will be hospitable to it. Let me know as soon as you feel you've a surfeit of my stuff, and I'll stop sending it.

It doesn't matter a whoop about the Phelphs' article, since you were nice to him in it. I was in hopes you had taken a whack at the damned Christian!

No—I don't think Dreiser is going to N.Y., but coming to S.F. And I suppose he'll bring the queen along. She's wasted on Los Angeles—and him.

I'll hang on to that vermouth till I find if you are to be here for the grove play on July 27th. You don't need to bring gin, as one can get plenty of it here. Gordon @ $10. a bottle.

My ode "To a Dancing Girl" has been privately printed, and I'm mailing you a copy to-night or to-morrow. An excellent job, I think. The Grabhorns came here from Cincinnati, I understand.

I've gone easy on the hooch for several weeks, but it means only sinking deeper into adultery. But the latter joy makes me write, while alcohol inhibits.

Wish we could have been at that Quatre Arts ball! With Sumner.

Remember me in your prayers!

George S.

[142] [GS to HLM] [ALS, NYPL]

June 14th, 1921.

Dear H. L.

Just a note, to accompany these clippings and to say I've mailed the ode. I think that the format is in very good taste.

As you'll note from the following headline, the old cats of Frisco are again rebelling against local vice conditions:

[Cocks and How They Are Pampered]

I think the climate is largely to blame.

Jack Newbegin announced proudly, today, that he had heard from you. The man has a quantity of excellent liquor, and parts with it with pathetic ease. I shudder to think what Dreiser, with his autographed books, will do to him. If you can possibly get out here for the Jinks, I'll have the police keep D. away until you get here. He is very vulnerable, what of his amours, and easily scared.

Don't laugh when you read the clipping about my being lectured on: leave that to me. I never expected to share the public ear with R.L.S. and Mark Twain. Another victory for the climate.

You needn't reply to this scrawl. Go back to your "American Language" and curse God, to whom I now commend your spirit.

Yours ever,

George.

[143] [HLM to GS] [TLS, BAN]

June 18th
[1921]

Dear George:—

I like the Everest piece very much, and I have no doubt that Nathan will agree. He is off next week for his first holiday in 7 years. This will tie me by the leg, and makes a trip to the Coast out of the question. I am, in fact, up to the Plimsoll mark[29] in labor.

The booze situation in New York is parlous, but I managed to pick up a case of Scotch, a quart of Pommery champagne, and some excellent red wine in the town last week. The red wine cost but 95 cents a quart. Here in Baltimore the malt flows like Niagara. I went to a noble beer party last night, and got down 10 or 15 Seidel. My stomach is skittish, and I am going slowly with hard liquor. But the Scotch in New York won me. No drinks are sold in restaurants, nor is one permitted to carry a jug. The thing must be done in private. So much the better. I like piano music with it, and the low hum of a gal's voice. I am preparing to have 20 or 30 gallons of wine made by an expert this autumn. The Scotch cost $96 a case—less than $8 a bottle.

Observe the enclosed.

Yours in Xt.,

M

[144] [HLM to GS] [TLS, BAN]

June 20th [1921]

Dear George:—

The ode to the dancing gal is here—a fine poem and a superb piece of printing. Please give my respects to the Grabhornii: they know how to do it.[30] The stuff is genuinely eloquent. You make me feel almost young.

I am about to smash my telephone with an ax. During the past hour no less than five damned nuisances have called me up. It is the curse of Christendom. I almost begin to regret that Christ ever lived and suffered.

Yours,
Mencken

[145] [GS to HLM] [ALS, NYPL]

June 2 , 1921.[30]

Dear H. L.

　　　Don't laugh—but "S.S." continues to be one of my monthly bright spots; though were I the New Nero, you'd go into a gilded cage and write fewer criticisms and more "Conversations." Little Georgie wants to be amused.

I've been on the wagon for several weeks. Don't jeer! It was the only way for me to get anything done, outside of dancing and adultery. I now arise at the ghastly hour of seven, reply to letters promptly, and let my poem a day! I'll be regaining the fame-illusion of the days of The Testimony of the Suns, next. Come out and redeem us from virtue, or Dreiser will get all Newbegin's hooch!

I've quit writing lyrics, for a time, though, and am at another dramatic poem I'm calling "Truth," showing the dear lady's reception by priest, potentate and populace. Having destroyed my youthful faith in democracy, you'll now have to share in the results! I promise not to protract them in any one volume.

I've had good letters lately from E. A. Robinson,[32] and one from Cabell. The latter wants to know how I got the notion he'd satirized Hergesheimer in verse, for joining the A.I.o.A.a.L. And I'm damned if I can recall whence I did get the idea. From you? Perhaps from Dreiser?

Cabell wants me also to give poems to "The Reviewer."[33] I've enough unsaleable ones to do *that*. Do you consider it ethical? You're already aware of my preoccupation with ethics.

I've been to luncheons and suppers with Ruth Chatterton this week and last, and have written another poem to her, in which I refer to her "seraph-tempting mouth"—not such an exaggeration as you think. (But I forget: you're not strong for labial stuff.) In return, she gives me tickets to "Mary Rose."[34] I haven't seen it yet!

I'm still "as those not without hope" that you'll come to see the grove-play. The Jinks part of it sha'n't cost you anything, but of

129

course the getting out here is frenzied spending. It's an experience, though, that you'd never *re*gret nor *for*get. And I can have a willing brat for you this time.

By the way, tell Geo. Jean that if he has more laundry bags than he can use, that I don't mind having one parcel-posted to me. I can reciprocate with scapulars, as fast as my one-out-of-six religious sister crowds them on me.

If I "repeat" things in my letters, remember that *my* memory is a cross between a disease and a joke, and forgive me. I sha'n't forget to stay single. Romance is safe enough for a poor man, over fifty. The Frisco girl is after one thing, and only one. As I've reiterated, "it's the climate." Come back and give it another whack at you! There'll be no Jane O'R. this time. (She's still in N.Y., is she not?)

Having prattled amiably on to this extent, I'll now be seen to cease. May the peace which passeth all understanding[35] be with your creditors now and for all days!

George S.

OVER

P.S. Let me thank you, sincerely, for your kindness to my friend George Hyde.[36] He had, I think, quite a gall, to communicate with you on the strength of a mere introduction by me in the Bologna; but after all, he's a bright boy, and worth knowing when he's in S.F. (as he is now, on the "Chronicle.") If you've any friends headed hither, don't hesitate to give them letters to me.

P.S. Your letter informs me that you can't come out this year. I'm horribly sorry! But of course George Jean deserves that vacation, which I trust he'll spend in a monastery.

Glad you liked the "dancing girl" book. I repeat that you've taken so many of my verses that I'm ashamed to send any more to you; but as soon as May Greenwood has touched up one she lately sent me, I want you to see it. It's a fine lyric, really.

I guess this makes an eyefull!

Yours ever,

George S.

[146] [GS to HLM] [ALS, NYPL]

June 29th, 1921.

Dear H. L.

This is so much a "S.S." poem that I can't forbear submitting it.[37]

One of my six (6) brothers-in-law just arrived from Honolulu with four gallons of *okolehao*. I'm praying for light!

Yours ever,

George S.

[147] [HLM to GS] [TLS, HUN]

July 3rd [1921]

Dear George:—

I didn't tell you that Cabell had satirized Hergy. In fact, I had never heard of it. Hergy deserved it, even though he didn't get it. He is now ashamed to wear the ribbon of the fraternity. I haven't seen him for several months. He is seldom in New York. Evidently, he is under espionage for having cast an eye upon La Gish.[38]

The Reviewer is all right, but the young editors are fools to pester you. They ought to try to dig up Southern stuff. I shall have a long piece about them in the August Smart Set.[39] We stopped the Conversations for fear that they were getting tiresome. I want to do two more—one on religion and the other on patriotism. If the book ever comes out there will also be one on women.

God knows I wish I could come out for the grove-play, but it is quite out of the question. Nathan won't return until the 17th, and I am blocked with work, and somewhat short of money. I think I'll take a look at Montreal during hay-fever. I hear that the law there allows one quart a day. But the price has run up fearfully. I am now looking for a likely gal to go with me—at her expense.

I have finished the revision of The American Language—all save correcting the copyist's MSS., revising the proofs, and making two indexes. Let me have your prayers. I shall now rewrite In Defense of Women, and then tackle Prejudices III. After that—my history of American Kultur—1914–1920.

I saw Jane in New York this morning. She is playing a sketch in the vaudeville theatres thereabout; there are enough of them to keep her busy. She has built a roof garden on the roof of her flat-house—very cool on hot evenings. But roof-gardens need beer to make them right. Here I have several new brews of great merit.

I hear that Nathan took a wench aboard ship with him. If so, he fooled me. He swore he was trying to get away from them.

Yours,

M

[148] [HLM to GS] [TLS, HUN]

July 5th [1921]

Dear George:—

I like the poem very much. Can you wait two weeks? Nathan will be back by then. Yesterday came a letter from Havana, reporting cocktails at 30 cents apiece. He says, however, that the gals displease him. I now hear that he took a colored girl with him.

Is the brother-in-law just arrived the incomparable Toots? I shall never forget him that afternoon in his room, lying out on the cooling board with ice on his head. The same night, at 10 P.M., he was soused again. A man of stupendous talents. He could knock out Jack Dempsey.

The beating of the Frog gave me great spiritual satisfaction. All the whores were for him, but Jack was the better man.[40]

Yours in Xt.,

M

[149] [GS to HLM] [ALS, NYPL]

July 14th, 1921.

Dear H. L.

Sure you may keep the poem two weeks. Longer, if necessary. 'Was pretty sure you'd like it. I wrote a better one to-day, but shall inflict no more on you for awhile. The Smart Set has earned a rest.

Yes—it was Toots who came up. He remained but a week, during which time he was perpetually soused, though he'd wake up feeling good enough, and eat breakfast. "It's a gift!"

He brought three gallons of okolehao with him, and he and the steamer's doctor got away with six (6) bottles of it that day! He showed up at the Bologna on his pins, but hungry and affectionate! As you say, "a man of stupendous talents." Some of the Roman emperors must have been made of such stuff.

I was for Carp., but bet on Dempsey to win in five rounds. Have lately discovered that the chap whose room is opposite to mine takes the Baltimore Evening Sun. So be careful what you write:

I'll see it. His name is Ned Greenway, our former social dictator.[41] He came here from Baltimore when a youth, and is apparently "well connected" there, as he has been left several fortunes by aunts in Virginia and Md.

I'm perfectly willing to give the Reviewer chickens some verse; but they'll have to wait until I see which of mine is going to sell and which isn't. Cabell wanted me to give them the enclosed, but I've a notion it's saleable. Put this copy with your archives.

God He knoweth that the Conversations were anything but "tiresome!" I'm damn sorry you've quit on them! Your energy is amazing. I wish I had a tenth of it, but the girls decree otherwise, or a weak will when one's in sight o' me.

I had Greenwood send you a lovely lyric, and hope you didn't turn it down. She's a good girl, and has left me alone for months. Fortunately, she abides in Oakland.

Our climate and women remain unsurpassed, but hooch grows daily scarcer, more expensive, and worse in quality. I envy you the trip to Montreal, with or without the heiress.

I was held up in Golden Gate Park last week, in broad daylight. We lost $68. and my silver watch.

George.

[150] [GS to HLM] [ALS, NYPL]

July 19, 1921.

Dear H. L.

Maybe you can use some of these epigrams. I've not sent any to "S.S." for a long time.[42] I suppose they should be typed, but my free stenographer has cut her business finger.

Yours ever,

George.

[151] [HLM to GS] [TLS, BAN]

July 25th [1921]

Dear George:—

I am trying the epigrams on Nathan. Some of them seem very tasty, indeed, to me. I accuse you of lifting them from the French.

New York has suddenly gone wet again, and with a bang. Cocktails are on sale in all the taverns, and very fair Chianti is to be had for $1.50 a bottle. I have actually bought a drinkable wine for 90 cents a quart. Such are the wonders of God.

Nathan reports Costa Rica is a very dull, but very wet country.
Yours in Xt.,
M

[152] [GS to HLM] [ALS, NYPL]

July 27th, 1921.

Dear H. L.

Here's a sweet little one-acter that I perpetrated last week.[43] Thought I'd take a chance at you, tho it's probably too low-browed for the "S.S." I suppose I could make it a little less obvious at the end: have them just look at the bed and yell!

I'm expecting Dreiser to appear this forenoon and go to the Grove with me, if he come at all. There will be a large attendance this year—about a thousand, I think. I wish I could trade a few hundred of them for you. Nathan should never have been allowed to go to Cuba. He'll probably acquire syphilis there, if he didn't get it on the out-going steamer.

Hooch seems to be omnipresent here, despite our aggressive Federal agent, the hated Exnicios.[44] The Grove will reek with it, every member seeming to take in an extra suitcase full. If anything will attract the megatherian Theodore,[45] that's it. As for me, let me brag that I'll be glad of four days of chastity.

Yours in the Sacred Heart,
George S.

[153] [HLM to GS] [TLS, HUN]
[The Smart Set
25 WEST 45TH STREET
NEW YORK]

July 31st [1921]

Dear George:—

An hour after this sociological piece appeared on the stands Nathan would be on his way to Sing-Sing, handcuffed to between two thieves, like the lamented J. C. Josephson. The Comstocks simply prohibit any such doings in bed. To change the ending would be to spoil it.

God knows, I wish I could be with you at the Grove. Dreiser will get drunk in half an hour, and fall asleep singing "Die Wacht am Rhein". He can't sleep alone. You will have to get in a colored girl to warm his old bones.

Today the temperature here dropped to 65, after five solid

weeks in the 90's. Result: I am so damned sleepy that I can hardly sit up.

Yours in Xt.,

M

[154] [GS to HLM] [ALS, NYPL]

Aug. 9th, 1921.

Dear H. L.

I survived the Jinks, though too intoxicated to witness the "Friday evening vaudeville" or the grove play itself.

Dreiser couldn't come; telegraphed his alleged sorrow. He'd have been sorrier if he'd attended, for we'd have murdered him with okolehau, of which we had six gallons; and he's partial to gin. It makes a very palatable fizz.

As it was, I had only "Dick" Tully and one, Dave O'Neil, a St. Louis chap addicted to vers libre, in my camp.[46] We slept little. The play is said to have been a huge success, and I ate five dozen écrevisse one day.

You were good to have taken so many of my epigrams. The more plaintive of them were written when I was a married man.

I gave the "Reviewer" a poem, and am wondering if any of its editresses are good-looking. If so, she may have others, as many of my things are too long to be saleable. You gave them some good advice in "S.S."

Raids continue on our Latin quarter restaurants, but the hooch goes on flowing. The Grove was *very* wet this year, as decent wine from the neighborhood was obtainable at $3. per gallon: Sonoma County is evidently beginning to unload some of its 25,000,000 gallons said to be in storage.

I hope to have another book out by Nov. 1st,[47] so please don't keep any of my verse in storage, or I'll have to buy it back, a painful procedure.

We're having a damned cold summer here!

Yours and His,

G. S.

[155] [GS to HLM] [ALS, NYPL]

Aug. 15th, 1921.

Dear H. L.

I've put in a refined evening reading "Smart Set," and hope it was Nathan and not you that perpetrated "The Ther-

mometer of Age."[48] Worse bosh I never read! "The challenge of
youth" is to one's bill-folder alone. As you know, I've more than
the average opportunity to rob cradles, aside from the disconcerting fact that young girls are attracted more to men of maturity
than to youths of their own set. Well, damned few of them are
worth sleeping with, for they haven't a tenth of the imaginative
sensuality of the woman in the thirties, and, indeed, seem to care
more for dancing, motoring and eating than for erotics. It's not
that they're trying to pull the leg of the mature man for what the
young man can't afford: God knows that they get little from me
in a material way! And a lot of the young men (at least in San
Francisco) have money and motors. No—their common cry is,
"Young men bore me!"

But, by Christ! young women bore *me!* Erotic sensitiveness is
largely cerebral, and education and development are necessary to
a girl. They actually lack in *feeling,* healthy as they usually are—
out here. But the woman in the thirties comes to physical love
with a sort of not-unnatural *desperation* of temperament. She re-
alizes what she's getting, and that the time is not for ever. Also,
her brain and sex have been trained to the flaming response. Result: she makes ten times as "good a push" as the youngster in
her late 'teens or early twenties. I've tried this many, many times
in the past thirty years, and I know what I'm talking about. The
vitality of our San Franciscan girls makes them more eager for
erotic experience than others, and one has a plethora of opportunity. I could have a new one nightly, if I wanted her *and* could
stand the strain. The girl wants the general excitement and fun
(aside from pushing) of a love-affair; the woman in her thirties
likes the same, but is really after the honest-to-God mattress
stuff. And she usually has the "challenge," both sexually, roman-
tically and intellectually.

No—take it from me if you need the taking: a kid is a bore and
a real woman a delight. And the latter certainly gives one all the
"conflict" one wants, in more ways than a few!

By the way, London came from good Rhode Island (I think)
stock. Charmian has data about his ancestry in her forth-coming
biography. There's a Sir John (?) London. The book as a whole is
sickening in parts—too much "mate" stuff. She seems to have
written it to prove how much he loved her. And he was "untrue"
to her on each and every opportunity that presented itself! But
he had a high respect for her nerve.

I think your appraisal of "Huckleberry Finn" is grotesque.[49]
The book goes all to pieces in the last two-fifths. I actually prefer

"Tom Sawyer." And when you speak of most of Poe's poetry being "hollow jingling," you go far to confirm a suspicion I've long held: that you don't really "get" poetry, notably on the "beauty side" of it. Poetry doesn't need thought, *as* thought: its highest value is in *imaginative phrasing. There* are the magic and the marvel, and a few lines of it are worth several volumes of prose to one sensitive to such thaumaturgy. I wish Bierce was here to take you in hand. You've a better brain than his in some respects; but not as regards literature. True, he greatly overestimated *my* merits; but then he did what he was always counseling others not to do: let the heart run away with the head.

Does all this sound ungrateful? Well, I rank you damned high, H. L.!

> Yours ever,
>
> George Sterling

Wow! I hear I'm Cabell's "favorite living American poet!" Wow!

[156] [HLM to GS] [TLS, HUN]

August 16th [1921]

Dear George:—

Thanks for the poem.[50] Why not a whole book of San Francisco, ending with an elegy? You have almost enough matter for it now.

Hay-fever has begun to nibble at my tail; in a few days I'll be very rocky. But as I grow older it tends to be milder. At 80 I'll be free of it. I have begun to draw up pians, by the way, for the national celebration of your 75th birthday in 1950. The Supreme Court agrees to adjourn for the day.

Work is hard these days. I am tired and in low spirits.

> Yours,
>
> Mencken

[157] [HLM to GS] [TLS, HUN]

August 22nd [1921]

Dear George:—

I agree with you absolutely. Nathan wrote that nonsense. He and I dispute over the matter endlessly. It is years since I have so much as spoken to a woman under 30. I detest all flappers. He is singularly naïve about women, for a man who spends so much time talking to them. You diagnose the case of the gal of 33 exactly right. That is the perfect age. After 35 they grow too sentimental. Before 30 they are idiotic.

As for poetry, I confess to holding various heresies about it. In Prejudices III I'll probably expound my notions.[51] They are not so far from yours as you think. But I maintain that much of Poe's verse is devoid of good phrases. He was greatest, I think, as a critic. The triviality of most literature constantly oppresses me. It represents the transient moods of third-rate men. I'll probably write no more about it after 1923.

"The Wiser Prophet" is capital stuff.[52] If it were shorter I'd slap it into type.

Hay-fever has me by the arse. I am middling uncomfortable. In a day or two I am going into Pennsylvania, to breathe the mountain air and try the 6% ale on sale there. Pennsylvania pays no attention whatever to Prohibition.

Yours,
M

[158] [GS to HLM] [ALS, NYPL]

Aug. 25th, 1921.

Dear H. L.

It's hell about the hay-fever! I'd not bother you with correspondence, if this weren't to ask you to send me a blood-specimen. I asked Abrams about the ailment, and he said he's not yet had a case to "try out" with. It is probable he can help or cure you—through one of his disciples in the east. Please send me a blood specimen, anyway. It sha'n't cost you anything. A few drops on a piece of white blotting-paper. The ear's the best place to take it from—the least painful. Don't let any *red* color be in the room when you take it, or approach the specimen afterwards. And don't send any animal's blood for a test or a joke: he's sure to detect it, and get angry.

Please do this, H. L.! It won't be much bother to you, and may result in future benefit to you.

T. R. Smith wrote to me about his anthology, at your suggestion, and I sent him six poems.[53] Of course he won't take them all. I suggested that he write to Clark Ashton Smith.[54] If he takes any of *his* stuff I want him to *pay* for it. Who makes the money on the book, anyhow? There ought to be some profit in it @ $15., unless it's needed to fight Sumner.

I've sent Cabell two more poems for "The Reviewer." They were too long to be saleable, anyway. Many of mine are.

Henry Holt & Co. want to bring out a book for me. I suppose

138

they're O.K. I tried to get my local publisher to bring out Jennings instead of me, this autumn; but he refuses.

Yours and His,

George S.

[159] [GS to HLM] [ALS, NYPL]

Aug. 28th, 1921.

Dear H. L.

I'm hoping that you're now in the hills, and in a mood to send me a specimen of your blood.

You're a good boy to take so mildly my comment on your estimate of Poe; though maybe you do not take me seriously as a critic. I've just gone over his poems again, and am surprised at the inequality there. It's usually a case of pure gold or pure lead. I'd no memory of his having written so much that was worthless. As you say, he was no maker of "good phrases," even at his best. What he did was a harder thing to do: he put over his aesthetic feeling by means of *atmosphere,* which represents hard artistic work instead of the immediate inspiration. Practically all great lines are the whisper of the subconscious mind. One gets them willy-nilly, without effort. Poe, by the more consciously mental process, made himself unique in literature. "The light that never was on sea nor land"[55] beats windily through, as if from a Beyond, all of his best work.

I enclose the list I just made when looking over his poems, and will give you *my* notion of the relative merit of the best ones, realizing that I'll probably find few folk to agree with me, unless roughly. I include "The Bells," that delight of the Kansan elocutionist, among his real poems, for it is all that he meant it to be: an extremely clever exercise in onomatopoeia. He spent years tinkering at the thing, and built it up from a few lines to what it now is, a rush of melody. But I suppose you know all that anyhow!

I can't rank "The Raven" very high. It's exactly what the boobery of his day would have fallen hardest for. And yet he has a wonderful passage in it—that about "an unseen censer." To me, "Ulalume" is unsurpassed for sheer art, for utter magic. After all, it *is,* as a whole, an imaginative feat, however deliberately he may have gone to work to create his atmosphere—as he did in "The Fall of the House of Usher," which seems to me the best of his tales.

You are right as to the triviality of most literature. I too find it increasingly difficult to find anything new that will hold me. Your suggestions are most valuable to me, and you're never wrong when you commend. I've read "Main St." (its author send me picture-postals from England), "Zell" and "Moon-Calf," and shall get "Dust" next.[56] I enjoyed "Main S." most, though "Zell" is better written. Carmel, you see, brought the small-town atmosphere home to me, especially as regards the tongues and hearts of women.

Sinclair was our "ugly duckling" at Carmel. None of us dreamed he "had it in him." But he has given literature and life a new and comprehensive turn, just as London did when he used the expression "the call of the wild." But again I'm telling you what you know already! Remember that this letter requires no reply.

I'll enclose one of my more fleshly sonnets in partial compensation.[57] It's one I hadn't quite nerve enough to let Smith have. 'Wish I dared send it to Harriet Monroe.

Here endeth this screed. May your shadow be long on the trail!
　　　　Yours in the Clitorian Guard,
　　　　　　　　George S.

[Enclosure:]

Real Poems

Sonnet: to Science
Fairy-Land
To Helen (the lyric) 2nd
The Valley of Unrest 6th
Lenore
The City in the Sea 3rd
The Sleeper 9th
Israfel
To One in Paradise
The Haunted Palace 4th
Silence
The Conqueror Worm 10th
Dreamland 8th
The Raven
Ulalume 1st
The Bells
Annabel Lee 5th
For Annie 7th

Al Aaraaf
Politian
　　　Chaff!

So are all the rest not noted here.

[160] [HLM to GS] [ALS, BAN]
[The Smart Set
25 WEST 45th STREET
NEW YORK]

[August 31, 1921]

Dear George:

Thanks very much. My hay-fever is so mild this year that I am taking no medication whatever, and need none. I was rocky yesterday, but that was due to a late party rather than to the pollen. I thus send no blood. I fear that Abrams might detect my diabetes, and so scare me.

Things are in a hell of a state here today. One of my partners died suddenly on Sunday, and there is a lot of business to engage us.

The poem is excellent. Has it been used anywhere?

In Xt.
M

[161] [HLM to GS] [TLS, HUN]

September 3rd [1921]

Dear George:—

Your Poe list is almost exactly as I should put it together myself. I'd probably put "Annabel Lee" in third place instead of fifth, but for the rest I follow you. Even more than atmosphere, it seems to me that Poe attained to sheer music—music devoid of content. Content is what ruins poetry. It is the bane of the whole vers libre movement. Poe showed clearly that beautiful words were their own sufficient justification. Swinburne learnt a lot from him. But all this I want to go into at length in "Prejudices III". And in a preface I hope to write to a new edition of Poe's critical essays, now unobtainable separately.[58]

The blood business for hay-fever is not new, and it doesn't work. At all events, not in my case. The damned thing bothers me for a week or two, but beyond that it is very mild. Today I am in the midst of it. I spent all afternoon working on my brick and concrete fence, a thing that will last long after my poems are forgotten.

What is the feeling on the Coast regarding a Jap war? I am rather astounded to find that it is taken quite seriously in Washington. Everyone believes that the so-called Disarmament Conference will bring it on.[59] I was told the other day by a man of very

141

high reputation, utterly seriously, that the Navy is preparing for the business, and that it expects England to give the Japs help. This fellow is no dreamer. Let the band play!

You should have sent "One Night" to Schmidt.[60] I think it is very good stuff. His book, I believe, is nearly done. He will be jailed for it.

God help us all.

Yours,
M

[162] [GS to HLM] [ALS, NYPL]

Sept. 5th, 1921.

Dear H. L.

I'm glad to hear that the hay-fever is mild this year. But you needn't have feared A's discovery of your diabetes: he cures it easily, and so his representative in the Bronx assumably can. I think that what you really feared he'd find is the high ohmage of your congenital syphilis. I've 35 ohmes, a dangerous quantity, as contrasted with Upton Sinclair's 5/25 of an ohm . . . 'Shall have it reduced to 1/25 this month.

You ask if some poem I sent you has been published. I can't answer, having forgotten what poem I sent. Probably it's one of those I've given to "The Reviewer" or "All's Well." I give them all my best work, as it's too long for "S. S.," and the termites on the other magazines don't want poetry, or don't know it when they see it.

Here's a new simile you may use if you care to: As homely as a girl-athlete. That's "inevitable" enough!

Well, dip your nose in the Gascon wine.

For Lion,
George S.

You don't have to waste time replying to these idle words.

[163] [GS to HLM] [ALS, NYPL]

Sept. 16, 1921.

Dear H. L.

Too damned bad—that hay-fever stuff! But I'd be willing to have it too, if all that Scotch were to accompany it.

Folks here refuse to take the prospect of a Jap war seriously, so far as I can make out. I think that that's because it seems impossible for one nation to get at the other one. And yet, the Jap is an odd fish. Who can predict what he'd try to do? Anyhow, I think you sized up the whole business correctly in one of your articles in your "Sun," this summer.[61] . . . The side that does the attacking is going to lose, on account of the aeroplane.

I didn't have enough nerve to give T. R. Smith that sonnet. Today I've a letter from him accepting all six of the sonnets and lyrics I did send! I thought he wanted only one or two, and was allowing him to select. So I shall figure prominently in his book, and only hope that the chaste Phelps sees it.

Don't imagine, Child of God, that your system is free from *congenital* syphilis! The very Esquimaux have it, and Abrams gets the syphilitic reaction from the bones of the very mummies of Egypt. He derides the Wassermann test, considering it a joke, and to be trusted about once in ten times. The disease is the base of almost all diseases: without a luetic soil, tuberculosis, cancer, paralysis, insanity, diabetes and all the other big ailments can't get a start. Lues, if not detectable in the blood, has its focus elsewhere, in various glands, but usually in the brain. If one have a high ohmage there, one is usually intellectual—or a criminal or idiot (Bierce says they're the same).

You must understand that all this stuff of Abrams' is absolutely *new*. I dare say it sounds like raving to you and your friends at the Johns Hopkins: I can't blame any of you for that. But you'll all have to "come to him" one of these days. I'm at his clinic several times a week, and talk a lot with the many doctors who are his pupils. Some of them are back from their home towns for a second course, and they all tell me that the thing's *proving out,* and that the cures they're making are (to the uninitiated) miraculous. And I can tell you myself that Abrams thinks no more of curing cancer or T.B., if not in the last stages, than another doctor would of lancing a boil. I've stayed with the thing too long, H. L., and interviewed too many physicians and cured patients, to have any doubts on the subject. I'll admit that it sounds like a huge hallucination, to *you*. I wish you could put in a week or two at the clinic. You couldn't doubt after that. I'm taking hostile doctors there and watching them give in, willy nilly. It's fun.

He has reduced my ohmage from 35 ohms to less than one, and that will be gone within a week. If you care to know what yours is, send me your blood, under the conditions noted in one of my late letters. Don't try any traps or tricks: he's sure to detect them, and then he'll get sore and refuse to diagnose.

My patriotism doesn't extend to my fellow citizens nor their form of government, but only to America's scenery, and not all of that. For instance, I'm of the opinion that all the country east of Denver would be better submerged, (except the Alleghanies) from December 1st to Sept. 15th. I exclude Maryland, where I escaped from the Sulpician fathers, and the graveyard in Sag Harbor. Yes—I love my country, the western part of it; but, as Bierce said, "tis infested of my countrymen."[62]

As you've probably but one of my poems in storage, I venture to enclose one more. It seems harmless enough.[63]

Beware of sin!

George S.

[164] [GS to HLM] [ALS, NYPL]

S.F.
Sept. 28th, 1921.

Dear H. L.

Our four-day summer is on us, with the thermometer in the eighties, and the S.F. Esquimaux are dying in heaps, feebly cursing God.

My silence in the Arbuckle case is that of counsel.[64] Charlie Brennan, his local attorney, came to see me about it, and I had to prepare the epigrams for the speech of defense. I sent Fatty "Rosamund," through Brennan, but he hasn't thanked me. Maybe he thought Alboin referred to him![65] My prediction is that he gets 2nd degree.

I had a bunch of clippings on the case, to send to you, but realized you'd get it all in the Baltimore papers anyhow, so sent them to my girl in Copenhagen.

Abrams found that he had entirely eliminated my "congenital," so I went on a five-day jag. Am now arriving daily, on faith. It doesn't seem to slow me up any.

I know his stuff seems "monstrous and incredible". It *should,* to anyone of intelligence. And yet it is all so. I am at his clinic several times a week, ostensibly to take doubting physicians and other acquaintances there, but really to watch the magic and marvel of the thing. He thinks no more of diagnosing and curing sarcoma and T.B. (unless in their last stages) than another doctor does of so treating a boil, or a mild case of piles.

I'll send you such of his "literature" as I can get, but it will be obscure to you, I fear. He prints it only to send to doctors who have been his pupils, to enable them to keep up with his discoveries, as he is going ahead all the time. I know I should have taken you out to see him work, but was afraid you'd think I was joshing you. Hc has put most of diagnosis and therapeutics quite off the map. Don't mind what the Johns Hopkins people say about him: they've not seen his late stuff.

Here is a poem that you may have gratis, if you want it (I think it's one of my best).[66] It was written too recently to *sell* to you, as it has to be in a book of my lyrics to appear early in November. But maybe you can run it before the end of the year; and few copies of the book will be in the east by then. It seems good S. S. stuff. Am also giving such poems (about to be in the book), too long for S. S., to Finger and The Reviewer. It seems a pity to waste them.

I expect to do a lot of writing this winter, but it may be in prose. Philosophical stuff.

A friend, physician on a Hawaiian liner, has brought up a lot of frogs legs from Hilo. I go to enfold them.

I think my youngest sister has a "sinus." Am taking her to Abrams tomorrow. If she have, he'll detect it instantly, and cure her in a few treatments.

Are you writing the article in Thc Appeal to Reason, signed John K. Turner?[67]

Dreiser sends me the enclosed. Rather heavy-footed irony.

Don't let your prophylactics run low.

Yours ever,
George S.

[165] [GS to HLM] [ALS, NYPL]

Oct. 8th, 1921.

Dear H. L.

Sir Henry is a pretty decent old scout, and really an asset to this club, as he gets in touch with all the big musicians visiting S.F., and entertains them here. His title is a joke; but he takes it with deadly seriousness. It was given him by Kalakana!

All I can tell you about the Abrams stuff is given in the "literature" I've sent you. Haven't you read Sir James Barr's article, and the five quarterlies I sent a couple of weeks ago? I'll repeat with the former. It seems certain that the man has revolutionized therapeutics, including especially diagnosis. IIe is now treating my youngest sister for a mild case of T.B.

Fatty will get a mild sentence, as you say. Anyone in the movies should have at least five years, anyhow; so justice will be preserved, and democracy made safer than ever.

I've just heard from Dreiser. The man is actually beginning to fall for Los Angeles! It's getting him! We'll hear next of his marriage to a widow, plump and older than he. And it's not as though he'd never been in S.F.

I enclose a rather solemn poem, just written.

Yours for devolution,

George S.

[166] [GS to HLM] [ALS, NYPL]

Oct. 19th, 1921.

O Friend of Poets!

You're wrong this time: I've been drunk on Swedish punch several times, with Genthe the photographer,[68] and the after-effects were not comparable in awfulness with those of a jag I once acquired (once and only once) on beer and benedictine. But that can't happen any more.

That Fatty case won't go to a jury for a long time: his lawyers are too wise. M'Nab is the downiest of old birds. But poor Fatty is ruined in all farming districts.

Thanks for the free advt.![69] But you've loosed on me a horde of local junkmen with tar for sale. Shall I send you a barrel, C.O.D.?

You are right: Abrams is enough to drive a hard head to temperance drinks! His injection of such nonsense as you specify is discouraging to his friends and pupils. It's as though Keppler or Newton went around reading palms. I beg you to overlook it, if you can, for he has really come on tremendous stuff. He may not have deserved to; but he did. I asked him why he didn't stick to his diagnosis and cure, and he said he was afraid some one else would come on the other stuff first! My name for it all is "circus stuff," a thing he often refers to jestingly in his clinic. I wish you could attend a few of them. I know of nothing more fascinating in the intellectual line. To see him infallibly run down and locate exactly *any* disease is to set one to pinching one's self. But he does it almost automatically, he has done it so many thousands of times. I never grow tired of watching him, and take many friends to be treated. Just had Clare Sheridan[70] there: her little boy has T.B. coming on. All the doctors I bring there become enthusiastic converts, though they go there utterly incredulous, which is only natural. So be patient with him, and overlook, if you can, his incursions into spookland. He has found 100% diagnosis. There's absolutely no doubt of that. And his oscilloclast is curing T.B., cancer, syphilis and all other *germ* diseases at the rate of scores a month. He is now handling about 80 cases a day. What he'll do

146

when the tide really sets in, God alone knows. He should have a hospital here, with internes. It'll come, some day. Meanwhile he's hard pressed, and I fear for his health. Still, a rest would fix everything. The trouble is, all the local physicians damn him violently, so his only near disciples are across the bay, in Oakland, and getting rich too fast, with their cancer cures, to wish to give him any of their time. Most of his pupils are from small towns, and are now making about $3000. per mensem. Hell! I wish you were here, to watch the clinics. It's terrific.

Glad you liked the last poem. I've plenty more, but shall have a heart and spare you for a few months; for surely you don't want to run me in every number.

I wish you and Jimmy Hopper could get together. He seems discouraged at his luck with our unspeakable magazines. He lives at the Brevoort. Is a Frog, but a live wire, and one of our very best short-story men.

I've been given four qts. of Perrier-Jouet!

Yours ever, George S.

[167] [HLM to GS] [TLS, HUN]

October 24th [1921]

Dear George:—

Certainly I want to have you in every number. Lay on!

Hopper sent me a story last week, but it was too fanciful for us—almost a fairy tale. I wish we could get him into the magazine.[71] I well remember his early work. I'll look him up in New York.

Abrams is an ass to add that transcendental trimming. No hard-boiled pathologist will listen to him while he spills it. Such fellows need managers, and the managers should be armed with clubs.

You mention a lady whose feats of gallantry are the talk of New York. I hope you took your turn on her couch. At the moment New York is drunken and happy. Prohibition has begun to go to pieces. Next week I am to receive several cases of Moselle and Rhine wines from a reliable bootlegger. Every incoming ship is loaded with it. The price of whiskey is falling, beer is now plentiful, and God is restored to His throne.

Yours in Xt.,

M

[168] [GS to HLM] [ALS, NYPL]

Oct. 30th, 1921.

Dear H. L.

If you can stand for me in every number, God He knoweth that *I* can't object! Is the enclosed ditty too frank for your chaste pages?[72]

No—I restrained myself with Clare. She's good enough for anyone but Nathan. However, I was otherwise involved, with a lady possessed of several bottles of the now almost mythical absinthe.

Of course Abrams needs a manager—or rather a keeper. He has fallen on the biggest stuff that ever went to the lot of a mortal—nothing less than the end of all disease and the race's physical regeneration. And he is queering it all, partially, temporarily, with stuff worthy of the Theosophists. I do what I can to restrain him, and he has agreed to let me inspect everything he puts into print in the future. I wish I'd got after him long ago. Pray don't let his divagations discourage you in your study of his work. His *real* stuff is inconceivably great and important. If you could only spend even one morning in his clinic with me and watch him diagnose, you'd be near to conviction. I'm luring doctors there, one by one. I've two lined up for next week.

It pleases me greatly to have you write you'll look up Hopper. It's a pity, and a fact, that much of his work can't be used by American periodicals of any paying ability. But he has several stories you should find available. He has been spoilt by high prices for his salable work, but should be reasonable in the case of his non-Pollyanic stuff.

Holy dreams!

Yours ever,
George S.

Dreiser proposes that I start a Little Theatre here! Great God!

[169] [HLM to GS] [TLS, HUN]

November 5th [1921]

Dear George:—

Egon's song caresses me; I shall steal it for my autobiography. Meanwhile, I see no reason why it should not be embalmed in our great family periodical. My best thanks.

The other night, in New York, I met H. G. Wells. He has an accent like an English waiter—pure Cockney. But he has done some sound work. New York now swarms with English pussyfooters, all bound for the Disarmament Conference. With their aid, Lloyd-George will frig poor Hughes to a frazzle.[73]

I'll dig up Hopper at the first chance. But it is hard to do any business with those Saturday Evening Post boys. They think it terms of 2,000,000 circulation. We have 50,000. Yet if we offer them 1/40th of their usual rate they yell for the police.

The whole East is drunken and debauched. Prohibition is a roaring success!

Yours,
M

[170] [GS to HLM] [ALS, NYPL]

Nov. 10th, 1921.

Dear H. L.

I don't think you'll find Hopper unreasonable in the matter of rates: he's beginning to be pretty badly scared, and is writing 2500 word stories for Leslie's. Make him go down into his portfolio: he has plenty of stories unsalable to that abortion, the average magazine. He really belongs to Smart Set, at his best.

Nathan didn't care to use "Egon's Song." I do not blame him, for it's pretty frank. Into your autobiography with it! You won't be lying.

'Wish I could have seen H. G. Wells![74] I like him for his "scientific" romances. He told Sinclair he was coming to California, and I began to hoard gin; but in the newspapers he's yearning for the Everglades, of all the swamp-holes on the planet! Malaria and moccasins to him!

Your pages from the Credo are kolossal, epoch-making![75] May I not have a couple more of them? I know several worthy young women who would appreciate them. Two of that kind took me to Carmel in a racing car, last week, and we shocked the natives, the more so as one girl looked about fifteen years old; but she's twenty. Dr. Nathan would like her.

From the enclosed clipping (the large one) you'll note there is still hope for you. But imagine anything of the sort being needed in this climate!

I'm being "sculped" by von Sabern. It'll be an awe-inspiring sight.

Another clipping, to show I've more ways than one of being a fool.[76]

Yours for more bastards,
G. S.

[171] [GS to HLM] [ALS, NYPL]

Nov. 21ˢᵗ, 1921.

Dear H. L.

I'm glad to learn your tastes concerning poems to poets, and am writing one to you as a young poet (you've confessed it), comparing you to Cale Young Rice.

'Just read your article on cancers in the "Sun,"[77] and again remind you that Abrams is curing them as fast as patients consult him—that is, unless the thing is very far advanced. He makes no more fuss about it than curing a headache. You or your medical confreres will say that the patients didn't *have* cancer. But the two or three hundred doctors who have been his pupils say he's *never wrong,* that every diagnosis of his is confirmed when an operation follows. Cheer up, as I have, for nothing can end us now but old-age, dissipation, or accident. Take your choice!

The Arbuckle trial is going to last till July 4ᵗʰ. Prayers are going up for him in all the Los Angeles churches, and the women convicts at San Quentin have petitioned the governor that he be put in their ward if convicted.

Yours for the reform of God,

George S.

[172] [GS to HLM] [ALS, NYPL]

Dec. 4ᵗʰ, 1921.

Dear H. L.

The heart of San Francisco is febrile with hope deferred. This (Sunday) morning the churches are packed, and the murmur of prayer is distinctly audible at my open window. The Dominican monks in Golden Gate Avenue are now on the fifth day of their Retreat, and the nuns of the Perpetual Adoration are getting in some good licks.

The dissenting woman-juror will undoubtedly hold out, the jury be dismissed and the Fat One discharged. The reception to Foch will be nothing to that awaiting Fatty.

I was asked to write an ode of greeting to Foch, but declined.[78] Am fed up on war-stuff; and the French begin to be disgusting anyhow. Your German cousins seem to have driven them hysterical with fear.

Am enclosing some pamphlets for your physical and esthetic good. Cherish them.

In His name,

George S.

[173] [GS to HLM] [ALS, NYPL]

Dec. 7th, 1921.

Dear H. L.

Get over the idea that a seven stanza (28 line) poem won't go on a page of "Smart Set." It will, with a space left for an epigram. I infer you did not care for "The Gulls,"[79] and wish you'd say so, for "this eel is used to being skinned," and is insensitive. But maybe you think it's immoral to pay ten bucks (listen to Le Gallienne!) for a mere poem. If so, you may have the enclosed for eight—provided you want it at all. I've not sent it out heretofore, and like "The Gulls," it's easy to sell.

My damned book is out at last,[80] and I'll be sending you one in time for the spring butchering, if you're going to hold one. It's easily my best book, always excepting "Lilith."

Fatty has fled south for the holidays, leaving a shamed city behind him. Archbishop Hanna[81] has already excommunicated the old hen who hung the jury, but as she's not a Catholic, that will do little good. She has been offered a position in the movies by D. W. Griffith, but is holding out for bigger money. If the next verdict isn't unanimous for acquittal, I look to see severe rioting in all the hotel district here.

"Ursula Trent" is a peach, isn't it? I hear George[82] is to lecture here, this winter, and I must begin to save gin, the British beverage.

That story, "The Three Kings," in the last "S. S.," is also a peach.[83]

Hope you've seen Hopper and lifted a little gloom from his monogamous heart.

I wish to Gawd you *could* get some of your local scientists to come out and "investigate" Abrams. He welcomes all comers, provided they don't come in a big committee, with murder in their hearts. And I'll bet a dollar to a pine-nut that he can convince any fair-minded man. I'll send you his last quarterly soon.

Yesterday I borrowed $250. from a local millionaire, and bought me one of his oscilloclasts for a physician friend. That shows what *I* think of it.

Yours ever,
George S.

[174] [HLM to GS]

[December 16, 1921]

[Text unavailable.][84]

[175] [GS to HLM] [ALS, NYPL]

Dec. 24th, 1921.

Dear H. L.

For you to be on a diet at Christmas time is, in the term I supplied Jack London with, "monstrous and inconceivable!" God must have used up all His mercy on Arbuckle.

I suppose Jack Newbegin, our best book-seller and MS-collector, wrote to you about the fuss the Fat One made over your mention of him in one of your letters to me. If he didn't, let me know.

I was talking to Charlie Brennan, one of A's attorneys, yesterday, and he swears to his belief that Fatty never even laid hands on the girl. I know that your prayers were mainly responsible for his near-acquittal, but still think that those of the local Dominican monks and your humble servant somewhat "affected the result." The next trial will be a sweeping victory for A. There are two members of this club on the panel, and if they fail to qualify (which will of course involve perjury), they'll be ostracized.

But to think of *you* on a diet! And in Baltimore, of all cities! Dr. Nathan is much more deserving of the penalty, for his views on marriage, of which I read he approves strongly, for all his acquaintances and you, his only friend.

Now say: isn't it about time you sent me that blood-specimen? I ask it as a favor. Only Abrams can tell you just what is the matter—and there may be something started that you're not yet aware of, such as that gentle thing, cancer of the stomach. Come on! Have a heart! Send me a small drop of blood and I'll do the rest. Don't waste time in sending some other animal's blood, for he's sure to detect it, and may then get so sore that he won't diagnose on the next sample from you.

One of my sisters-in-law is now singing his praises for curing her of mastoditis, from which she'd been having frightful headaches for years.

I note a disconcerting phenomenon about our local bootleg: it raises Hell with one's ability to sleep. I don't mind a good honest headache: I've a vast capacity for aspirin anyhow. But I like to sleep between the hours of 12 M. and 7 A.M. I've a notion you're getting much better hooch on the Atlantic coast, as compared to the Pacific. In between it must, of course, be awful stuff. Friends bring down splendid Scotch from Seattle, but they can't bring much, naturally.

Thanks for the kind words about "Sails and Mirage!"[85] Yes—it's much my best book, always excepting "Lilith." I like my "Testimony of the Suns" poem, too; but only Bierce and I seem in accord on the matter.

I doubt if Nathan cares for "The Killdee," so am sending a bird of another plumage.[86]

Now for Christ's sake, Old Scout and humble follower of Him, send me that blood-specimen, if only to keep me quiet! I swear to tell no one of the trace of lues he's sure to find!

Yours in ever-lessening respect for God,

George S.

[176] [HLM to GS] [TLS, UCLA]

December 29th [1921]

Dear George:

I am a Quaker and am forbidden by my bishop to shed blood. But some time soon I'll sneak behind the door and get that specimen for Abrams. He will diagnose Asiatic cholera, I am sure, and probably the great pox also. But I believe in Wassermann. Eight times he has pronounced me pure.

Now you tell me that Fatty didn't touch the girl! And I spent weeks praying for the scoundrel! Take a message from me to him: tell him I hope he breaks his neck. I was absolutely confident that he had given the wench a herculean service, and busted her bladder by the sheer power of his backbone. If he is a fake, then let him rot in hell.

I like the poem very much. It puts me in a sentimental mood. The name of mine is Mathilde.

Yours,

M

1922

[177] [GS to HLM] [ALS, NYPL]

Jan. 7th, 1922.

Dear H. L.

I recovered from the holidays at the small penalty of two days in bed. I'm now ripe for crime again, and hope you are the same. It was a disappointment to receive no blood-specimen from you. Probably you're waiting to get a drop of monkey's blood. That might fool Abrams, but no other kind would.

I have a raging letter from Scheffauer in which he demands that I recant in public for writing "The Binding of the Beast," under penalty, unless I do so, of being roasted to a cinder in one of your forthcoming books. All I have to say is, H. L., that you would better do so if you think the truth demands it. It will hurt, not because of what you may write, but because it is written by a person I like. Written by a stranger, it would mean less than nothing to me.

I don't mind telling *you* that I'm sorry that I had those poems published in permanent form. Not that I recant on any of them, but because it is a finer thing to get in and fight than to stand on the side-lines and merely curse.

My advice to Scheff is to let sleeping dogs lie. I was just beginning to feel sympathetic for the Germans, by reason of the way the hysterical Gaul is putting on the screws, and now Scheff bobs up and wants to stir up the late stinking mess. Worse, he goes about it in a haughty and arrogant manner. Well, if he wants worse invective than that book he may have it: I haven't *begun* to exercise my talents in that direction yet.

He's an odd Scheff. Bierce once told me: "Scheff argues with froth on his lips."

Here's to your gastritis!

George S.

[178] [GS to HLM] [ALS, NYPL]

Jan. 30ᵗʰ, 1922.

Dear H. L.

You're not going to get into any argument with *me* about the war; so I meekly accept your qualified noun and pass on to higher things.

It *snowed* here yesterday, to the intense joy and interest of San Franciscans. Being used to the stuff, *I* stayed in-doors. But many school-children saw snow for their first time.

Scheff must have meant some one beside you—I read his letter carelessly. Very likely he is going to write the book himself. He may go to Hell!

There's a fine old San Franciscan lady now in New York who has to make a few extra bucks to augment her small monthly income. Her name is Ina Coolbrith,[1] and she was an intimate friend of Bret Harte, Ambrose Bierce, Stoddard, Miller and all our old writers out here.[2] She seems to be writing pretty fair stuff yet, and if you find any of it in your mail I hope you'll be as kind as possible to the old girl. (She has drunk more than we two "put together"!)

I'm editing a lot of Bierce's letters, for publication by the Book Club of California. Will send you the volume when it finally appears.[3]

Newbegin, I, et al. will take good care of Hergesheimer if he ever shows up in S.F. But I fear he'll stay in Hollywood. I admire his work decidedly, and should be glad to see he got decent hooch.

W. L. George, another of my favorites, will lecture here in two weeks. Do you know him sufficiently well to let me have an introductory note to him? I should like to get him lit. If you don't, I'll butt in anyhow.

I've read every page of your monumental "American Language," and can only say it's an amazing work. I was almost entirely unprepared for such a thing. You await that deluge of new sewage a damned sight more calmly than I do. But not my will but thine be done!

Yours ever,
George S.

[Enclosure:]

To an Irate Father
(But dedicated to H. L. Mencken)

You say I have deceived her;
    You say I made her fall;
You say I have bereaved her
    Of maidenhead and all.
Oh! rightly you pronounce me
    A wolf within the fold,
And justly might you trounce me,
    The bad, the base, the bold.

I know that monsters like me
    Are foes of innocence;
I know God's wrath shall strike me,
    When I am taken hence.
My honor is in hock. I
    Am ruin to the chaste.
But—your daughter's gonococci
    Are little to my taste!

                    George Sterling.

[Separate enclosure:]
P.S. California disgraced herself over the Wright act,[4] but that
was the fault mostly of Los Angeles County. San Francisco is
flooded with import Scotch @ $8.50 a bottle. It's rather "green,"
however.

                    Sterling.

[179] [GS to HLM] [ALS, NYPL]

                                    Feb. 25th, 1922.
Dear H. L.
        Thanks for the introductory letters! George lectures
here next week; Hergy hasn't put in his appearance yet. I suppose
Hollywood has got him. At any rate, I'm glad he wasn't here for
the past fortnight: "the incomparable Toots" is dead! His mother
died of the flu, and he came up from Honolulu to take back her
body, got the flu himself, and died in four days: his kidneys quit
on him. My sister, his wife, was with him, and returned to Honolulu last Tuesday, with both bodies. Hell!
    I got the flu from him, and had to stay in my room all last week,
in bed part of the time. Am all right now, but on the wagon and
feeling rather blue. Toots was a dear boy, and my sister was de-

voted to him. She left in charge of a nurse, and semi-hysterical. Once more, Hell!

Here's a sonnet I wrote this morning, one of the best things I ever did. I know you've two poems of mine on hand, but feel you'd like to have first look at this one.

No more now. God is disgusting and the local bootleg sheer poison.

Conspuez le bon Dieu!

George Sterling.

[180] [GS to HLM] [ALS, NYPL]

Mch. 8ᵗʰ, 1922.

Dear H. L.

May the here-to-fore merciless God deliver me from reading any worse drivel than that in "The Triumph of the Egg" volume![5] It outjabbers Jim Joyce.

Hergesheimer hasn't appeared yet. I'll do my best for him when he does, but intellectual females are not on my list, and he'll have to take a chance on a passionate bonehead in the early thirties.

How is this for a hard-luck tale? One of my friends had been operating on a fair young thing for months, without apparent progress. Then, one night, he took a bottle of good brandy up to her apartment, and after a while had her so well advanced that she went to her bedroom and lay down. He followed, lay beside her, got to the stage of intimate kisses, then to feeling her shapely calf, then a velvet thigh, and finally—found out she was menstruating, at which instant she threw up on him!

I'm encouraging him to go back and try again.

I'm not going to present your introductory note to George. He has shown up here with a young wife, and I am broke and on the wagon till I can get something beside bootleg. But I'll meet Hergesheimer on his own terms.

That's a fine bust that von Sabern has made of me. But don't hang my picture near Mary MacLane's.[6] She's a Sapphist.

I've just finished a 200 line ode to Shelley—very poetical and highbrow.[7] Of course it won't sell. You seem to have peeved the gentle Jennings, who moans of sundry refusals of his perfectly good lyrics. But he sells more verse than anyone *I* know of.

I haven't heard again from Scheff. When his letter comes it will probably be a sixty-page one, containing all the vituperative adjectives in the language. And *I* got all the wrath out of my system while the war was on!

I've a standing grudge on God over Toots' death. Now I don't care if I *ever* visit Honolulu. Four other brothers-in-law could have been so much more easily given.

May the angel of the flu pass you by!

George S.

[181] [GS to HLM] [ALS, NYPL]

S.F. Mch. 21, 1922.

Dear H. L.

Of course you're right as to Anderson's work. But I'd just been driven crazy by his damned style. There are abundant guts in his creations. Joyce is another cuss that gives me the willies. I dare say I'm too old-fashioned.

I enclose a letter written under the influence of dago red, on Sunday evening. I was not "seeing things." Had I been, they'd have been animals and not birds. (I can see I should leave the stuff alone.)

No Herg. in sight yet. Why must the successful literary gent always pack a wife around with him? Even Sadakichi did, who is a success only as a grafter. I sent Wilton Lackaye[8] home to his wife once, close to extreme unction, and maybe I can ingratiate myself to a like degree with Mrs. Herg.

"Cytherea"[9] *did* delight me. I suppose you noticed the knocks it received in the radical and old-hen periodicals. Of such is the K. of H.

A lustful Hawaiian girl is on my trail. As she's not quite good-looking enough, I'm coyly retreating, with the aid of our switchboard boy. Sometimes I wish I was young again. Why should we become more fastidious as we grow, personally, less eligible for the tilting-yard? Of such are God's mysteries.

His child,

George S.

[182] [GS to HLM] [ALS, NYPL]

Apr. 1st, 1922.

Dear H. L.

If I laugh any more over the Wilson-Criley fight I'll have tonsilitis.[10] Plainly, Wilson has a true jealousy-complex—is actually a bit insane on the subject, as he broke with Jimmy Hopper the same way, though he didn't dare challenge him to a fight. Aw God! it's comical!

I heard from the Great Herg this morning. He's at the St. Francis, and is motoring down to the Santa Clara Valley to-day, having dinner with some millionaire to-night, and playing golf to-morrow morning. But I get him for part of the time after that. I'm damn sorry I couldn't have him for to-night—we're having a costume party over at Lafler's, on Telegraph Hill, and no one will be allowed to leave the place except on a stretcher. I plan to remain one-fourth sober, and grab the prettiest girl—an anti-social act.

Why in the Name do chaps like George and Herg. have to travel around with their own wives? I suppose that's what they "have" to do. I *was* hoping Herg. would prove an exception. No one should be permitted to marry till past the age of seventy, when one needs watching.

I had no copy of that "Things Worth Doing,"[11] so, unless you foolishly save my letters, I'll have to imagine some further atrocities. And I think I can do "something more worth while" anyhow.

Aprop. of saving letters: cast an eye on this clipping! It must refer to a whole letter, or, more likely, to a lyric in my handwriting. I am offering either at cut-rates—four for a dollar. Better get in on the ground floor.

I've sold my "Ode to Shelley" to Scribner's—**204** lines, count 'em! I sent it only as a joke.

Angels guard thy sleep!

Geo. S.

[183] [HLM to GS] [TLS, HUN]

April 7th [1922]

Dear George:—

The Wilson-Criley affair belongs to psychopathology. I am genuinely amazed that Wilson should have gone in for such buffoonery. Why didn't he simply hire a slugger, and have Criley murdered? As for Hergy, I hope you will fill him to the nozzle with trade gin, and destroy both of his kidneys. I have heard nothing from him, save a telegram, since he left the East.

God forgive me for burdening you with letters of introduction, but a very good fellow, Dr. Paul H. De Kruif,[12] of the Rockefeller Institute, will be in San Francisco shortly, and you may be able to give him some information. If he shows up, will you please tell him what he wants to know? I don't know precisely what it is. Some business in which Norman Hapgood is concerned.[13] De

Kruif needs no steering in the matter of refreshments. He can smell alcohol through 18 feet of oak.

Hopper came into the office lately, and we had a long gabble. I had an idea for him, but he said he was too busy to tackle it. He is at the Brevoort, and working hard.

In Xt.,

M

[Enclosure:]

Dear George:

This is Dr. Paul H. De Kruif, of whom I wrote to you lately. He is an earnest Christian man.

Ys

M

[184] [GS to HLM] [ALS, NYPL]

Apr. 12ᵗʰ, 1922.

Dear H. L.

I'll be delighted to see Dr. Kruif, and hope he wants to look up the Abrams' matter. A. is going right ahead, and his clinic is full of physician-pupils, *all from points outside of S.F.* The medical gang here will have to eat a humble pie of vast dimensions, within a few years.

I go to the clinic almost daily. A. is *never wrong* in his diagnoses.

Hergy has passed on to brighter scenes. I'd hoped to see more of him; but he promises to return in time for our forest Jinks. That's from July 15ᵗʰ to 29ᵗʰ, the play being on the 29ᵗʰ. Why don't you come out too? I know it's expensive; but it's worth it.

I had a kike friend all ready to give Herg. a dinner with profuse pre-prohibition stuff. It is to weep.

Hopper's on Hearst's International.¹⁴ That should fix his financial woes.

Use all the letters of introduction you want to with me. That is, **you** may.

Yours ever,

George S.

[185] [HLM to GS] [TLS, HUN]

April 17th [1922]

Dear George:—

Hergy, I suspect, was rescued from you and your gang by Mrs. Hergesheimer, a most intelligent and charming woman. She knows that a few more bouts in the grand manner with the higher alcohols would bring him to the fits.

We celebrated the Arbuckle verdict Saturday night with noble ceremonies. They were really most impressive. When the list of jurymen was read, the whole crowd leaped to its feet and yelled "Hoch, hoch!" We have applied for permission to put a bronze tablet commemorating his acquittal upon the wall of the City Hall. God's ways are mysterious, but trust in Him is never betrayed.

Yours,
M

[186] [GS to HLM] [ALS, NYPL]

May 10th, 1922.

Dear H. L.

As I noted on the clipping, De Kruif called; but he didn't appear till the last day of his visit here, and I'd been on a two-week bend, and *had* to be on the wagon. However, I ran him up against a man with a bottle of Scotch, which they demolished up in my room.

De K. seems to be a very likeable chap, and I'm hoping to see a lot more of him when he returns (as he promises to) at the end of the month. I'm hoping, too, to get him up to our Midsummer Jinks.

Two young women whom I know well (though they're otherwise respectable) are going to open a boot-legging parlor! It will be fun while it lasts. Heaven help me!

Saw Hergesheimer only a few times, but he too promises to return. I'm told you purpose going to Europe for the summer. I don't wonder: it must be fascinating now. Drink to me in Liebfraumilch, which used to be Jack London's favorite tipple—and mine.

I'm inflicting no poems of mine on you, as you've two already. But here is as lovely a lyric as I've seen in many a moon.[15] 'Don't see how you can resist it—pure poetry! "Smart Set" is the only magazine fit to print Smith's work. As for me, I've just written a twenty-five stanza "poem" about trapping a mastodon![16]

In His name,

George S.

[187] [HLM to GS] [TLS, BAN]

May 15th [1922]

Dear George:—

Thanks for the Smith poem. I like it very much, too, and am sending it to Nathan forthwith.

I have not heard from De Kruif for weeks. Evidently he is pursuing a career of drunkenness and dissipation on the Coast. Well, I warned him to be careful. Hergy, I hear, is on his way home. I heard from him but twice during his trip. He wore out two dress suits and five plug hats. He is a doggy fellow.

I hope to escape on August 15th, not sooner. My plan is to go to England, look into the logrolling camorra there, and then proceed to Munich and immerse myself. God knows how long I'll stay. It is a curious fact that in 1914 I didn't know a single man in Germany save the British consul at Munich, whereas now I have at least 20 good friends there, scattered in all directions. I may make a grand tour of the country, testing the various wines. The reds are bad, but the whites are superb. I doubt that I'll go to France. I dislike the Frogs, and don't have much fun in Paris. But I may go to Pilsen, in Bohemia, with a Bohemian friend.

The Second Coming is at hand—and Will H. Hays is the Man![17] Whisper this everywhere.

Yours,
M

[188] [GS to HLM] [ALS, NYPL]

May 26th, 1922.

Dear H. L.

So we're not to have you at the Jinks. I'm sorry—we'd have done our best to kill you. I'll have to take it out on De Kruif, if only he keeps his promise to appear.

I don't blame you for preferring the European trip. Imagine vintage wines @ 50¢ a bottle! If I thought Scheffauer wouldn't have me jailed, I'd sell out and make the trip myself. I have his last pamphlet, supposed to be by one, F. Hansen; but the style is inescapably Scheff's.[18] Bierce was correct when he wrote to me: "Scheff argues with froth on his lips!" Oh, well! he's no crazier than the damn Frogs. I begin to wish they'd been licked.

I'm glad you felt hospitable to that beautiful lyric of Smith's. As you have but one poem of mine now on hand, I venture to submit one more.[19]

Was at a place on the water-front last night called "The Mermaid Cafe." They were serving wine, whiskey, gin and cocktails openly and in profusion. I tried only the claret, and found it good. A friend of mine is getting a 5 year old burgundy for $2.²⁵ a gallon—really decent stuff. But I'm longing for some benedictine or chartreuse, stuff one never sees here any more. Anyhow, good Haig and Haig now retails over our bar here for $14. a bottle. A stiffish price, but it's worth it.

I still read, and marvel over, your amazing "American Language."

Here's to Valentino!

G. S.

All Germans should bow down and adore you, Old Scout!

[189] [GS to HLM] [ALS, NYPL]

June 7ᵗʰ, 1922.

Dear H. L.

Don't jump on Scheff and the alleged Hansen: they're doing what they think is the big thing. But they're going about it stupidly. Start in by calling a man a son of a bitch, and he'll allege your fondness for wife-beating.

I'm enclosing a poem that I wrote for *you,* this morning.²⁰ That interrupted my shaving at least twice; but don't thank me.

Your details on the booze of Gotham make me drool with envy. Here it's nothing but gin, Scotch and rye, and I like things that taste good, like chartreuse, benedictine, absinthe, etc. However, we have port. I went on a five-day system of interlocking jags, last week, and am barely back to normal yet. It was all on Haig and Haig. I awake to find myself owing our head barkeep $65. for my share of it—a considerable sum for a poet.

I'm sorry you can't be at the Jinks. I suppose Hergesheimer won't come either, though he swore he would. My last hope is De Kruif. Heaven help him if we get him past the gates!

You'll have a grand time in Europe. I suppose I'll never see that land, unless I let someone keep me. But one has such a hell of a time here—I mean a good time—that all else seems immaterial. My present girl would have landed St. A.²¹ in seven seconds—or six.

I've just signed the contract with Holt & Co. for my book of selected poems. Holliday thought that "Selected Poems" isn't a "striking title," so I've suggested "Neglected Poems" to him. But it's dishonest to sell a book of selected poems unless it's so specified. I don't much care whether or not the thing comes out. Poetry is a joke, anyhow.

Knopf sends me a leaflet with Nathan's picture on it. I've pinned it alongside of Nora May French's.[22] He's a handsome cuss, and she'd have fallen hard for him. Of such are the kingdom of Heaven.

I'm reviewing "The Poetic Mind," by one Prescott of Cornell, for our "Bulletin."[23] The poor cuss has worked hard, but the book (so far) is full of absurdities. It takes a thief, etc. If he'd written any poetry himself he'd not get that way.

My friends are reading your "American Language," and go through it (two of them so far) from cover to cover. That is going some, considering the subject.

Abrams continues to horrify the local shamans. I'm taking a rich and aged friend there to-morrow. He has arthritis. A. will find the pus-pocket in two minutes and eliminate it in two weeks. All that reflects credit on my selfishness, as said aged friend tells me I'm mentioned in his will.

Nearly 300000 "Shriners" are about to descend on this devoted town. I'm wishing old Ambrose were here. He soaked that gentry hard, as do you. But you are elsewhere.

I hear you're keeping Jane, in Baltimore.

> Yours ever,
>
> G. S.

Do you suppose "Snappy Stories" would run this poem?[24]

[190] [HLM to GS] [TLS, BAN]

June 12th [1922]

Dear George:—

The poem has a sweet and affecting smack. I am having it engrossed upon vellum and shall hang it upon my office wall, between the portrait of Hoover and the Italian lithograph showing the Battle of Izonzo.

God knows I wish I could come out to the jinks. My stomach is in very fair shape again, and I now eat and drink ad lib. I am tenderly grooming it for the heavy work ahead of it. I shall strike London about August 15th, and put in two weeks eating at Simpson's. Then for Bremen, Berlin and Munich, and some beering in the grand manner. The stuff has excellent effects upon my system.

I shall try to dissuade Scheff from his crazy jehad. Every time he looses one of those indignant blasts he makes new enemies. But, as you say, his heart is pure. I wish he'd do more articles on the new German books and plays. Some of them are very interesting, and he knows them better than anyone else. I may drop down into Bohemia to see what the Czech-Slovaks are making of liberty. The country is probably a wreck.

I haven't heard of or from Jane for months. Now and then one of her creditors waits upon me in New York, but my stenographer knows how to get rid of them.

The hotel-keepers in New York are bawling that they are being ruined by the fact that all the restaurants are now wide open. Hence the boobs avoid the hotel dining-rooms. Last night the cops raided Rogers' at Sixth avenue and 45th street, and pinched Robert, the head-waiter. I am glad to hear of it. He had been selling gin at $15 a case above the market. It will give me some pleasure to loose a sneer when I see him next week. Meanwhile, I have sent him a Bible to read in the calaboose.

I wish I could get some liqueurs to you. Day before yesterday a customer here gave me six bottles of chartreuse, kümmel, goldwasser, etc.

Upton Sinclair is in Baltimore, and I shall meet him tonight. He is staying with his cousins, who are 100% Americans of the Kiwanis Club species.

Yours, in Xt.,
M

[191] [GS to HLM] [ALS, NYPL]

July 7th, 1922.

Dear H. L.

I'll fire one more poem at you, before you escape to peaceful Europe.[25]

De Kruif showed up once more, for a day only, and as luck would have it, caught me again on the wagon. I'd been on a six-day tour, and wound up with a mean congestion of the stomach; so I had to behave. However, I ran him into a bunch who were celebrating the divorce of the Holy Ghost; so he got a snout full. He was here only a day, then left for Truckcr, promising to return for the Jinks.

Hopper got here yesterday, from New York; but he has a return-ticket. His views on American magazines are instructive and highly entertaining. He speaks well of the "Smart Set," however, on which he evidently has designs.

I wish I could have been present at your meeting with Sinclair, and hope your breath was strongly alcoholic.[26] Do you expect to see H. G. Wells when in England? He's a sort of super-Sinclair. But perhaps you met him in Washington. I wish he'd go back to his "scientific" romances. That "Time Machine" is hard to forget, even if one wanted to.

My best girl has taken an apartment only two blocks from this club. I hope to be alive on your return from Europe, where I hope you'll have a real Neronian tour. Remember me to Wilhelm and Scheff.

> Yours ever,
>
> George S.

[192] [GS to HLM] [ALS, NYPL]

Nov. 22nd, 1922.

Dear H. L.

I'm damned glad you're back; and I've a hunch that your trip was a disappointment to you, for which I'm sorry, though you must have got lots of "material." If you'd come to S.F. and tried grappa again, your right kidney also would be out of whack.

This is sad news about Jane. I felt, however, that retribution impended, for her five-year repulse of all my attacks on her virtue. Poor Jane! There's an Armenian here whom she could easily have vamped. But the girl isn't without her sense of humor: imagine her asserting a deep interest in the Armenian race! The little devil.

Nothing exciting has happened here since I went into the lake for lilies for Dreiser's girl. I think I sent you the clipping of that.[27]

I sent only one poem to "S.S." in your absence, and Nathan sent it back, saying they had too big a stock on hand, and to wait till Dec. 1st. As he seemed to have no objection to the verses otherwise, I've held them against your return, as they seem to me the kind of thing you want. I enclose them.[28]

Wish to Hell I could drop in on you and hear what you have to say of Europe. Would it bother you too much to send me some of the "Suns?" Am wondering if you saw Scheffauer. He never replied to the very mild letter that I wrote him. I know you'll be busy, but drop me a few lines anyway.

> Yours in sin,
>
> George S.

This is shaky writing, but I'm recovering from a double periodical.

[193] [HLM to GS] [TLS, HUN]

November 28th [1922]

Dear George:—

I'll be delighted to have the Bierce letters. Some
time ago a man in Cleveland, named Loveman, printed a small
volume of Bierce's letters to him. Hollow and polite stuff. I am
slating the book in the Smart Set. The Clark collection looks to
be the real thing.[29]

What has happened to Jane God knows. The whole episode but
teaches us once more that it is imprudent to violate God's holy
ordinances. But I am glad that it was an Armenian who was
stung. Jane has Turkish instincts. If I ever hear from her I'll let
you know.

I have written nothing about my European adventures. The
truth is that I have been too busy. Moreover, there is nothing to
say. Another war is inevitable, and the sooner it comes the better.
I had a high old time in Berlin. Scheffauer, of course, is a very
mild fellow, but there were others of larger capacity.

The Abrams stuff seems to me to be pure piffle. His handwriting magic reminds me of the feats of my old friend, Mme. Rosie,
the colored psychic. He will end by convincing you, Dreiser and
Sinclair that you are down with the great pox. Dreiser now believes that even black eyes are caused by syphilis.

I like the poem very much, and am passing it on to Nathan. I
believe the bars are lifted.

New York is wetter than ever. It is dangerous to life and limb
to go to a party there.

Yours,
M

[194] [GS to HLM] [ALS, NYPL]

Dec. 14th, 1922.

Dear H. L.

I'll be sending you the "Bierce letters" in a day or two.
I fear that there also you will find more or less of the "hollow and
polite," but enough remains to show the "human side" of the
man, besides much that is variously interesting. Had I had the

publication of the book, I'd have cut its contents down by half. But Bender[30] (who has most of the letters) wanted as fat a volume as possible. It's a pity it couldn't have been enriched by Bierce's letters to Scheffauer, which abide, probably for all time, with the British government, which seized them long ago.[31]

The hooch out here is getting worse monthly. My last sampling of it put me in bed for five days, with a doctor calling three times a day. I got a real scare. What in hell is one to do? Emigrate to Italy or China?

As to Abrams' stuff, all I ask is that your kidneys last ten years more. By that time it will have gone through the same course as Lister's, Pasteur's and many others'. If it's the bunk, why are his diagnoses invariably correct? And why can his pupils put over the same stuff? Let's declare a ten-year truce on it, anyhow.

One of my old flames is down in the city jail, accused of murdering her young husband. I go to see her almost daily, bearing delicacies. I fear they have the goods on her; a pity, for she's a good-looker. (You met her at the Bologna.)

> Yours ever,
>
> George S.

[195] [HLM to GS] [TLS, Mills College]

December 19th [1922]

Dear George:—

The poem is prime Winter goods. I am sending it to our laboratory to be assayed.[32]

My best thanks for the Bierce book. I have gone through it at a gulp. Your memoir is excellent stuff, and so is the preface by La Pope. Who is she? It is true, of course, that some of the letters are trivial, but they all throw some light upon the man. I shall do a review of it. I am writing to Bender.

I have not sent you Prejudices III for fear that parts of it might be offensive to you as an Americano.[33] Friends are far more valuable than books, especially as the embalmer draws nigh. I lost an old and good one last week: called to God via an ulcer in the belly.[34] A capital fellow. We had been boozing together for 20 years. Have your chaplain pray for him.

My personal ecclesiastical valet is instructed to batter and befoul Heaven with prayers for the gal in jail. I hope they don't accuse you of putting her up to the crime.

My stomach is somewhat frayed by the bootleg concoctions of

this latitude, but in the main I am still drinking sound stuff. The danger lies in going to parties. I have a mind to withdraw from society altogether, and become a solitary drunkard. Two weeks ago I went to a party, and had to get down some rye that left me quaking for three days. In the end, my system mastered it. Down here there is no excuse for feeding such garbage to guests. Good stuff is still plentiful.

The other day Jane called me up from Philadelphia, the first I had heard of her in six months. She said she was bound for the coast and would wait upon you.

God help us all in 1923!

Yours,
M

[196] [GS to HLM] [ALS, NYPL]

Dec. 26th, 1922.

Dear H. L.

I suppose it's my Berserker war-sonnets that give you the impression that I'd resent criticism of this country. I sha'n't apologize for them, as they still seem to me the natural reaction of one whose ancestry, however far removed, was English. I may even go so far as to say that I love my country; but, mark you, it's *scenically* that I love it. As Bierce says, "But 'tis infested of my countrymen," and their antics and shortcomings do not infect me with the sense of hilarity that you get out of "the monstrous pageant." Rather is it a case of "the madness of man and his shame." I feel depressed and disgusted by the contemplation of God's little show, and nothing you wrote could offend me. You are right oftener than any other censor morum with whom I'm familiar, among the living.

So send me your book—inscribed. I don't love America politically nor esthetically, though I'm going to write the national anthem, words and music, with the customary exaggerations!

I'm glad you liked the Bierce book. Bender is the secretary of the Book Club, and its main-spring. He's an ultra-benevolent little Hebrew in the fire-insurance business, and when he found I was going to buy the book for you, he insisted on sending you one.

La Pope is the ex-wife of a U. of C. professor. She's a woman about 35 years of age, blonde, good-looking, writes pretty fair poetry. She lately made a whacking big killing, selling some apartment houses, and has betaken herself, poor wretch! to Europe.

My old flame is out on $20000. bail. The coroner's jury voted unanimously for acquittal, but she'll have to stand trial, of course. She's guilty, all right, but they'll never convict her. The jade promised to ring me up as soon as she got out; said it was the longest time in twenty years she'd gone without a push! But she didn't: I suppose her bondsman got her. Even murderers are ungrateful—to *me*.

Your little roast of Loveman was pleasing, and correct in all respects. He's a young Jew with an eye on Fame. I used to correspond with him, but quit on account of his lavish and indiscriminate praise of my work! An unusual reason for a poet, you'll allow.[35]

I'm still on the wagon, but shall fall off if Miss Loos[36] wants me to. Am eagerly awaiting her appearance. Nathan refers to her as a super-cutie. I'm not strong for kids but then . . . .

Who said I can't review books? Sample enclosed.[37]

How can 1923 be any worse than 1922?

Patriotically yours,

George St.

1923

[197] [HLM to GS] [TLS, Mills College]

January 2nd [1923]

Dear George:—

The book goes to you by this mail. If it makes you heave and fart, then throw it to the sealions. It disquiets me to hear that you are still on the water-wagon. It is against nature and the public decencies. If old Abrams is scaring you again, give him a kick. A couple of stiff drinks will do you good. I find 18 empty bottles on my cellar-table. It was bare on December 24th.

Your dithyrambs to La Taggard almost make me sob.[1] She must be a fair one, indeed. Give her my love La Loos I know only slightly. A very amusing gal. She is full of capital movie stories—that is, tales about the morons at Hollywood.

My dinner club, which has been meeting regularly since 1910, and in that time has got down more than 400 carboys of alcohol, is about to die. One of the members was unexpectedly summoned to Jesus a few days before Christmas, and another has fallen upon a complex of misfortunes. These two were the hosts: we dined at their houses. Now we are homeless. The funeral of the dead brother would have delighted him. Two widows showed up, and the family of the second sent three Methodist preachers to pray him out of hell. But his friends had hired another cleric, and the Methodists were shouldered out. One of his old friends showed up stewed, and followed the funeral in a taxicab to a country graveyard 15 miles in the country. Altogether, a most pleasing affair. Now the two widows are hiring lawyers and preparing for battle.

Yours,
Mencken

[198] [GS to HLM] [ALS, NYPL]

Jan. 15th, 1923.

Dear H. L.

Lay abed this morning to finish "Prejudices III." I find myself agreeing with you on almost everything—bad news for you, no doubt, as I am often "the dupe of this world's sounds and odors." But I'm still far from perfection: the spectacle of my country's folly or misery afflicts me unpleasantly. Nausea to pity nearly is allied. I feel more and more impelled to write my treatise on the cosmos, which will at least enlighten Dreiser on several points.

Abrams didn't put me on the wagon. He advocates alcohol, probably regarding it as conducive to carcinoma. No—it's the quality, the greenness of the awful stuff that's proffered to one out here that deters me. I find my friends' breaths redolent of ether, on a morning after. One would not be sure they'd not been operated on. Guess I'll have to marry money and hie me to France, if the insane Frogs aren't at war by that time.

Jane hasn't appeared yet, nor has that damn murderess called me up. Her trial's on the 25th, and I think of going there in full mourning.

If you want some more errata for Prej. III, here they are:

page 17, "digitation"

"   142, "lamasery"

"   159, "cherishing"

"   165, "even"   line 14

"   186, "whomever"   line 16
"   264, "sedentary"

Guess you did your proofreading by proxy. Oh! and on page 129 occurs the word "catachumen." I can't rid myself of the vague impression that the "h" is superfluous. But I can't find the word in dictionary nor thesaurus—probably because it's pure Greek. Enlighten me.

Do you care to use the enclosed poem? If so, you may have it gratis, as it's of the unsalable type. I dare say, though, that you prefer to stick to the soft stuff for "S.S." However, it would do no harm to run verse, occasionally, with a bit of sense in it. Despite your notions, poetry sometimes states "truth" appallingly and vividly.

Yours and Hisn,

George S.

P.S.

My national anthem is nearly ready to be published. I think of asking Hearst to spring it on my fellow citizens. What a revenge for their neglect of "The Testimony of the Suns!"

G. S.

[P.P.S.] Yes—La Taggard's a peach, but (so far) happily married.

[199] [HLM to GS] [TLS, BAN]

January 23rd [1923]

Dear George:—

It should have been catechumen. The h belongs in there but not the second a. I am the worst proof-reader ever heard of. The new edition is almost as dirty as the first. But the third, if it ever comes, will be clean at last. My best thanks for your corrections. You have an eagle eye.

This poem, unluckily, is a bit too stately and long for us. We have to stick to lyrics.

Jane called me up in New York last week. She said she had just returned from California, and was about to start on a vaudeville tour. I didn't see her. She said that she was leading a virtuous life still. God help us all.

I am in the doldrums and can't work, and so I have taken to making bookcases. Result: five large splinters in my hands.

I am off to Washington to take a snout into politics. The newspapers never publish the truth.

Yours in Xt.,

M

[200] [GS to HLM] [ALS, NYPL]

Feb. 1st, 1923.

Dear H. L.

I hope that the winds of wine have broken up your doldrums. An alleged friend proposes to store fifty gallons of seven year old claret in my room here—as great an insult as has been proffered in years. He must think I'm pretty damn safe! (I have accepted.)

Served you right for *making* bookcases! It is your job to *fill* them.

Behold the enclosed picture, giving the first verse of a "poem" I was asked to write for our annual charity covering all charities![2] 'Wish I'd met the girl!

You'll not care to run these refined verses on our friend Lorimer,[3] but the cat sarcasms seem to be in line with your epigrams on women. Pardon its being a carbon: I mailed the original, by error, to the original of the poem, an old sweetheart.

Your comments on D. H. Lawrence, in the last S.S., are correct to the last period mark.[4] He's a tubercular erotomaniac, and his books and the Spoon River Anthology[5] owe their vogue to the same cause—their raciness.

Here's to the damnation of mankind!

Yours ever,

George Sterling.

[201] [GS to HLM] [ALS, NYPL]

Feb. 14th, 1923.

Dear H. L.

That picture of the bill-board was sent to amuse, not impress. But wait till you hear (if you ever enter school houses) my "American Hymn!"[6] You'll break off all diplomatic relations.

So the invincible Jane has bobbed up again. If she paid any visit to these regions, she let *me* know nothing of it. My murderess is still out on bail, and the trial is postponed regularly—the same old stuff. I am wondering how Ben Hecht will fare.[7]

The local police have been pretty rude in their hooch-raiding, lately. "Bigin," of that Wop restaurant we went to, has been hauled in three times. I was in his joint last week, and two big bulls came in and searched the kitchen thoroughly. They found nothing, at which he actually taunted them, assuring them that they'd overlooked it! Of course they'll return, some wet evening.

I was out at the ocean beach with a crowd, last night, but was dissuaded from entering the surf. Too bad you and Dreiser weren't there! I'd have had a run for my money.

Yours for the reform of God,

G. S.

[Enclosure: Invitation by the American Academy of Arts and Letters to attend the formal opening of the permanent home of the academy, February 22, 1923.]

[202] [HLM to GS] [TLS] [HUN]

February 19th [1923]

Dear George:—

The sonnet bathes me with appreciative sweat.[8] I am sending it to Nathan. He is, I hear, sober temporarily.

Ben Hecht seems to me up against it. All the Chicago literati have deserted him. His wife wrote to me last week, asking if I'd come to Chicago to testify for him. I said yes, of course, but it will do him no good. They have offered to let him off with $100 fine if he will plead guilty. He has refused. His book clearly violates the law. The interesting thing is that the Chicago swine have all run to the sewers, and left him high and dry.

Your tales of Prohibition raids appall me. Here in Maryland all the wops are selling all the known drinks, and no one seems to molest them. As for New York, it is dripping wet. I suspect that the Christian influence of Los Angeles is responsible for the troubles of San Francisco. Why doesn't some one burn down that town?

The invitation of the literary Babbitts gave me a good laugh. Kick them, and they kiss you. It would be a good idea to go to the meeting soused and give three cheers for Hearst. They are Anglomaniacs of the crawling, snivelling variety. Imagine having a ninth-rate Englishman as guest of honor on Washington's birthday.[9]

Jane looks about 47. What she is up to I don't know. I saw her for a few moments only, and two other gals were present, one of them very fair.

I have a low flu, not bad enough to take me to bed. I shall assault it tonight with some Scotch.

In Xt.,

Mencken

[203] [GS to HLM] [ALS, NYPL]

Mch. 3rd, 1923.

Dear H. L.

I hope that the Scotch proved a specific for the flu. I've a cold incubating, myself, but shall knock it, as usual, with bromo-quinine.

175

That's depressing news about the Chicago literati—I had imagined them as made of sterner stuff. One could understand such weakness in New York writers, with their horror and dread of what's not respectable. But Chicago! Sandburg[10] should re-write some of his poems. I introduced him, by the way, at his reading here a couple of nights ago. I have small use for his manner, but there are entrails in his matter. Here is one of *my* few incursions into vers libre.[11] I had a mind to entitle it "A Lamb of God," "One of His Flock," or something of the sort. If you've the nerve to do so, go to it—provided you care to use the squib at all. Maybe even "Blah!" is a better title than "Bah!" The latter smacks a bit of indignation.

Our police here are going on with their rough work. And yet I know of a small French restaurant where apparently real absinthe retails @ 50¢ a drink.

I'm the gainer by the fact that you go on publishing the only readable (throughout) and intelligent magazine we have. You've a strong team in Suckow and Winslow, and this last one-act play is a smasher. "Dashiell Hammett" puzzles me: I find it hard either to believe or to disbelieve in his existence. Some of the items sound incredible; and it seems impossible to have *invented* others.[12]

I've been working for a week on my essay on the cosmos.[13] Don't laugh! It's briefer and less dull than you imagine, and the cognoscenti will extract small joy from it. I expect to publish it as a pamphlet, with "The Testimony of the Suns" included.

> Yourn and Hisn,
>
> George S.

[204] [HLM to GS] [ALS, BAN]

[early March 1923]

Dear George:

I am laid up with a damned laryngitis, bronchitis, etc.—nothing serious, but my voice is gone and I feel very low. Let me see that essay on the cosmos. Why not embalm it in the S.S.?

The enclosed things somehow miss me. "Bah!" is too indignant—and Nathan is bawling that he has too much long stuff in type. What else have you?

Hecht, I assume, will be jailed. I had hoped to go to Chicago to stir up some defense for him, but the germs have floored me. Scotch seems to do no good. I am switching to rye.

Let me have your prayer.

Ys

M

[205] [GS to HLM] [ALS, NYPL]

Mch. 14th, 1923.

Dear H. L.

I can easily sympathize with you about the laryngitis, for that was *my* weak spot until Abrams used the oscilloclast on it, three years ago. "Great is faith!" I can hear you say. But a specialist had told me my tonsils were "putrid," and twenty minutes of the oscilloclast seem to have cured them permanently. By the way, I'd think hot rum would be better than rye.

'Sorry you didn't like my "Bah!" It seemed in line with much of your stuff and the title could have been changed. Well, here's a sonnet. Most of my short poems are too serious for "Smart Set." Which brings me to that essay on the cosmos. I'm printing it myself, as a pamphlet, and have no idea that any magazine will run so black pessimism. But if you want to use parts of it, you're more than welcome to—gratis. It's too long (over 8000 words) to run in toto. Besides, its altruistic ending will awaken your jeers. I want you to glance at it, anyhow, and shall be sending it to you in MS. in two or three weeks, when I'll speak more in detail of it.

The cops are getting more and more sassy here, and restaurants are raided every night. How Bierce would grin (or rage) at the way "votes for women" is working out—in this case via the Wright act. All his old mistresses hereabouts seem to have turned to Christian Science, or gone crazy—if there's any difference. He was like London—so virile that homely women looked all right to him.

In His name,

George S.

[206] [HLM to GS] [ALS, BAN]
[The Smart Set
25 WEST 45th STREET
NEW YORK]

[March 22, 1923]

Dear George:

Nathan reports that no verse is to be bought at the moment: too much in type. But next month!

I defy you to do your damndest with your "Sceptic's Fate". Skepticism, in fact, is the only comfortable philosophy. One is never disappointed. But very good verses!

New York grows better and better. All of the most respectable restaurants—for example, Delmonico's—are now booting. God knows where it will end. I begin to despair of public virtue.

I have been laid also, along with my whole family. But God has delivered us all.

Ys

M

[207] [GS to HLM] [ALS, NYPL]

Mch. 28th, 1923.

Dear H. L.

I seem to have got your goat, slightly, with the "sceptic" jingle—an amazing thing. Of course I was only jesting, and used your renowned name only on that one carbon-copy.[14] I'm a sceptic too, on most things—Conan Doyle's fairies make me smile.[15] But von Schrenck-Notzing's book seems to "prove" ectoplasm.[16] And I know that Stewart Edward White[17] and some of his newspaper friends have experienced some amazing phenomena (the stuff hasn't been given publicity yet.) Well, 100% scepticism is as foolish as 100% faith. I'm willing to be shown. Telepathy has been proved to me a dozen times.

Have you run into the amiable Jennings yet? He seems to be trying to make a living in New York on poetry alone, an attempt that elicits my horrified admiration!

Ford got after Abrams in his "Independent."[18] Abrams was about to sue him for libel, but Sinclair dissuaded him. Abrams is taking in $2000. a day!

My essay is now with the fair typist. I'm going to send you a copy, tho I know you won't care for the last fourth of it. Anyhow, give it the once over, and tell me if you think I'm guilty of gross error anywhere (except of course in my altruism. I accept my softheartedness there.) It isn't pleasant reading; but such truths have to be told sooner or later; and some of them haven't yet, so far as I know, been thus collocated—or synthesized.

Day by day in every way my friends make fools of themselves: who am I, to expect exemption?

Yours in Faith,

George S.

This letter seems to require no reply—so don't bother.

[208] [GS to HLM] [ALS, NYPL]

Apr. 12th, 1923.

Dear H. L.

Another good (and undeserved) letter from you. You're a Spartan of correspondence, and I have that guilty feeling whenever I fire my fool letters at you.

My bright and bad young friend George Ilyde writes to tell his joy over your acceptance of something of his.[10] A glad and ruthless sinner, one of the exceedingly few men I'd trade skins with.

I wish to "Christ-and-Him-crucified" that anything remotely resembling "perfect" Scotch was obtainable *here!* All our S.F. booze must come from British Columbia, where it's being mixed hastily, like swill for swine. It's a depressant, not exhilarant, and must be full of "green" poisons, like other immature things.

As time goes on, I find myself more and more puzzled by Abrams, whose greed for coin and unwillingness to "demonstrate" before a committee is disconcerting. It all smells of quackery. On the other hand, there are his amazing accuracy at diagnosis and his incredible cures. He cured every person with T.B. I ever took there—and they *had it,* and *stay cured.* About ten in all, well within a month. I give it up; nor do I attend his clinic any more.

Your praise of "The Goose-Step"[20] pleases me—it's sane and justified. But Dell's made me want to puke, so I roasted poor Upton (in a letter) for taking it seriously. The "G-S" is a formidable document—why insist that it's art as well? And now Haldeman-Julius blurbs Upton's "Hell,"[21] a crude and childish drama. But I become indignant—so "Hush!"

In nomine Domini,

G. S.

Hoch to the predatory Jane!

[209] [GS to HLM] [ALS, NYPL]

Apr. 15th, 1923.

Dear H. L.

Here's my fool essay, which begins not so badly, but peters out, like most things human, in the illusion of mercy and hope. Well, cast your eye over it some rainy night, and let me know what weak spots you find in its first two-thirds—I know the weak spots in the rest.

I know too you'll have no time to say much about it—a few brief comments are all I'm asking for, and not those if you think it would be a waste of your time.

I've not read the philosophers, but have picked up a smattering of some of their ideas, and it seems to me that there are a few ideas in the first part of the essay (the implications of infinity) that haven't been put into print yet. At least, they seem to have left no impress on modern thought, or Dreiser would have come on them in his explorings, and would not have had to ask some of the questions in his "Hey Rub-a-Dub."[22] And it seems to me that they are important implications, fatal to all superstitions that *I* know of.

If you think it's worth it, I want to issue this essay as a pamphlet, with "The Testimony of the Suns" added. I've deliberately made it as simple as I could.

Yours till He come,

G. S.

[210] [HLM to GS] [TLS, BAN]

April 17th [1923]

Dear George:—

This poem is too damned indignant. We bawl so much against godly men in prose that I hate to take another hack at them in verse. They are moved by the Holy Spirits; the Saints operate in them.

The fact that Abrams cures patients with tuberculosis is not surprising. Such patients always get better under a new cure. Perhaps half would get well anyhow, even if they took no cure at all. No medicine can help them. Meanwhile, don't forget that many diagnoses of tuberculosis are incorrect. A number of other diseases look like it superficially. To establish its presence beyond a doubt is a very difficult matter technically, and takes at least a week of observation, with constant laboratory tests. I incline to believe that A. will blow up with a bang. His literature grows more and more absurd. The "eminent physicians" who use his machine are chiefly osteopaths, homeopaths, etc. Not a single genuinely competent man has one.

Your news that honest Scotch is unobtainable on the Coast fills me with sadness. Have the Methodists actually won? Down here they are having a very hard time of it. New York is flooded with whiskeys, wines and beers. Last week I spent three successive evenings at the beer-table, drinking out of big steins. One night Nathan and I and another fellow went out to Union Hill, N.J., and found an archaic German beer-house of a sort theoretically extinct—the town bakers playing cards at round tables, lace curtains at the windows and the pickled herring made by the proprietor's wife. We drank so much that we could scarcely stand. Next morning we felt like two-year-olds. A superb light beer, running about 4% alcohol. The Dutchman charged us 40 cents for a large stein: it was worth it. Come East!

I am still trying to start my book, and still stuck. Well, it will come soon or late.[23]

Yours,
M

[211] [HLM to GS] [TLS, BAN]

April 21st [1923]

Dear George:—

This is excellent stuff: a persuasive argument, very well presented. I see no way of sawing an article out of it for the Smart Set without hopelessly botching it, but in a pamphlet it should be very effective. I think it will cause a lot of discussion—and maybe get you some invitation to address women's clubs, universities, etc! Demand your pay in 120 proof Scotch! The title, it seems to me, is a bit bald and pretentious. You can think of a better one.

Who are the Bookfellows? Who gets the profit when they make any? I have a feeling that the organization is not altogether altruistic. Some of the leading members send me MS.—always cheap, amateurish stuff. It is amusing to find "Frederick Coykendall" giving his imprimatur to George Sterling. What next, in God's name? Who in hell is Coykendall? The whole organization has a dubious smell. I'll be delighted to have the book.[24]

It turns out that my recent tip about the Second Coming was a false alarm. Nothing has actually happened.

Yours,
M

[212] [GS to HLM] [ALS, NYPL]

Apr. 23rd, 1923.

Dear H. L.

Sorry that the sonnet seemed "indignant" to you. 'Sent it to you first because it seemed just the kind of thing "S.S." wanted to run! Here's one of another caliber.

That Jersey beer-joint of yours has an almost mythical sound, and is almost enough in itself to bring me to New York. I should expect to board there, for beer is one of my many weaknesses.

The Methodists haven't "won out" here. The trouble is that the Canucks seem to have found out that we'll buy anything they're kind enough to offer us; so they offer green stuff. It's our own fault: why should they keep it years to ripen, when we're so eager to take it off their hands at once? Damn the late war!

By this time my cosmic profundities will have landed in your mail-box. Take your time. I sent it also to Sinclair, as it hit re-forms, and have to-day a silly "reply" from him, showing that either he read it carelessly, or, what's more likely, cannot reason. I shall dismember him at my leisure, if I can get my sister to take in stenography what I have to say.

There was a grand free-for-all fight at the Bologna Thursday night, just after I'd left, curse it! One girl pulled another's hat to remnants, and was rewarded with a plate of hot spaghetti on her own bean. Then the male consorts and their friends took a hand. Fifty squares of mosaic knocked out of the wainscoting. Coises!

Yourn and Hisn,

G. S.

[213] [GS to HLM] [ALS, NYPL]

May 4th, 1923.

Dear H. L.

I'm delighted to find you approving of my essay, which I'll call, I think, "The Will-to-Pleasure." If I've given you the notion that this poet isn't entirely moronic, it will not have been written in vain. Some of the intellectuals think that your "blind spot" is poetry; but you are correct as to nine-tenths of it. Don't forget, though, its great possibilities for condensing "truth," for etching it in with the imaginative acids—also its power of suggestion. Sometimes I think it's the bunk; at other times prose seems feeble and tawdry compared to it. But despite the ability of E. A. Robinson et al. to make it "intellectual," it is at its best when pure moonlight, as in Poe and parts of Coleridge. The magic of words—that's more *fun* than "the truth," anyhow.

Sinclair didn't like my essay—I knew he'd not. He came back with a foolish "answer," which he said he'd publish as a reply to the essay when it appeared. When I tore *that* to tatters, he wrote declining to go on with the argument, adducing that his "work would be utterly meaningless and absurd" to him if he thought that "mind and conscience were the accidental product of warm slime." He is enormously an egotist, with a real appetite for pleasant delusions.

The Bookfellows are an association of over 3000 alleged souls in Chicago, held together by one George Steele Seymour et ux. They seem to be, mostly, rather stupid, well-meaning critters. Seymour is honest, I have been led, so far, to believe, and no one seems to be getting anything but kudos from the books he gets out. He has some sort of soft job on one of the big railroad systems, and has impressed Cabell, Starrett[25] and others favorably. I joined his association out of good nature, long ago, and last winter he wrote asking me if they couldn't print something for me. I was just about to bring out "Truth" at my own expense, as I'd done in the cases of "Lilith" and "Rosamund," and thought it a good chance to save money: all I want is to see the play in print. Then it's off my mind and I no longer give a whoop what becomes of it.

No—Seymour is evidently out for fame, not coins. When the book's out I've a notion of asking Holt, or Liveright, to bring all three dramatic poems out in one book. A certain Miss Thoda Cocroft, by the way, is trying to sell the movie-rights of "Rosamund." She was Margaret Anglin's secretary once, and seems a nice girl. Which reminds me that I've just stolen a sugar-daddy's pet. Pushed her in a chair at "Gobey's," yesterday. Of such are the kingdom of Heaven.

"Who in hell is Coykendall?" is right! Some New York Brahmin of whom I'd not heard till Seymour mentioned him.

I was at a dinner last week with Maugham. Everyone got decently drunk, the ladies more so. I've been around a bit with Walpole, too, and old Ham Garland.[26] He's a gentle old boy, from whom I got a sense of pathos. I wonder what he thinks of Ben Hecht!

Enclosed clipping will show we're doing what we can.

    Yours ever,

                Sterling.

[Enclosure?]

"The Liberator" is actually going to run the "Lumberjack" thing![27]

I hope you saw my metrical insult to Lorimer in the same journal of uplift.

George.

[214] [GS to HLM] [ALS, NYPL]

May 16th, 1923.

Dear H. L.

The memorial to Arnold is a noble conception,[28] and I bespeak the privilege of writing a quatrain or couplet for its pedestal. My mother's ancestors grew wealthy in Revolutionary times through the sale of provisions to the British fleet in Gardiner's Bay. That, it seems, makes me especially eligible to this honor. And I am much in favor, generally, of any plan that promises a free trip to the Wetlands. Let the good work go on!

All right, dear heart: I'll stop the flow of verse or worse Smartsetwards. Sometimes I wonder why I ever do send out poems, for a girl who doesn't need the money usually gets the small change resulting. I suppose it's just the natural, and commendable, vanity of the poet. When I read my prose I'm as vain as the next one.

Seymour writes: "Coykendall is a member of the Grolier Club, a collector, reader and appreciator of books, and, from my point of view, a man eminently well fitted to say whether he does or does not like them." So now shall we be good?!

I think you'd do well to *intellectualize* your poetry department. You've done that for your prose. I'm sure no "blowsy dames or cartilaginous virgins" buy S.S. for the sentimental quality of its verse. You should use less of it, and invite contributions for such hard-boiled poets as Elinor Wylie, Edna Millay, Robinson, Bodenheim, Untermeyer, et al.[29] Lots of their stuff isn't just what I call poetry, but readers eat it up. And the world loves being puzzled, anyhow.

Just congratulated Dreiser on his come-back in the Authors' League-Zukor affair. The old elephant reacted just as I'd have predicted. The League termites rallying to the help of the movielice—I hope the cootie press comes in too![30]

I hear that Ben Hecht and Harriet Monroe are going to Europe together. Am mailing Hecht some boro-tons and a whirling-spray.

Yours for the Reform of God,

George Sterling.

Holt & Co. have brought out my book—do you care for one?[31]

[215] [HLM to GS] [TLS, BAN]
[The Smart Set]
25 WEST 45th STREET
NEW YORK]
May 23, 1923

George Sterling, Esq.,
The Bohemian Club,
San Francisco, Calif.

Dear George:
I have put your name down for the Arnold commit-
tee and shall send you your certificate of manuscript and silk ro-
sette anon. The Hon. Charles Evans Hughes has consented to
serve as Honorary Chairman and we hope to include a number of
the Anglo-Saxon Chauvinists, especially Otto Kahn, Henry Morgenthau, Oscar Straus, Rabbi Stephen S. Wise, Horace B. Liveright and Judge Brandeis.[32] I'll see that you receive bulletins of
news from time to time.

What you say about the Poetry Department has not failed to
make its impression upon me. As a matter of fact, we are planning to reorganize the whole magazine in various ways. We took
to the sweet and lovely stuff eight or nine years ago at the height
of the free verse movement, and for several years The Smart Set
was the only magazine in America printing any actual poetry. But
now even the free verse fellows have begun to snuffle and sob,
and so I rather incline to letting them in. But that they write any
actual poetry, I deny absolutely. There is no more poetry in the
whole published work of Bodenheim than you will find in any average college yell.

Nathan is going abroad next week, and I'll have to sit on the
job here in New York. A very powerful yearning to come out to
the coast again is upon me. I'd be willing to serve twenty extra
years in Hell if I could only hop a train tomorrow. Maybe I'll do
it when he gets back.   .

Yours in Xt,
M

[216] [GS to HLM] [ALS, NYPL]
May 30th, 1923.

Dear H. L.
I wish to Gawd you *would* come out again! Couldn't
you fix it so you could get here late in July? Our Grove Jinks lasts

from July 23rd to Aug. 6th, the play being on the night of Aug. 4th. Gawd! I wish I could get you up there! It's a scream!

Also I hate to think of you stewing in Gotham all this summer; though, come to think of it, Baltimore must be just as hot. Let Hopper or young Chanslor run the magazine for you for a month, and come out where men are men and have to be to stand the bootleg. I'll begin to save prescriptions at once.

I ran into some 20 year old Scotch, Sunday, that put me down and out for that night. Have also met a Baltimore girl whom you'd find amusing. She's not pretty, but impish looking and stimulating. About 27, divorced. She is one of the Carrolls of Carroltown: guess she is, for I cross-examined her on the topography of the plantation, and she was 100% correct. Shall I give her a letter to you? She'll be back in Baltimore this summer or autumn. 'Wish I could hold her here.

You're right about Bodenheim's stuff. It's not poetry—he'd hate my kind of stuff, for instance—but it's often acrid and penetrating comment on life, so I'm for Bodie. He and Hecht seem to be having a joyous time. I take their paper, and trust I'll not appear in it.

Marky, editor of "Pearson's," is out here, to make Abrams reform or to get his scalp.[33] A. is unhappy, as who wouldn't be when an income of $2500. a day begins to be threatened?

Shall give your love to Sir Conan to-day.

> Yours ever,
>
> George Sterling.

[217] [GS to HLM] [ALS, NYPL]

June 16th, 1923.

Dear H. L.

Rotten! I actually had hopes that you might be able to get here by Aug. 1st. Maybe next year: we may have another convention. Won't it be grand if Ford runs! I shall make a score of women vote for him.

Am feeling rather shaky to-day, thanks to red wine reinforced by grappa and a red-headed girl reinforced by her great-great-uncle, the Devil. There really seems to be something in the notion that they're in a class by themselves. I wish I'd found it out when younger.

You speak of some difficulty in getting prose stuff. Here's a nondescript collection that has piled up on me during the past six months. Maybe you can use some of it. You'll note I've a nom de plume for certain cynicisms, the same to save me from feminine wrath.[34]

Hopper is still in N.Y. I hear he finally admits that "there's something in Dreiser." Am sorry I can't witness the conversion. How's the Jersey beer-joint holding out? The Canuck Scotch grows worse every week.

His Child,

George S.

[218] [GS to HLM] [ALS, NYPL]

June 28th, 1923.

Dear H. L.

I go forth covered with honor and glory, thanks to your proposed selection in "S.S."[35] No less than nine friends have torn out the page and sent it to me from the four quarters of the U.S.! I think Willard Wright should have the Treasury, but am too happy over my own fame to be captious. I think I can guarantee a solid delegation from northern California, with southern votes split. Let Sinclair do his duty there.

I'm not going to brag about local weather: you've enough to bother you now. Let's hope it's hell-hot in Paris. I'm wondering if S.F. gets a convention. It's a wonder they don't both go to Detroit, or Niagara. The A.M.A. convention is here now, all cursing Abrams. I wish he were either worse or better. In view of the cures he goes on making, I'm afraid to take sides. 'Wish I'd become a doctor, after all.

I went on a bad tear Friday, winding up at the tavern atop of Mt. Tamalpais with an expectant girl. She was badly disappointed. That was on Sunday. I recall little "in between" except a fist-fight with a total stranger in "Bigin's." He was smaller than I, and the aggressor: so I won. 'Was trying to steal his girl. Gawd! I'd like a movie of some of my lunacies when I'm lit—it would cure me.

The enclosed is better sense than Bryant's poem, but poorer poetry.[36] I doubt if you care for it.

Remember me to God!

Yours ever,

George S.

[219] [HLM to GS] [ALS, BAN]

[The Smart Set
25 WEST 45th STREET
NEW YORK]
[July 5, 1923]

Dear George:

I shall look into the matter of the Macdougall poem at once. The chances are that the steal was unconscious. That sort of thing, in fact, happens very often.[37]

I am taking the water-fowl piece. My best thanks.

I am off to N.Y. to meet Nathan, who is returning from London.

Ys

M

[220] [GS to HLM] [ALS, NYPL]

July 14th, 1923.

Dear H. L.

I'm not going to pester you with any more verses till next month, and am writing now only to ask if it's not possible for you to come out for the Bohemian Jinks, since Nathan has returned so soon. I know it's an expensive trip, but it sha'n't cost you anything while you're in California, and you may have my room here in the club. We'll keep you lit, and there'll be a better consort for you than the grafty Jane.

I hear Bodenheim has it in for you for your summary of "Black-guard."[38] It struck me as a finely accurate criticism of the book. He's an arid beast, and he seems to be "living on his nerve" in more ways than one. Why "The Dial" doesn't support him is a mystery.[39]

I've discovered some ten dollar port here that seems to agree with me, though it's not so good as that which once sold at a dollar a gallon, Ay Di Mi! None of the heavy drinkers here at the club has died yet, tho some abstainers have.

I took a sort of preparatory trip to San Quentin, with Sinclair, last Sunday. It seems to be about as liveable as the outside world, and a good time seemed to be having had by all. The ropes, stretching with weights in preparation, were the most impressive feature. I selected mine, a manila of about the same hue as my third-best girl's hair. A dozen ropes, and the men not even murdered yet!

In nom. Dom.

George S.

[221] [GS to HLM] [ANS, NYPL]

[Postmarked Montrio, Cal.,
Aug. 3, 1923.]

You were lucky in not coming this year. Grove-play given up and
everyone returning to Frisco to-day. Such is life in the far West.

Sterling

[222] [HLM to GS] [TLS, HUN]

August 9th [1923]

Dear George:—

I only hope that you are not charged with having
poisoned the poor fellow.[40] His passing has plunged the whole
East unto grief, so that no business goes on save that of the bootleggers. As the funeral train passed through Baltimore today the
Elks were lined up to either side of the track, and when the train
came to a halt each Elk removed his hat with his left hand,
clapped his right hand to his brow, and murmured: "God, what a
tragedy!"

Yours,
M

[223] [GS to HLM] [ALS, NYPL]

Aug. 18, 1923.

Dear H. L.

Note from the enclosed my latest activities. I fought
hard for my girl, but the winner was a 110 lb. cutie with the hips
of a 140 lb. woman. What's the use?

After staying on the wagon for God knows how long, I went on
a ten day tear with an older scoundrel possessing a cellar full of
vintages of unknown antiquity. I recall much Benedictine, and
bet he's remorseful now. Have had no word of him; but *I* got three
days in the hospital out of it. Am joining the dry force next week.

I consider your letter in re our late venerated leader in exceedingly bad taste, and am turning it over to the American Legion
with full explanations. Expect a visit from your local branch
within a month, sir!

Did you see the roast I got in the "Freeman" of Aug. 15th?[41] I
am preparing a dignified reply, which made, I expect to begin my
to-be-famous "Hymn to Caligula." All my girls are out of town,
and I feel creative.

Harding's body left S.F. at 6:30 P.M. By 7:30 every dance-restaurant in town was crowded with calloused beings who betrayed not a sign of grief. Whither are we drifting?

Did you see John Head's illustrations for my ballad in the July "Century?"[42] Good in themselves, but absolutely nullifying any possible esthetic impact of the poem. Such is life back where the kale begins.

Remember me in your prayers!

George S.

[224] [GS to HLM] [ALS, NYPL]

Aug. 29th, 1923.

Dear H. L.

The tracts for the bathing-beauty came too late: she had already yielded to the persuasion of a prominent rabbi, whose sacrificial port seems to have been convincing.

Of course I've heard of the new review, and await it impatiently.[43] Hope it's not subsidized in marks. Are you to indulge in "verse and worse"? And who in Hell will run "S.S.," the one bright spot in my monthly reading?

Running over the mental list of possible inducements to go east, I find you're the only one! I mean that. By long odds enough; but the fare is lacking. If John M'Cormick[44] sings some of my songs for the Victrola people, as I am assured he will, you may yet find me demanding your bootlegger's name.

"Bigin's" was raided again, Monday night. I was absent, at confession. Bigin has now five indictments to face, which means they'll fine him all he has made and give him a year in jail to boot. "Sweet land of liberty!"

Yours ever,

George.

[225] [GS to HLM] [ALS, NYPL]

Nov. 8th, 1923.

Dear H.L.

The reason for my not pestering you with letters is my visit to Los Angeles, whereof the pleasantest part was the return trip. The only man there who'd take more than ten drinks with me couldn't "hold his liquor," and wept violently on the street! Only God's mercy prevented our arrest.

I was in Mexicali, but it was too insufferably hot for anything but beer. Good beer at that, @ 15¢ per stein. I went there actually to shoot ducks, but didn't get a shot. Saw the northern end of the biggest cotton ranch in the world—226000 acres. It's an odd sight to see turbaned Hindoos driving huge wagon-loads of the raw cotton. The owners are scared stiff that the I. W. W. are going to bring in the boll weevil, as Chandler of the "Times" is chief owner.[45]

It looked funny to see ripe dates. They have to put cheese-cloth over the bunches to save 'em from the birds.

I was urged to become an inhabitant of Hollywood, but declined on grounds of premature senility. Was at Upton Sinclair's, but they refused to introduce me to Mary Miles Minter, who was in hiding near by with a married man. She is getting fat, drinks like a fish and says openly that her mother shot W[m.] Desmond Taylor. Just the same, I think we should have met.[46]

I won 1st prize at our Poets' Ball at the Fairmont, last week, for my seductive appearance as Dante. My girl won 1st as Beatrice. We think of opening a road-house.

Every third person I meet asks what's to become of S. S. What *is?* Any use to send them poems?

Good luck with the "Mercury!" I hear there's Ku Klux money back of it.

With all the major beneficent wishes,

George S.

[226] [HLM to GS] [TLS, BAN]

November 13th [1923]

Dear George:—

At this writing the plan seems to be to continue the S.S. at a reduced price and to aim at the booboisie. I have washed my hands of it completely. My stock is sold to Warner,[47] though the transaction is not yet completed. But I'll be out teetotally in a week or two, and damned glad of it. The Mercury is a hard sweat, but the chances seem to be very good that it will go over. Knopf is taking in subscriptions at the rate of 50 a day, and we have six weeks to go before the first issue.

Los Angeles must be dreadful. I'll never go there. The movie wenches all come to New York soon or late. Very few of them, at close range, measure up to the average stenographer. The booze question here in the East seems to be settled permanently. Last night Carl Van Vechten was here.[48] After dinner with cocktails,

Spanish red wine and liqueurs, we went to a beer-house, and sat in an open table drinking a capital 6% Dunkles for three hours. The government crooks still raid a few poor Jews and Italians, but they apparently let all first-class places alone. I believe that this will last. If prohibition were actually enforced in Maryland there would be a revolution. Last Tuesday there was an election, and all the wet candidates won by enormous majorities. The politicians are now all becoming professional wets. Incidentally, the Ku Klux got its tail pulled off: it supported the Methodist drys.

Why don't you come East again? I'll be moving around during the Summer; I'll certainly go to both national conventions. But neither, I hear, is to be held in San Francisco. A great pity.

A man at the Johns Hopkins has lately perfected a new aphrodisiac. I am ordering 100 lbs for you.

Yours,
M

[227] [HLM to GS] [TLS, HUN]
[The American Mercury
220 West Forty-second Street
NEW YORK]

November 24th [1923]

Dear George:—

Who in hell is Stuart X? He sends me idiotic letters now and then. I take it that he is full of Los Angeles metaphysics.

We made up the first number of the Mercury this morning. Tomorrow my pastor, Dr. Himmelheber,[49] will mention it in his morning prayer.

Yours,
M

[Enclosure: Statement by Mencken and George Jean Nathan, dated Oct. 10, 1923, on why they are resigning from *The Smart Set*.]

[228] [GS to HLM] [ALS, NYPL]

Dec. 1ˢᵗ, 1923.

Dear H. L.

My fifty-fourth birthday, God help us all! But it shall be celebrated with the customary vinous and amatory details. A gift of fifty four bottles of good Burgundy decorates my clothes-closet. "Come back and redeem us from virtue!"

The nut you refer to is "Harry" Stuart, a big, bearded buck who joined this club in '84, but who has been in South America for most of the intervening years, building railroads. Now he's back here, an affable old cuss, fond of his tipple, but stung, patently, by most of the bugs.

I told Newbegin about the Mercury some time ago, and he has ordered several copies weekly; so I'm to get mine at his store. Am eager to see it, knowing your affection for this fair land and its political lords. I shall miss S. S., though. By some miracle, you were able to make it readable from cover to cover, and I feel lucky when I can find one item that interests me in the other periodicals. The Dial is especially vain and idiotic: I'm hoping you razz them.

Yours for the reform of you and God,

George S.

It is my brightest dream to introduce Sinclair to Stuart.

[229] [HLM to GS] [TLS, HUN]
[The American Mercury
220 West Forty-second Street
NEW YORK]

December 29th [1923]

Dear George:—

The San Francisco booklet makes me homesick. I met Fanny Hurst the other day and she told me that she disliked the town.⁵⁰ Is she insane? Murder the Methodists and it will be perfect.

The enclosed clipping shows the latest operations of the fair Jane.⁵¹ I haven't seen her for months. This is the third time she has gone through the same business. How she manages to escape very time I don't know. A talented gal!

The Mercury has cost me a kidney and three ribs, but it seems to be doing very well. We have had to go back on the press with the first number. Your prayers were not unheeded!

May God preserve us to do His will in 1924!

Yours,

M

[Enclosure: newspaper clipping, "Charge Fraud, Hold Woman."]

1924

[230] [GS to HLM] [ALS, NYPL]

Jan. 31ˢᵗ, 1924.

Dear H. L.

This letter is a rather belated expression of gratitude for your bringing to birth The American Mercury. So pardon— I've been in Hollywood all the month, writing the captions for D. Fairbanks' new movie, "The Thief of Bagdad!"[1] A queer job for me, but, like the great and good Benedict Arnold, I needed the money. My conviction as to the essential moronism of movies is unchanged. Fairbanks, however, has turned this time to the real province of the movie, a fairy tale, for that is what this Arabian Night stuff is, and the result will not be displeasing, I think, even to ice-domes like you and Nathan.

The only woman "stars" I met were Mary Pickford[2] and Mary Miles Minter. The latter is a luscious thing, and is much enamoured with Upton Sinclair's brother-in-law. The Sinclairs sent him on a tour of the U.S. to save him from her wiles, but the fair youth is back and hitting, apparently, on all eight cylinders. I think she'd marry him if he asked her. He asked *me* if I thought a man should marry "for looks or character!" I was at her house with him two evenings. She has pre-Volstead stuff, extracted from a rich admirer. Is hard-up for ready money, though she used to get $11000. a week. Is to go into vaudeville @ $1800. a week as soon as her lawsuit with Ma is over and she can escape from southern California, which naturally she hates.

I met Chaplin too.[3] He's getting very grey. Wants me to go on a tear with him when I return to Hollywood, as I have to do soon, for a few days.

I missed our annual Quatre Arts ball here at the Fairmont. It was a drunken orgy after 2 A.M., some of the girls tearing around practically naked. They unleashed the fire-hose in one corridor and turned the stream into all accessible transoms, and now the hotel says they're to hunt a new caravanserai for the next ball.

But about the Mercury: it's great! Here at last you have a free, full swing, and may have to send it to S.F. via the canal: the middle West may bar its passage. Shall I send you a pome? I don't like to knock Dreiser, but really his stuff was valuable for publicity only.[4]

Abrams died and was buried in my absence. I'd not called on him for a year, so he cut me from his will, where I was down for $10,000. My poor creditors!

I'm wondering if they jailed Jane. Would not mind occupying the same cell with her.

Yours for the redemption of Hollywood,

George Sterling.

[231] [HLM to GS] [TLS, HUN]
[The American Mercury
220 WEST FORTY-SECOND STREET
NEW YORK]

February 6th [1924]

Dear George:—

Do you know the name and address of Ambrose Bierce's daughter? Vincent Starrett says that she has the incredible name of Mrs. Isgrigg and that she used to live in Alvarado street, Los Angeles, but he can't remember any more. I want to get hold of her, if possible. Some Bierce letters loom up, and it will be necessary to get her permission to print them. Is she Ambrose's heir?

Poetry, at the moment, is rather under the ban. We shall use relatively little of it, and several long things are already in type. But what of prose? Would you care to do an article on San Francisco under the Methodist Terror? Various spies send in clippings of church advertisements and tales of moral endeavor. What is the net effect of all this? A detailed article would be excellent. Or what else do you suggest?

What has become of Jane I don't know. She calls up my office now and then, but I have her on the "out" list. She seems to be pursuing a lamentable career, and I fear for her soul.

The American Mercury has dam nigh killed me—80 hours work a day. Your prayers!

Yours,
M

[232] [GS to HLM] [ALS, NYPL]

Feb. 14th, 1924.

Dear H. L.

Wasn't sure I was to hear from you again, after my be-trayal of higher things, so your letter comes like ancient Scotch to a more ancient member of this club.

Bierce's daughter's name is actually Isgrigg—Mrs. Francis Is-grigg! *He* is a Los Angeles lawyer, and she a large and joyful Christian Scientist. Just what her address is none seems to know. I asked Bierce's nephew here,[5] and he thought that a letter sent to Atascadero, Cal. would reach her. I'll go to the telephone com-pany here and if I can find her name in the Los Angeles 'phone book I'll enclose it.

Don't see what you want her permission for—we didn't ask it when we published the Letters of Ambrose Bierce. She's a very amiable woman, and his heir, of course—although he left no will, I am told.[6]

You're right about poetry—use it sparingly, and then only rather long and "intellectual" poems. Lyrics will get you no-where, unless they're the hard-boiled stuff that Madame Wylie and Millay are delivered of. As to doing any prose work, I must decline with thanks, not having time to spare from my love-mak-ing. And it's too much of an effort. I never make a mental effort. The verse arrives painlessly, which is, no doubt, the reason why it's no better. I'd not mind your running the essay I once sent you. It's the only *complete survey* of man and matter that I've ever seen, and its altruistic end could be omitted. I think it would arouse much protest, especially among socialists, optimists and reformers, for it is truly a grisly vision of the universe—infinite and eternal diffusion of horror and injustice; but such facts have to be faced sooner or later.

Hopper left for N.Y. two days ago. I gave him the Mercury with Anderson's story,[7] which has Hopper as its "hero!" Watch for a scrap.

Yours for the Rhineland Republic,

George Sterling.

Have your picture in the "boss" derby. You're not the only one, as behold!

[Enclosure? Written on Pacific Telegram stationery]
I find only Daphne Isgrigg,
353 S. Tremont St. Los Angeles.

You might try her, though it's not "our" Mrs. Isgrigg, nor her daughter. But she might know, the name is so uncommon.

G.

[233] [GS to HLM] [ALS, NYPL]

Apr. 26th, 1924.

Dear H. L.

In the evident valetudinarianism of Doctor Nathan, your labors must be heavy, and I hesitate to inflict letters on you. I can't help commenting, however, on two things in the last "Mercury." One of them is McClure's theory of poetry as sound—as absurd an idea as ever I've encountered![8] I agree with him as to poetry not depending on ideation. But sound—why, I could give you musical lines of sheer gibberish. McClure is himself a fine poet, and I've noticed often that poets can function without knowing what poetry is. Old Ambrose, for one, was on to the fact that it's the magically imaginative expression, to be found in prose as well as in meter or rhythm. It must give the sense of strangeness, the thing being said as it was never said before. Where's the sound when a thing isn't read aloud? A "poem's" wisdom or music is one thing, its poetry another. There one has to have magic of imagination.

The other matter is your anthropomorphism in asserting that force has to be an application of will.[9] Your metaphysics has a kelp leg, but perhaps mine has too when I claim that the universe is *absolute*, that it's the nature of matter to act as it does, and that it cannot act otherwise. Will implies a dualism.

The matter is too vague for me to express exactly what I want to, without writing reams. Your time, too, is limited, so it's best for us to wait till I can discuss these things with you over real beer, as I'm hoping to do within a year.

The hand of the Lord has been heavy upon me, doubtlessly for my many impieties. But thanks to Him, I've found out what has been slowing me down for over a year and causing liquor to hit me so hard that occasional rides on the wagon were necessary. I had eight (8) abscessed teeth! They're out now, and already I begin to feel far more pep, slightly diminished at the thought of what my bill for bridge-work will be. One abscess had been there over two years. It was the size of an olive! But what a miracle dentistry has become, when one can go through such an operation (?) not only without pain but with actual interest!

Thanks, for being willing to take a look at an amended version

198

of that essay of mine! I may get around to it one of these days. Just now I'm contemplating a new dramatic poem to be called "The Gardens of Caligula." The trouble with it is that it won't be printable—not with a real Caligula.

Would it be any use for me to send you some of Clark Smith's epigrams, enough to make a page or two? I think some of them are wonders.[10]

Just finished reading "The Goslings."[11] Scratch this country and pus gushes out. But I fear I'm in wrong with Upton for roasting his last play (an I.W.W. affair) in my last letter to him. Upton doesn't hate himself.

In Xt.,

George S.

[234] [GS to HLM] [ALS, NYPL]

May 13th, 1924.

Dear H. L.

Here are those Smith epigrams—some he just sent me on request, and others that I've culled from lists he has heretofore sent. Pardon the graphite: I'm in a hurry to-day, being about to motor over to Yosemite. My companion is an old Arizonan ex-sheriff who is *dumb*. He has lately had his pharynx removed for cancer. However, he's very chatty with his pad of paper, and we hope to break the booze-law every five miles. This old chap's body has more scars on it than come from the surgeon—scars from bowie-knives and bullets.

My eighth (and final) tooth departed this jaw a few days ago—a big wisdom tooth. I'm keeping it for mother Church: they will have it in a shrine, performing miracles, when they learn how many drinks I refused during the past twelve months.

By the way, I begin to experience already the good results you predict. And I've a cannibal grin that would ensure me high rank and honors in the Solomon Islands.

As to my coming east, it depends on whether or not Fairbanks puts on sale the lyrics for songs that I wrote for him. Hopper informs me it wasn't done in New York; but I'm told it's not the custom there, but in cities farther west. Here's hoping. I'd sure love to see you! Four years is a long time, and hooch has deteriorated; but we have become braver, having less to lose. Here's to God!

I've not written "Caligula" yet. I await leisure and royalties. But it'll be a shocker, all right.

Here's hoping Nathan will pension some of his flappers and get to work.

      In His name,

                  George S.

[235] [HLM to GS] [TLS, BAN]
              [The American Mercury
              730 FIFTH AVENUE
              NEW YORK]
                    May 17th [1924]

Dear George:—
      Some of these Smith epigrams are excellent (particularly the ones inspired by Bierce!) and if I were still running The Smart Set I'd buy at least half of them, but I have a doubt that they would hold up if printed together in a formidable series. Too many of them run in obvious directions. I know only too well the art and mystery of making such things: I once wrote 88 in one day.[12] Most of them can be nothing but variations upon standard ideas. Why doesn't Smith try them on Morris Gilbert, the new editor of The Smart Set? He is still using epigrams.

I shall depart for Cleveland in ten days to see Cal given the red hat.[13] He is, I believe, the greatest man ever produced by the Republic—greater, even, than the martyred Woodrow. So long as such men are thrown off by Nature democracy will never die.

Once you get in your new set of china teeth the gals will begin to be full of Freudian suppressions. They like a fellow with a flashing smile. Relieve them!

            Pro Christo et Ecclesia,
            Mencken

[236] [GS to HLM] [ALS, NYPL]

                    June 15th, 1924.

Dear H. L.
      By this time you've seen God's will exhibited in Cleveland, and are back before the Himalayas of your postponed and accreted work. I don't want to add my mite to it, and you needn't reply—or briefly. Here are a few clippings that may interest you—also a poem. I've been trying, since its appearance, to note what kind of verses, if any, you can use in "The Mercury," and am merely guessing that this might approximate the quality. Maybe not; it doesn't matter, though I'd like to be in your civilizing periodical sooner or later.

Do you ever see Dreiser? I wonder what the old pachyderm is writing, and if he's still true to the peach he brought from Hollywood. The enclosed tract should go to him at once, if his soul is to be saved.

I was in the Yosemite a few days, last month, and damned near came home in a wooden dress-suit, owing to my views on the scalability of certain cliffs. My host was *dumb,* and had much Scotch with him. On the way in, we had luncheon at a hamlet with the romantic name Coarse Gold. In the dining-room was a big sign, red, white and blue, WELCOME, ROTARIANS! The history of the state at a gulp. I have also to report that the inner side of the door of the privy at Inspiration Point (in the Valley) is covered with the full names *and* addresses of sundry persons, most of them hailing from Los Angeles—none from San Francisco. Also I heard a woman in a tent exclaim: "No—we didn't like San Francisco, but Los Angeles is heavenly!" She was playing solitaire, with her back to the scenery.

Yours ever,

Goorgc S.

[237] [GS to HLM] [ALS, EPFL]

June 27th, 1924.

Dear H. L.

By the time this reaches you, I hope the Pope will have gotten the upper hand in N.Y., though I may be hoping in vain.

You're dead right as to the inherent absurdity of a "woman" poem being *signed,* at least, by a man, though the writing of it might be justified as an exercise of the imagination, and has been done so often and by so big chaps that your idea never even occurred to me. I'm damned glad you gave me the notion.

I've nothing now that you might want to use except some outrageous things in free verse that I want to have some magazine print in bulk (say two pages), signed by a girl's name. If the idea interests you at all, let me know. They won't get you in jail. I enclose a sample or two.

Am feeling rather low today—not quite recovered from a six-day spree that put me to bed for two more days. Again I say that Vancouver Scotch can't be trusted.

Here's a somewhat exaggerated record of one of our parties on the Hill. You should have seen Lafler's upper lip!

Yours for the League of Nations,

George S.

[238] [HLM to GS] [ALS, BAN]
[The American Mercury
730 FIFTH AVENUE
NEW YORK]
[July 3, 1924]
Dear George:

The public prints here report that Scotch is now selling in S.F. at $35 a case. Can it be that the Second Coming is actually at hand?

The free verse, I fear, is out of our line. But why don't you do an article, in prose, on the San Francisco of today? It would fit into the American Mercury perfecty. The old S.F.—and the new!

This Democratic national convention is so obscene that it makes even a Methodist Conference seem dignified.[14]

Ys

M

[239] [GS to HLM] [ALS, NYPL]

July 18th, 1924.
Dear H. L.

If Scotch is selling in S.F. @ $35. per case it must have been made in the Mission. We are paying $8. a bottle for it, a reduction of $2. I'm not sure what that figures out per case. Even at $8. it is green stuff, full of headaches. I'm sticking to the drugstore Bourbon.

Just returned from Los Angeles, whither I had to go to attend the funeral of the wife of my oldest friend[15]—I was to have been at the wedding of my youngest sister!

One has to hand it to L.A. for one thing, anyway: it must be the greatest concourse of feminine beauty since the Rome of the empire—and there they were mostly under lock and key. One sees a score of pretty girls on every *block*. I saw Mary Miles Minter several times, but she was on the wagon. She's to leave for New York next week. A damned bright girl, who will tempt Nathan when she has lost 20 lbs. She crowded her photo. on me, though I'd have preferred the original.

I'd like to do that S.F. article for "The Mercury," but am too lazy for prose, at present.

Our grove Jinks begins on the 19th. Pray for me unceasingly!

Mrs. Gerould has an article on S.F. in the July "Harpers."[16] Enthusiastic enough!

Yours for La Follette,[17]

G. S.

[240] [GS to HLM] [ALS, NYPL]

July 19, 1924.

Dear H. L.

Here's a poem that seems suitable for The Mercury. I meant to have enclosed it in my letter of yesterday, but lacked a typewritten copy.

Our Jinks at the grove begins to-day. I wish you were to be with us. How about 1925?

With pious ejaculations,

George Sterling.

[241] [HLM to GS] [TLS, HUN]
[The American Mercury
730 FIFTH AVENUE
NEW YORK]

August 1, 1924.

Dear George:

This is an excellent poem and it tempts me very much. But after long prayer we have practically decided to cut out poetry altogether and so I hesitate to take it.

I certainly hope that you will change your mind and do that prose article. Prose, I admit, is much harder to write than verse. It sucks out the very essence of the human soul. It is very fatiguing to the muscles. Nevertheless it must be done.

The Moose are holding their annual convention in New York. And yesterday they had their annual parade up Fifth Avenue. More than 800 bootleggers were in line.

Sincerely yours,
M

HLM:L

enc.

[242] [GS to HLM] [ALS, NYPL]

Aug. 8th, 1924.

Dear H. L.

I agree with you as to the non-necessity of poetry for The Mercury. No one takes a magazine for the poetry in it.

I don't want to do that article for two reasons. The first is that prose is a man's job, and if I'm to go to the exertion (non-existent in verse-writing) of writing it, I prefer to concentrate on a short-story—: I can get real writers to publish them under their own names, after a little revision or padding, and go halves with me![18] That means real money, and I've just finished one.

The other reason is that there hasn't been so much change in our night-life as one might think, at your distance. Over in our Latin quarter are half a dozen big, ornate restaurants, with fine orchestras and dance-floors, crowded with revellers every night. Many more go out to the big restaurants at the beach, or down the Peninsula to the road-houses. I should say that the difference is mainly in the *cost,* as compared to the old days. Some of these restaurants will serve booze to known patrons, others send out for it, by the flask or bottle. Of course it's pretty poor stuff. One sees a good deal of plain drunkenness, especially among women.

So the effect of prohibition seems mainly to be that the average person has to cut down on the number of weekly, or monthly, parties. When, however, he does turn loose, he becomes more hectic. And on the nights he stays home, there are others to take his place. Wherefore "anyone seeking for trouble can always find it," and forbidden things are sweetest.

I'm mailing you a copy of that "Dirge" of Mrs. Travis' that you took a fancy to. Also her "Lord's Prayer," to which she has been first to give (I'm told) a lyrical accompaniment.[19] Should you be overcome by a messianic impulse to supply them to all the churches in Baltimore, you may have them by the hundred!

I wrote to the titanotheric Dreiser lately, trying to interest him in your former contributor, Whit Burnett,[20] but he avoided all comment on the young man. But Whit will go a long way, I think, if he don't have to do too much reporting.

Dreiser says his girl is in Los Angeles, but I suppose he wasn't half an hour in finding her successor. He still babbles of coming to San Francisco to live, but of course he won't. It's a hard town to write *from.*

There was some damned hard drinking at our annual Jinks. One chap is still out of his head from it, with three attendant physicians.

If you don't see Haldeman-Julius' weekly, for Xt's sake get it and read the Sinclair stuff called "Mammonart."[21] S. is anesthetic to beauty, and is going to make an awful ass of himself. But the book may create an uproar, which, of course, is exactly what he's after. If he had to do his reforming anonymously he'd do no reforming.

Jimmy Swinnerton[22] tells me a soldier of fortune in N.Y., one Col. Tex O'Reilly, has the dope as to Bierce's death, and is to have it published in "Liberty."[23] He was with four different Mexican armies, and so learned of B's execution as a possible spy. Keep an eye out for the article.

Yours for more and cheaper prescriptions,

George S.

[243] [HLM to GS] [TLS, BAN]
[The American Mercury
730 FIFTH AVENUE
NEW YORK]

August 13th [1924]

Dear George:—

Thanks very much for Mrs. Travis' two songs. I like her setting of your dirge very much. The Lord's Prayer is too soft and flowing. I greatly prefer to sing it to the old tune of "The French They Are a Peculiar Race, Parlez Vous, Parlez Vous!". My pastor gives it as a college yell: very effective on a hot Sunday morning.

I shall soon take a hack at California, denouncing it as the anus of Christendom. Clippings flow in from Los Angeles, describing almost incredible things. The whole southern half of the State seems to be in the grip of Babbitts and New Thoughters. What a pity! I look for a revolution and a massacre. On to the barricades!

The heat here in the East is still infernal. I have almost sweated to death.

Yours in Xt.,
Mencken

The Roosevelt poem was written by Joe Hergesheimer.[24]

[244] [GS to HLM] [ALS, NYPL]

Sept. 12th, 1924.

Dear H. L.

It's a month since you wrote, so maybe you can stand another of my letters. God in His infinite wisdom has seen fit to afflict me with boils, and I'm in a vindictive mood.

You're dead right as to the condition of the southern part of the state; but for God's sake pray specify that it *is* the southern part! Up here we have little such muck—only an occasional dry raid, for the most part on obscure Wops.

About "The Lord's Prayer." Mrs. T. has been told it's the first time it ever had a lyrical accompaniment. As sung by her, I can imagine nothing more tenderly reverential. It would be in every Jesusric in America if she'd give it to a live publisher instead of bringing it out privately.

My "Mercury" hasn't yet arrived, and probably won't, now. When my subscription runs out, I'll let it stay so, as it's a lot more convenient to buy the magazine in a drugstore. I hear only praise of the periodical: we are imperfectly patriotic in S.F.

Viereck sends me the two booklets of his poetry that Haldeman-Julius brought forth.[25] Too reminiscent of Wilde and Swinburne, but full nevertheless of real poetry. Our literature sorely needed such a hot shower at the time it originally appeared.

I went swimming (naked) with a girl in a lake in G. G. Park, last month. We were arrested, but routed the superintendent out of bed, and he made the cops release us. But the papers got it, and I've been heavily joshed.[26]

In His name,

G. Sterling.

[245] [HLM to GS] [TLS, BAN]
[The American Mercury
730 FIFTH AVENUE
NEW YORK]
November 20th [1924]

Dear George:—

I have lately read a MS. by Paul Jordan-Smith, in which he describes the failure of his efforts to gather materials for a life of Bierce.[27] Among other things, he describes two meetings with you. The general burden of his tale is that he planned to buy some Bierce letters from you, but that you had sold them to some one else in the interval between the two meetings. What is in this? He deals with you very politely, but I don't want to print any such stuff unless you approve.

Why don't you do an article on Bierce yourself—not a solemn critical piece, but a chapter of your recollections of him? You knew him better than anyone. You could do 3,000 or 4,000 words that would be very charming. La Isgrig is apparently hot against printing any of Bierce's letters. Scheffauer has been unable to make any progress with her, and Jordan-Smith seems to have failed completely.

I am gradually breaking up.

Yours,
Mencken

[246] [GS to HLM] [ALS, NYPL]

Nov. 26th, 1924.

Dear H. L.

I've owed you a letter for weeks, but have refrained from writing it, being well aware of the burden of your labors. As for me, I labor not, and the yarns I spin seem imperfectly salable. Is marriage for money permissible after the age of 55? I reach that sublime crest on the 1st of Dec.

As to Jordan-Smith, I'm sure I told him the truth—that Albert Bender already had the letters, and that I'd try to buy them back for him (J.-S.) But Bender was hot for bringing them out in book-form, which he soon did, through the Book Club of Cal. Surely I sent you that book, and for it I wrote just such an "easy-going" memoir of him as you now propose my writing. Why not use that, or such portions of it as you think available? It will save The Mercury money and me toil, and I can guarantee you permission from the Book Club.

I'm sorry B's daughter objects to the publication of his letters. In a conversation with Bierce himself, he gave me permission to use any he wrote to me—said it was *his letters to women* that he drew the line on! It's a pity Scheff. cannot get his back from the British Govt. Bierce wrote him some fine ones; also some angry ones, toward the last. One of them is printed anonymously at the end of the Letters.[28]

My tearful gratitude for the tract, which will alter the whole course of my few remaining years or months. The author seems to have it all sized up correctly. Sin is fierce.

Our cafe life is receiving body-blows: *patrons* are now being arrested, and fined $500. each! They got around it by showing up pretty full, eating and dancing, then going back to their apartments for more drinks, then re-appearing after ten o'clock. But it all costs money, and our little group of serious thinkers can't indulge oftener than twice a week. It all came out of a row between the local police and the federal men—a row over the spoils. It may end, any time, though.

I note your progress toward fame and wealth, and genuflect at a becoming distance.

Esoterically yours,

George S.

That (black) bird Cullen is O.K.[29]

[247] [HLM to GS] [TLS, Dartmouth]
[THE AMERICAN MERCURY
730 FIFTH AVENUE
NEW YORK]

December 1st [1924]

Dear George:—

I misunderstood Jordan-Smith. I thought he referred to a quite different set of letters. Your introduction to the volume, I fear, is not quite the thing. It is rather too much an estimate and too little a portrait of the man. Moreover, there would be copyright difficulties. Spit on your hands and do the piece: Bierce as he actually was, warts and all!

I have been lame in both legs, and full of a bilious distrust of God. The cause: senility. But the gong-beater is still functioning. When it is stilled at last I shall quietly drown myself in the baptismal tank of the First Baptist Church.

New York goes dry intermittently, but only for an hour or so. I have transferred my trade to Union Hill, N.J. It is but 25 minutes away by the 42nd street ferry, and its saloons are all wide open. It is a great comfort to see the bartenders at work, cutting the foam off the beer with ivory paper-cutters.

Yours in Xt.,

Mencken

1925

[248] [GS to HLM] [ALS, NYPL]

Mch. 24th, 1925.

Dear H. L.

Here's a howler for your "Americana."[1]

Went on a three-week boom in December. It put me in the hospital with gastritis, and I've been on the wagon till lately, when one can get some old sherry from up-state.

De Casseres was here, and a great surprise to me—as human as any Babbit, whom he facially resembles. Lewis sends me his "Arrowsmith," but I've not yet done with it.[2] Masters was here for the better part of a week, and we got on beautifully together, though I'd not join him in his hard liquor—and there was nothing else. Like De C., he was nuts in this city, and swore he'd be back in Oct., to stay all winter. But no such luck, I fear.

You asked me to do an article on Ambrose, and I'd have done so if I'd not gone on that boom. I suppose it's too late now. That was some tear: the club is still talking about it and my "lady-friends" still cussing me.

The Mercury keeps up its high quality. I had this club subscribe, as I dropped out. Have you seen Sinclair's absurd "Mammonart?" He terms my criticism of it "savage abuse!" Upton doesn't savvy the artist, nor get "pure beauty."

If you keep a cat, kiss him for me.

Yours ever,

George S.

Thanks for your own most interesting article on Bierce. I'd seen it.[3]

[249] [HLM to GS] [TLS, UCLA]

March 30th [1925]

Dear George:—

Where is the bust to be put? I suggest a lofty knoll in Golden Gate Park. Notify me of the time of the dedication. I'll come out for it, and make a speech.

De Casseres is an amusing fellow—full of the delusion that he is a new Schopenhauer, but otherwise very decent. He has an immense capacity for malt liquor. Masters is a quieter fellow, but with a good gizzard.

You deserve all your sufferings for going on the water-wagon. The cure for alcohol is more alcohol. When I got back from San Francisco in 1920 I, too, had gastritis. The faculty put me on well water. I kept getting worse. So I returned to malt and was quickly cured.

I surely hope you do the Bierce article. Don't bother about his books in it. Give us a picture of the man!

Red Lewis, at last accounts, was drunk in Munich.

Yours,

Mencken

[250] [GS to HLM] [ALS, NYPL]

Apr. 9th, 1925.

Dear H. L.

I'm working on the Bierce article, and shall observe, at least in part, your admonition to say nothing of his books. Evidently your estimate of my critical acumen is low.

How many words can you use? Can you stand for 7000—a little over 9 pages, I calculate? I warn you that I'll have to use some (quite a bit) of my material in my memoir in the "Letters," as they present the high points of my relations with him. But hardly more than 200 copies of the book have been sold so far, I estimate, and almost all of those locally. So it can make practically no difference.

I enclose a few clippings, and trust that their saddening effect will be but slight. The Bulletin man is George Douglas, one of their book-reviewers—Australian. I doubt if you are greatly loved in the English colonies, or even in Texas.

You were pretty nearly correct when you wrote me that you weren't going to use any more poetry in the Mercury. Perhaps the enclosed verses are unpoetical enough. Excuse the carbon. Here's a quatrain submitted (I swear it!) to the poetry section of "The Bookfellows," to which I attend in a Radamanthic capacity:

The Optimist

However deep the shadows stray
Upon the seven hills,
We know that they must creep away
When Dawn unpacks her frills.
(Anne Mathilde Robinson.)

I cruelly returned it to the dear girl.

The shadows lengthen in the vale, here. Scotch (I won't drink it) has gone up to $9. a bottle, and the legislature is getting after the rabbis who dispense sacramental wine. Compulsory attendance at church looms in the offing.

Yours in Caligula,

George S.

[251] [HLM to GS] [TLS, DAN]

April 14th [1925]

Dear George:—

I'd rather have the article about 5,000 words long, if you can make it so. But do it as it comes to you. I haven't the slightest objection to the use of the material in your preface. What I'd like to get is a picture of the man as he was in his prime. His daughter, unfortunately, still prohibits printing his letters in the magazine, and under the law she is within her rights. A most unpleasant woman.

I have been trying hard to get an article on the Methodist conquest of San Francisco. The latest candidate for the job is a newspaper man whose name I forget. I believe that publication of such an article would inspire the local bigwigs to meditate resistance. Here in the East, despite the lofty gabble of the Prohibition Bureau, enforcement is almost forgotten. In New York last week I bought two cases of prime Moselle and some excellent Scotch. The Scotch cost $54 a case—$4.50 a bottle. Beer is openly on sale in 100,000 saloons. Red wine has been as low as $3 a gallon. Come East, young man!

This poem, for some reason or other, leaves me chilled and pallid. Haven't you something else?

Yours in Xt.,
Mencken

[252] [GS to HLM] [ALS, NYPL]

Apr. 16th, 1925.

Dear H. L.

Here's your order on Bierce. I've been as little high-browed as possible.⁴

I figure I've wasted on it, in energy-ohmage, at least seven (7) good screws, so make my check for as much as Knopf will stand for.

Fell off the wagon with an awful crash last night, and am a nervous wreck to-day.

Yours ever,

George.

[253] [GS to HLM] [ALS, NYPL]

June 15th, 1925.

Dear H. L.

I don't give a letter of introduction once in a coon's age, but am now on one of my periodicals and in a mellow mood. I promise not to do it in cold blood, and give you an equal privilege.

This may serve to introduce to you one of our bright young San Franciscans, Raine Bennett.⁵ He once ran a magazine of his own here, called "Bohemia." I understand he was on terms of undue intimacy with the girl who solicited subscriptions. It ran six months! Bennett will make almost no demand on your time—he merely wants to be able to come back here and brag of having met you. However, you might try out some dubious bootleg on him. If it have disastrous results, we can very well spare him.

If he survive it, you ought to have him play the piano a bit for you.

I am well, and still retain a little of the handsome check you sent me for the Bierce stuff.

(Warning: Bennett is a Fundamentalist!)

George.

[254] [HLM to GS] [ALS, NYPL (Berg)]
[The American Mercury
730 Fifth Avenue
New York]

[c. June 25, 1925]

Dear George:

Your treatise on Bierce was scheduled and advertised for August, but now I find that I must hold it over for a month to avoid a conflict with another San Francisco article. The latter is a chapter from a book to be published in September, and we must work it off before the book comes out.[6] Such are the ways of God!

How are you?

Ever yrs,
H L Mencken

[Envelope postmarked New York, N.Y., June 25, 1925.]

[255] [GS to HLM] [ALS, NYPL]

July 1st, 1925.

Dear H. L.

It doesn't matter a whoop when the Bierce article appears: the longer deferred will be the wrath of his fat daughter. If she assails me, I'll tell her a few of the things I *might* have told on the venerable chaser.

See how our friend Irene has come up in the world (and in looks) since that night you slept with her. I intend to look her up as soon as disengaged.

Have barely recovered from my last periodical, which sent me again to the St. Francis Hospital. I put it over on sherry, this time, as our Scotch is too green. A month out of Canada.

Where do you go for your vacation? I wish it were to be in California, where you could be my guest at our midsummer Jinks. The grove-play will be on the night of Aug 1st. Come on out!

Next year they're to use my third dramatic poem "Truth" as the grove-play. It will have to be cut down some, but not drastically.

Did Masters send you his two josh advts., "Sinful Sensations" and "Fem Vigiro"? For a man who takes himself so seriously he's some josher.

The chap who's "acting editor" on "The Workers' Monthly" (Communist, Chicago) wrote asking me to be a contributor. (as I am a subscriber.) I sent him "A Lumberjack Yearns"! Do you recall it? "A whore in her perfumed bed." I fear his clientele won't care for it, if run.

I like Santa Barbara's nerve, trying to get a reputation as an earthquake center! Los Angeles will be butting in next. Well, it was bad news for Florida.

When do you start for Dayton?[7] And when do Geo. Jean and Lillian break up?

Yours ever,

George.

[256] [GS to HLM] [ALS, NYPL]

Aug. 6th, 1925.

Dear H. L.

I'm glad you got out of Dayton alive. Is it true that you worried the K.K.K. so much that they warned you to leave? Such is the rumor here.

I like Jones' "Elegy" immensely. Didn't know he could write as well—a very vital narrative. And he did a lot of digging for it—had plenty of stuff that was new to the present generation, including me.

Your magnificent diatribe on Bryan is before me, and I think you've sized him up to a hair.[8] How many, though they were as acute as you, would have the courage to depict the old cuss, now, as they see him? You are indeed Bierce's sole heir.

I'm not surprised that Mrs. Isgrigg has given Scheff. her permission to print her father's letters to him. He was always solid there. I've just learned of an elderly woman in Mendocino Co. who used to be a pupil of B's, and who apparently has letters from him. More of that anon, as the Hottentots say.

I was up at our Midsummer Jinks, and managed to keep out of the local hospital. Our gang there still has pre-V. Scotch. Wrote two comic (?) songs for us to howl, the latter one entitled: "Meet Me in the Morgue at Midnight." There was little sleep in the grove those last two nights. Also I rubbed poison-oak in the crotch of the pajamas of a member who displeased me. Haven't heard results.

My friend Mulgrew, an ex-reporter (now) whom you met at "Bigin's" one evening, wants me to send you the enclosed note referring to Professor Gilman. "Mul" is going to pass out with a big aneurism and leaking valves. Has been on his back for eight months. I never knew a hospital patient to have so many woman visitors—he must have screwed 5% of the feminine population of Northern California in his day. They're mostly his age. I go out to see him often, and he's never alone.

This caricature by Major isn't bad, though I've not that *vengeful* expression, I trust.

You want long poems, and I hope this longish one, lately finished, will be satisfactory.[9] The theme is of no great importance, but the incident is really funny, and was related to me by my mother concerning her father, the old whaler who killed more whales than anyone that ever lived. I remember him distinctly, as I was at least ten when he died (apoplexy) sitting in his chair. The poem could fill at least two pages, with perhaps an overflow.

What's the matter with Willa Cather? She goes all to hell with this rubbish of hers in "Collier's."[10]

Dreiser heard from you that I was in hospital, and not knowing it was but for a day, wrote me a most sympathetic letter, enclosing a check! The dear old megatherium!

Hopper has gone to N.Y., to mend his fences. Hope your trails cross. A good man, that Jim, though a bit quarrelsome. I think he'll give Sherwood Anderson a bad quarter-hour if they meet. A. used him despitefully in his autobiography.[11]

Finger was with me for a day—an enjoyable chap. He's two years younger than I and looks ten older. Has had much responsibility, I suppose.

I'm writing a prospectus for a "dude ranch", of all possible jobs. Will send you the circular when it's out. The "Covered Wagon" ranch.

> Yours in Mohammed,
>> George.

[257] [GS to HLM] [ALS, NYPL]

Aug. 29th, 1925.

Dear H. L.

I know you'll want this. Don't want to make The Mercury the lyre of a single string; but you could run it with the Swab ballad—that would be but four pages. If you think that "nudity" is a bit strong, we can go back to "scant attire." I did have "nakedness."[12]

"The Shadow Maker" seems to have made a hit out here. I'm receiving congrats. from all over the state, and four dealers reported the magazine sold out on the second day. I've not heard from his daughter, though, nor from the lady who idealizes him, a la Stevenson, in the August "Bookman!"[13]

Mulgrew is beginning to suffer badly—angina. I must give him the euthanasia soon. I went to four hospitals yesterday to see sick friends!

Things are beginning to go from bad to worse here. They now search automobiles coming in from the wine counties—grabbed 70 bottles from a friend of mine last week.

I had too much tokay last night, on Telegraph Hill, and my hand is a trifle shaky; but I wanted to get this ballad to you at once. The Gang here is crazy about it.

Scotch is getting scarcer, but better.

> Yours ever,
>> George.

[258] [GS to HLM] [ALS, NYPL]

Sept. 29th, 1925.

Dear H. L.

You're doomed to another letter, tho God He knoweth I've little to write.

The Shadow Maker seems to have made a big hit here: I hope there'll be no "returns" to the news company. I've had more congratulations on it, by mouth and letter, than from any *poem* I ever wrote. Had a letter even from a rabbi in Galveston who used to know Bierce.

I suppose the article infuriated Mrs. Harding, who has him idealized—he had a way of showing his *hurt* side to women. You have probably read her own article in the Aug. "Bookman." I think the man whom she describes Ambrose as slamming there is Scheffauer! Whomever Bierce happened to be sore at at the time was always "the most detestable of men!"

You gave me the shock of my young life when you turned down my "Ballad of the Grapes." I thought you'd fall on it with a yell! I dare say you're right, though: it's too flippant for your stern pages. But what a kick in the faces of the righteous!

I'm running it in the Overland Monthly, having taken an interest in the rejuvenation of that long-moribund magazine.[14] What a howl their old lady subscribers will raise!

I wonder if you'd care to have some such article on Joaquin Miller as I wrote on Bierce. I could make it pretty snappy, involving the names of Bierce, London and others.

The Mercury grows ever in grace. I was amazed to find how many Babbitts here in the club read it. And some of it is a bitter pill for the hundred per centers.

I dine to-night above an immense pre-war cellar. Pray for me!

In His name,

G. S.

[259] [GS to HLM] [ALS, NYPL]

Oct. 11th, 1925.

Dear H. L.

All right—I'll do the Miller thing in a week or so, conditional on your allowing me to use the term "the consecrated John Gould Fletcher!" It'll be as interesting as the Bierce one, echoes of which still resound from sea to sierra; though he was a smaller man than B.

I'm wondering just what Neale's howl was about. Can you give me an abridged notion? As for Danziger, he was the bird on whom Bierce broke the cane![15]

I wish now I'd remembered to refer to B's "three B's" essential to perfection in woman: brains, beauty and barrenness! The thing clean slipped me.

O God to have been at the Dayton reunion! My last bout with the daughter of the vine put me in bed for three days—all right now. You see, I got hellish gas-pains. I suppose that's all that saves me from a drunkard's grave—I have to quit early: after five days.

I wish we could have a piece from you for our rejuvenated "Overland," but we can pay only 2¢ a word. If you've anything you're too wise to print, Sumner living, let us have it. I aim too high, though.

In the name of the Prophet,

G. S.

[260] [HLM to GS] [TLS, Mills College]
[THE AMERICAN MERCURY
730 FIFTH AVENUE
NEW YORK]
October 17,
1 9 2 5

George Sterling, Esq.,
The Bohemian Club,
San Francisco, Calif.

Dear George:

Go as far as you like with Fletcher. He is a dreadful fake and makes constant efforts to get money out of The American Mercury. Neale's complaint was so idiotic that I have forgotten it. He is an ill-humored and nasty fellow. Sometime ago he sent me a manuscript with a long and very polite letter. I returned it with a rejection slip.

God knows I wish I could write something for the "Overland" but I am worked so hard that it is a sheer impossibility. What with The Sun, The Chicago Tribune Syndicate and The American Mercury, I turn out so much stuff every month that it is absolutely disgraceful. My next book should have been started two years ago. I have yet to get beyond the dummy.

Law enforcement is scoring fresh triumphs here in the East. Last week I bought a dozen bottles of excellent Rhine wine at two dollars a bottle. Red wine is so cheap that the Italians now use it to poison rats.

Yours,
Mencken

hlm:r

[261] [GS to HLM] [ALS, NYPL]

Nov. 7th, 1925.

Dear H. L.

Here's my article on Joaquin, just recd. from the typist. I'm sorry that that chap in the Lit. Digest "beat me to it," but you'll see that our two tales seldom coincide.[16]

About your writing for the "Overland": I never hoped, even, that you'd be a steady contributor. My notion was that maybe you had something already in cold storage that you thought injudicious to print in Sumner's and Straton's commonwealth.[17] The "Overland" is willing to take chances.

I told the damn fool girl[18] editor that I was asking you if you'd anything we could run, and the imbecile promptly put you down as a "contributing editor!" I've had her eliminate *that* proud boast.

Am feeling better since the removal of my tonsils, but am bothered by a sore throat and have an idea the doctor thinks it's something serious. So I'm having dreams of a new operation, this time for cancer!

Decent booze is becoming scarcer here every month, as winery after winery is raided or intimidated. I've already stated that the Scotch is impossible. Our one best bet is drug-store brandy. Three dollars a pint and fifteen years old. I'm beginning to save it up for holiday egg-noggs. But think of Rhine wine (one of my favorites, as it was London's) at $2. a bottle! It is to take the eastward trail.

Joaquin had also a half-breed son, but I'm sparing him on that.

Yours ever,
G. Sterling.

[262] [HLM to GS] [TLS, NYPL (Berg)]
[The American Mercury
730 Fifth Avenue
New York, N.Y.]

November 14,
1 9 2 5.

Dear George:
            The Joaquin Miller article is here and I am putting
it into type at once. My best thanks for a capital piece of work.
The proof will reach you anon and also a check.

I have a notion that it would be better to strike out the present
title of the article and substitute simply the name of "Joaquin
Miller".[19] The old boy is less known than he ought to be but there
is still considerable curiosity about him. You can decide this question when you get the proof.

God knows I wish I could write something for the "Overland",
but the fact is that at the moment it is a physical impossibility. I
am worked so hard that I can scarcely get through the day. My
book has gone to pot and Knopf is bawling

Sincerely,
Mencken

[263] [GS to HLM] [ALS, NYPL]

Nov. 20, 1925.

Beloved in the Lord:
            Propped up in bed, with a watch announcing
the hour of nine A.M., I salute you from the purple mirage of fif-
teen-year-old brandy. Prosit, H. L.! May the land be filled with
your bastards!

My tonsilar operation was a spectacular success: I have had
thirty drinks a day for five days and no gastritis yet. Wept on the
shoulders of three doctors last night at our Thanksgiving Dinner,
and all three promise to appear to-day with pints of brandy.

Old Thing, it's a damn shame we can't get together. You need
me and I need you. You are a 99% human proposition, lacking
only a realization of the concentrated virulence of poetry, for
beauty or "wisdom." Somehow that escapes you.

But we really ought to get together. When you were here I
never really had a heart to heart talk with you. Perhaps you
weren't scared of me, but I was a bit scared of you. Since then, the
haze has cleared a bit, and I am ready to inform and be informed.

Red Lewis wrote to me in regard to entertaining one, Lord

Thomson, and I had a passionate young animal ready to go to the mat with the dear lord, but he was out when I called and I was out when he called. So the great rosy thing took it out on an Italian. So much the worse for the lord, who was beguiled by the idiocies of reform.

I am glad that the Joaquin article satisfies you. Entitle it, of course, whatever you think most appropriate. My first heading was "Moonshine and Memory!" I shall make a few changes in the proofs, recalling certain repetitions of adjectives.

Am having a lot of fun these days, singeing the tail-feathers of our governor, F. W. Richardson, which the same is a pig-headed old chuckwalla.[20] I'm writing in no very great sincerity, but it's fun to deposuit potentes de sede, and the rich men in the club gape at me as at a new freak of nature.

My girl won't believe the report of our boy at the switch-board that I'm out of town, and sends up deputations to pound on my door and rescue me. But to hell with all such mercies. Me for the whole wrath of the katzenjammer!

Again I remind you that you are to be my guest at **my** grove play in our grove in 1926.

G. Sterling.

5 P.M. Worse, if possible. Am entertaining delusions as to the great H. F.'s mistress, a sullen Chino-Portuguese whose orgiastic outcries are said to be audible a block away.

How about the enclosed ballad of days that all he-men must regret? I sold it to "Sonnet" two years ago, but they seem scared to run it, and would probably be glad to get their money back. It seems to me it would be a good offset to the serious matter that occupies so much of your space. But God He knoweth the editorial heart.

The sonnets are of course rhetorical bunk. Just the same, the old bird will simply detest them, and it's no easy matter to penetrate his ancient hide.

Oh! Hell! Hen! I'd love to have a good long talk to you over four gallons of beer. My girl has just miscarried. I've only a swallow of brandy left, and suppose I must dress and go down stairs. God help us all and make us deserve well of the republic!

Yours in His maltreated name,

G. Sterling.

Poetry is the bunk—and is greater than all wisdom.

[264] [HLM to GS] [TLS, BAN]

December 19
1925.

Dear George:
You will be sorry to hear that my mother died last Sunday. Her illness fortunately was brief and painless. This house, I hope and believe, will go on. My sister is here and we plan to remain in Baltimore.

Obviously you ought to do an article sometime on Jack London. Also there must be many other such notions in your head. I see an excellent book in the distance.

I surely hope that you are completely well again.

Sincerely,
M

[265] [HLM to GS] [TLS, BAN]
[The American Mercury
730 FIFTH AVENUE
NEW YORK]

December 22, 1925.

Dear George:
Sometime ago I wrote to you suggesting that an article on Jack London would be excellent. William Marion Reedy also occurs to me. My impression is that you knew him well. Is it a fact? If so, he certainly ought to be done. My private impression of Reedy was that he was 92% fraud. But perhaps I am wrong.

I have suggested to Knopf that a book of your literary recollections would be interesting and he is very much taken with the idea. If you do it, he'll undoubtedly be glad to publish it.

Sincerely yours,
Mencken

HLM:L

[266] [HLM to GS] [TLS, BAN]

December 29
1925.

Dear George:
Thanks very much for your telegram which did not reach me until this morning. My sister and I went to Pittsburgh where my brother lives for Christmas and have just come back.

Does the project of an article on Jack London interest you? If so, I'll be very glad to do it in the spring. The Joaquin Miller article will probably be used in March. There are also many others: for example one on Charles Warren Stoddard.

Sincerely yours,

Mencken

1926

[267] [GS to HLM] [ALS, NYPL]

Jan. 6ᵗʰ, 1926.

Dear H. L.

      I went on one of my interlocking jags for the holidays, got three days in bed with gastritis (?) for it, as usual, and am only now tackling my correspondence.

Your mother's death has been an awful shock to you, I know. When mine died, several years ago, I was ill in the hospital, and could not even attend the funeral. One has at least the consolation that the loved one is forever beyond the reach of pain.

You're most kind to suggest these articles! I never met Reedy, so can give no estimate worth having as to his actual sincerity. Naturally, I was inclined to like him, for he professed, at least, a high regard for my verses. As you know, he died here in S.F., and I was to have met him on the very day he passed out.

Chas. J. Finger could give you an article on him, but it would be in the nature of a panegyric!

My fingers ache to do the London article, but I won't do it unless I can do it right, and so long as his elder daughter Joan lives (a dear friend of mine) and his widow, I *can't* do it right. The least breath of dispraise would wound them, and where they are concerned I'm not in the wounding business. Pass the job on to a sterner soul than mine!

I *could* do a brief sketch of Stoddard, but there is so little to write of absorbing interest that I hestitate to try it. His life wasn't especially eventful, though he went to Europe and the South Seas. He was one of the wittiest men I ever knew, and a sex invert.[1] I'll take a hack at the thing if you really want me to. Would run about six pages.

I'd feel like a supcrannuated ass were I to write up my "literary recollections!" Wait till I'm twenty years older. Just the same I'm greatly obliged to you for mentioning it to Knoph, and to him for his complimentary attitude. Why in Hell are you so kind to me, Hen? Are you heaping this grey head with embers because I was so nasty about Germany in war-time?

223

By the way, your remarks in the Sunpaper about the sweet side of war give me a new kind of pip.[2] I suppose you visualize yourself as an officer, but even to most of them war couldn't have been any "bloomin' violets." I've talked to a lot of them, and have yet to find one who has any real yen for the job. As to the common soldier, I've gone into the matter with all kinds, even Germans, and one and all look nauseated when I suggest they got any fun out of it.

Of course I refer to war as it's waged at present: the Civil War variety seems to have been better; at least Bierce liked it, apparently.

What gets the officers' goats is to see men whom they liked dead or in agony. The privates object to losing their pals, and to the general discomfort.

I believe, of course, in preparedness: that's crowded on us by the other gang, I suppose.

I did more screwing and less drinking in 1925 than in 1924. Even at that I had over a thousand drinks. I predict fewer in 1926, as our wineries are slowly being throttled. The Scotch gets greener and greener, the gin never was much to boast of. You of the East have it all over us as to quality and variety. I suppose I should migrate, but hate to give up the eternal comfort and incessant stimulation of this city.

I've signed the contracts with the Macmillan Co. "Lilith" this spring and a volume of poems, selected and otherwise, to follow six or twelve months later.[3] There won't be much money in it, and I'm indifferent to "fame." But it will peeve such enemies as I chance to have.

In nomine Prophetis,

G. S.

The Mercury continues to be readable from kiver to kiver. Prosit!!!

[268] [HLM to GS] [TLS, NYPL]
[The American Mercury
730 Fifth Avenue
New York]

January 11th [1926]

Dear George:—

It is too bad you can't do London. Who could do him so well? Nobody. But I think you are right. Is Stoddard really worth an article? I don't know, and leave it to you. You'll have to put the soft pedal, of course, on his inversion. He may have relatives, and the libel laws are very harsh. Finger is hopeless. He writes only rhapsodies.

Despite your evidence, I still believe that war is good sport. I think of it, of course, only from the standpoint of a correspondent, seeing it from the grand-stand. To hell with the other fellow! What has he ever done for me? The American Legion denounces me every time it meets.

The New Jersey towns opposite New York now swarm with accomplished booters. I have been buying good German wine there at $2 a bottle.

Yours,
Mencken

Why not a dozen of those capital fables for the Mercury?
M.

[269] [GS to HLM] [ALS, NYPL]

Feb. 2nd, 1926.

Dear H. L.

      I think that Stoddard *is* worth an article, and will try my hand on one some time. It would have to be rather brief, however. He lived a very quiet life. His "South Sea Idyls" is worthy of being a classic, and I wonder at its obscure place in American literature. Ever read it?[4]

Can you stand for a five page article on Pete M'Coy, one time welter-weight champion.[5] It would be mostly an account of how he influenced the lives of two boys of 18 or thereabouts, with side-anecdotes of his relations with John L.

As to the fables, I'm agreeably surprised to find you liking them, but think them hardly up to "Mercury" standards. I wrote those you saw over 33 years ago, shortly after meeting Bierce.[6] Of course they were imitations of his. (He quit writing such things as soon as he noted he had a disciple!)[7]

Did I tell you that I signed contracts with the Macmillan Co. for the publication of my "Lilith" this spring, to be followed by a book of short poems six or twelve months later. I hope you'll give "Lilith" a review, even if it's a roast, when it appears. I am not hot for money and fame, but should like to see the book sell, to justify my own faith in its merit. They wrote that dramatic poetry is even harder to sell than the lyrical kind. I've asked the Megatherium (Dreiser) to write a preface for the thing.[8] He may do so: he did one for a poorer dramatic poem. Have lately finished his "American Tragedy."[9] Of course his style is bad; but the story is unforgettable, and that counts a damn sight more than style. How many hundreds of novels doesn't one utterly forget!

As in the case of the Bierce article, I've had numerous congratulations on the Miller one. And his widow hasn't shot me yet.

In His name,

George S.

[270] [GS to HLM] [ALS, NYPL]

Feb. 11th, 1926.

Dear H. L.

This is probably the best thing I ever wrote, and I'm sending it to you first, hoping you'll like it.[10]

"Red" Lewis is here for two weeks, and dragged me from the joyless wagon. Some crash!

Yours ever,

George Sterling.

[271] [HLM to GS] [TLS, BAN]

[The American Mercury
730 FIFTH AVENUE
NEW YORK]

February 17, 1926.

Dear George:

I think you are quite right. "The Pathfinders" is an eloquent and excellent piece of writing and I shall put it into type at once. The usual check and proof will follow.

I am as usual up to my ears in work. But I still find time to go to mass every day.

Yours,
Mencken

HLM:L

[272] [GS to HLM] [ALS, NYPL]

Feb. 24th, 1926.

Dear H. L.

Delighted to find you can use my "Pathfinders," for the Merc. is the one magazine I am eager to see it in. You may make the price as low as you wish.

I am grateful too that you'll mention "Lilith" in your chaste columns. The point is this, so far as I am concerned: Macmillans accepted the drama with misgivings, and only with the proviso that I give them a book of lyrical poetry to follow up with, saying that dramatic poetry sold even more slowly than lyrical. So I'd like to give them a little surprise, and am asking some of my more famous friends to boost the book a bit. Dreiser has consented to write an introduction. I'm not at all sure that he savvies poetry as such, but there's a good deal of thought in the penultimate scene of the book; and of course collectors will buy it just because they'll have their Dreiser matter complete.

You were a bit rough on the dear old megatherium in your review of the "Tragedy,"[11] but it certainly *is* a human document and *not* a work of art. However, as to its length, I'd no demurring, for I found it all interesting. But ach Louie! some of those sentences!

I've been knocking around with that sot Lewis for over two weeks. He dragged me from the wagon, and he drank so much that he was impotent on at least one occasion; but he's good fun unless he's asleep. We went to Pebble Beach, near Carmel, a week ago. I'm just back, while he has gone on to K.C., via L.A. He was lit about all the time when at Pebble Beach, and when at a dinner at Gouverneur Morris' tried to vamp Pola Negri![12] She was nice to him, and he joshed Valentino so intimately that now he (L.) thinks that he made Valentino jealous![13] I'll say that's going some for alcoholic imagination.

I'm glad you'll try a piece on Pete M'Coy, and shall start it soon. To do the Stoddard one rightly I'll have to interview Ina Coolbrith and one or two other old-timers. Of course I'll not say anything about his inversion.

Our Scotch doesn't improve. It looks as though gin is to be the only safe stuff. Wine gets scarcer every week, with port and sherry at $15. a gallon.

I.H.N.,

G. S.

"Pathfinders" seems to have made a tremendous hit with my *friends*.

[273] [HLM to GS] [TLS, BAN]
[The American Mercury
730 FIFTH AVENUE
NEW YORK]
February 27,
1 9 2 6.

Dear George:
What shall I say about you in the Author's Note to
go with "The Pathfinders". The exact names of the Macmillan
books ought to be mentioned and the dates of publication.
Sincerely,
H L Mencken

[274] [GS to HLM] [ALS, NYPL]

Mch. 5th, 1926.

Dear H. L.
A bit shaky this morning. Some one gave ex-Sen. Phe-
lan[14] a bottle of fifty (50) year old whiskey, and he shared it with
me, I getting about 7/8 of it.
As to "Lilith"—the Macmillan Co. ought to have it out some
time in April: I sent the proofs back to them yesterday. As to the
book of lyrics that's to follow, I'm uncertain about the date of
publication. Either in the autumn or next spring.
It's damned fine of you to treat me so handsomely! I got a real
thrill when I saw the size of the check you gave me for "The Pathfinders." Half that much would have satisfied me, as what I really
wanted was to see the poem in a really civilized magazine.
Louis Untermeyer gets here Sunday, and I hope to get him
soused that evening: am taking him out to the home of some Jew-
ish friends who have a huge cellar of pre-war stuff, including even
absinthe.
Harriet Monroe lectures here on the 22nd, but she's too old to
"seduce" or to waste good booze on. The old cat hasn't much use
for me anyhow, as I won't send her anything for her magazine.
Dreiser promised, as I've already told you, to write me a preface
for "Lilith," but he hasn't yet done so, I think, and may put it off
till it's too late. If you happen to see him, ask him how about it.
I've not heard from Sinclair Lewis since he left me at Carmel
"with never a farewell." He ought to be as far as Santa Fe by this
time, if the bootleggers haven't put him in a hospital. He's a great
little drinker, but he can't carry it well.

I'll have a pretty seditious poem in the first number of "The New Masses."[15]

In Nomine Prophetis,

G. S.

[275] [GS to HLM] [ALS, NYPL]

Apr. 7th, 1926.

Dear H. L.

Hurrah for you! I wish I could have been there. Now if we could get you, Dreiser and Sinclair in the same cell it would be some exhibition. Well, guts is guts.

About this "yahoo" stuff at Joaquin's funeral: an old woman in Oakland also raised a howl, and they may be correct—I got my own dope from what I actually read in the "Examiner" at the time, though. Also in the "Oakland Tribune."

I've not begun on the M'Coy or Stoddard articles yet. Had a terrific cold, the only real one I ever had, made worse by my going on a five-day jag. So I went to the country to recuperate, and it damned near killed me: no sleep for four nights, on account of deluded roosters and dogs barking at coyotes. Also my bed was as hard as the floor of a tomb. No more country for me till I'm strong enough to stand it. By the way, they *shoot* salmon up there, after they've spawned. Use a 44 cal. rifle.

I was at Stoddard's grave in the old Catholic cemetery in Monterey on Monday. A ground-squirrel was *burrowing* for him, I don't know with what luck. Bierce would have liked that squirrel as a pet.

The straw-vote on prohibition was a glorious surprise. S.F. went 46 to 1 for beer and light wines. I fear Sinclair will get infantile paralysis before all's over.

In nomine Patris, et al.

G. S.

[276] [HLM to GS] [TLS, BAN]

[The American Mercury
730 FIFTH AVENUE
NEW YORK]

April 27, 1926.

Dear George:

Herewith a dozen copies of our circular.[16] If you can hand them quietly to discreet and Christian persons, I'll be greatly obliged. The more our case is understood, the better for it.

> Yours,
> H L Mencken

HLM:L
enc.

[277] [GS to HLM] [ALS, NYPL]

May 4th, 1926.

Dear H. L.

My last boom endured for but a day, or rather four; but it put me in bed for six, as I tried to taper off. The M.D. who came to give me the once-over said I had the heart of a bull, but that my nervous system was too sensitive. I dare say it's best that way, if in any way.

The circulars came, and will be judiciously distributed. A glorious victory indeed; but the godly seem to be at you from a new angle, or why this clipping from the "Examiner"? If there's really such an article as "Sex and the Co-ed," and it's not to appear in the "Mercury," how am I to have a look at it?

Your May number is a strong one, and in your review of that book on the Bible[17] you say something that I've been asserting for years: that we non-believers have been taking it lying down, and what this country needs is a good hot religious war, with the pen, not the sword. Just for the present I wish I were rich enough to flood the country with pamphlets showing what asses the religious are.

Pertinent to your remarks, the article in the March number, on America's need for a new God, shouldn't have appeared.[18] That too was a sop, in its way, to the superstitious.

At the request of a young friend, a *Russian* from Russia, I've enclosed one of his short-stories. I think it amusing enough, but hardly of your metal.

"Lilith" is out, and you've received a copy by this time, I dare say. When I go to N.Y., via steamer, in Sept., I'll drop in and write in it for you.

Don't reply to this yet, as I'm writing again tomorrow.

Pox vobiscum!

> G. S.

[278] [GS to HLM] [ALS, NYPL]

May 5th, 1926.

Dear H. L.

Do you care to take a chance on running this? The theme is exceptional, and I've not seen it in print before—at least, lately, locally and conspicuously.[19]

It is *expressed* modestly enough. Whether or not the P.O. people will object to the story itself is of course another matter.

A huge demand for the April number here. Have you one to spare? Mine was stolen and the copy in our library was gelded.

I was interested in Babette Deutsch's article on poetry—an odd mixture: she's wrong more often than she's right.[20] For one thing, never was there so much interest in poetry before, in America. The very high-schools boil with it, and business-men are writing it secretly!

In nomine Diaboli,

G. S.

P.S. A most enthusiastic letter from Ben De C., about "Lilith." I hope you can stand for its ("Lilith's") optimism. I had to let the other side have their say, such as it is.

George.

[279] [HLM to GS] [TLS, NYPL (Berg)]

May 11th [1926]

Dear George:—

I have so much fiction in type that I am buying no short stories, and I fear that the Lesbian poem is not for a great family magazine: it would simply get us bumped off again, and so put us to more and worse expense. The combat with the comstocks has already cost a pile of money. We are paying our own way, and taking no help from anyone. Hays often works for nothing, but when he is paid he is expensive.[21]

The news that you will be East next September is excellent. How long will you be in New York. I bespeak the high honor of introducing you to the Christian life of the town. I always have hay-fever in September and so devote the whole month to drink. I may go abroad myself in October. Phil Goodman[22] and I are thinking of going to Constantinople, to get out of Christendom for once in our lives.

I am sweating through two books, and hope to finish them both by the end of July.[23] They were delayed by the Boston business, which kept me jumping for three weeks and put me out of the mood. But now they are moving.

Yours,

M

[280] [GS to HLM] [ALS, NYPL]

May 24th, 1926.

Dear H. L.

I was almost certain that you couldn't run a poem with such a theme, but I wanted you to see it, anyway. It'll have to be "for private circulation." Have sent a copy to Dreiser.

Your paragraphs on sundry poets in the June "Mercury" are very interesting, and, it seems to me, adequate so far as you have room for such remarks.[24] I was glad to find you speaking respectfully of Jeffers.[25] He's the biggest of the lot, I think.

Yes—I hope to be in N.Y. late in September, but it's no sure thing. Naturally, I'd hunt you up, the first thing I did, for I'd go for the main reason of having a gabfest and hooch-hoisting with you. Didn't have a chance to talk half enough with you in 1920. Jesus! it doesn't seem six years ago!

I have to go to Los Angeles in a day or two—pleasure, not business—and when I'm back and convalescent, will turn out those two articles for you, as I think you'll like them. Am already hearing kind words for "The Pathfinders." The sense is slightly skewed, in the first paragraph, by incorrect punctuation that I should have caught in the proofs.

I suppose you've come on "Count Bruga."[26] I wonder what Bodenheim thinks of it, and to what extent it's a caricature of him. Have he and Hecht fallen out, or are they so hard-boiled that that's their notion of conferring friendly publicity? My Gawd!

The San Franciscan girl whom I wanted you to meet, last summer, is back here, and has just had a ten pound boy. Just think, H. L.—you might just as well have been its father! But doubtless you've plenty of other descendants. There are many locally attributed to my humble but earnest efforts.

Yours ever,

G. S.

[281] [GS to HLM] [ALS, NYPL]

June 27th, 1926.

Dear H. L.

Why in hell don't you put to sea every September, and so avoid that hay-fever? It must be a woeful thing to look forward to. The only ailment, aside from writing poetry, that I can confess to is the jag-headache, and even that is submissive to acetanelid.

Masters writes me from Santa Fe that he'll be here on the 14th, so I'm already hunting up a girl for him and collecting prescriptions. One can get an excellent brandy, 16 years old, at one of the local pharmacies.

I'm taking Masters down to Carmel, to see the stormy-eyed Jeffers, and I hope he can be here long enough to see my grove-play.[27]

A "lady-friend"[28] is having my Lesbian poem printed—just 200, in paper covers. I hope I won't have to go to San Quentin for it. It is modestly expressed, and only the *theme* is hazardous. Also one can "get away with murder" in verse. How many copies may I send you?

Here's some enthusiasm for De Casseres, done in his own style. On reading it he wrote that the coming decade belongs to you, Cabell, me and him! Wrong on three of the counts!

Have you an interest in the Ionaco?[29] It is like Abrams' oscilloclast, in that it's a miracle-worker.

In His Name,

George S.

[282] [GS to HLM][30]

July 27, 1926

Dear H. L.

This will introduce to you my very gifted young friend, Bert Cooksley.[31] I know of no other poet of corresponding years and ability.

It is rumored that he left this city because of news as to the quality of New York hooch; but *I* think he is merely trying to escape his harem, and to found another where girls don't expect miracles in the line of fidelity.

Get him drunk (if it can be done) and turn him over to the nearest cop.

Your venerable brother in God,

George Sterling

P.S. He can't do the Charleston.

G. S.

[283] [GS to HLM] [ALS, NYPL]

Aug. 2nd, 1926.

Dear H. L.

The grove play was a tremendous success, its series of "pictures" being unbelievably beautiful. I'll be a long time regretting your absence.

Masters appeared on July 1st and stayed till the 9th. We were lit all the time, and after his departure I kept it up till the 20th, finally landing in the Franklin hospital for two days of recuperation. Masters *is* a fine chap, and I wish he would live in S.F.

About this sonnet: you ask where I'm publishing it. I can't see any of the Braminic or Kiwanian magazines taking it, and if you care to run it, you're welcome to it gratis. As I remember, you don't care to run "fillers," so if this sonnet "The Restoration" can accompany it, they'd make a full page.[32]

We've let about two hundred chaps of the twenties into the club, during the past year, and the result was a wet and songful Jinks. I was there six days, and averaged three hours a night of sleep. The last night none at all. But it doesn't hurt one, apparently, even at *my* advanced years.

If you don't mind, I'll tell Cooksley he may meet you. Roberts has made him his assistant on The American Parade.[33] A wild youth, but one with a fine future.

Yours for the Resurrection and "the life,"

George S.

Lesbian poem will be out this week. I'll send you half a dozen copies.

[284] [HLM to GS] [TLS, BAN]
[The American Mercury
730 FIFTH AVENUE
NEW YORK]

August 10th. [1926]

Dear George:

God knows what has happened to me, but both of these sonnets somewhat let me down. Even "The Seventh Veil" on rereading leaves me cold. I hesitate to do anything which doesn't knock me over completely and so I pass them up. I hope you will forgive me.

When are you going abroad? It is conceivable, though by no means probable, that I will get to the Coast sometime during the next three or four months. I am going South on a newspaper enterprise in October and if it takes me to Texas, as seems likely, I'll probably jump over the mountains for another look at San Francisco. Certainly, I must see that gaudy town again before I die. All of this for your private eye. My plans are still somewhat vague.

Sincerely yours,
Mencken

[285] [GS to HLM] [ALS, NYPL]

Aug. 15th, 1926.

Dear H. L.

I'm sorry you couldn't "see" "The Seven Veils" sonnet. I sent it in only because you asked where I was going to print it.

I sent you, last week, ten copies of "Strange Waters." It was vilely printed, but I had nothing to do with that. They didn't even correct it from the proofs, which I did get a look at.

One of the copies I inscribed. Do you mind sending copies to T. R. Smith and Nathan?

I forget whether or not I sent you the book of my grove-play, "Truth." I've one in cold storage for you, if you want it.

If ever I do go abroad, soon, it will be next spring. For Gawd's sake come to Frisco if you get anywhere near California! A delegation will await you, wise in the location of pre-Volstead medicaments and anodynes. Irene Millier is still here, and far more presentable than in the past. Red Lewis says she's passionate, which is more than she ever was for *me*.

Fog here morning and late afternoon and night; but it makes for eternal comfort.

Peruse carefully these moving words of Dr. Jordan!

In nomine Diaboli,
George S.

[286] [GS to HLM] [ANS, NYPL]

[August 1926]

Dear H. L.

Enclosed has come to me in a round-about way, but bears strong internal evidence of Masters' authorship.[34]

G.

[287] [GS to HLM] [ALS, NYPL]

Aug. 28th, 1926.

Dear H. L.

Of course I'll be in S.F. in November, if only to see you. If I had the price I'd go to N.Y. to-morrow, for that reason only. I *shall* be there by next March.[35] I think you'll find the town not too much changed for the worse. Most of our hooch is gin, but I have several friends, "multis", of the pre-Volstead age. And there's a delightful joint up on Telegraph Hill, run by a Wop named Joe and called "The Cellar." One sits at a rough table (a long one, the only one in the place) and sips a palatable though young Tokay. There are usually ten or twelve young folk in the place, from the Hill's Greenwich Village. But I fancy that old-time Martinis in clean surrounding will be more to your taste.

I'll ring Irene up in a day or two. If she has moved, there are others, notably a big girl, a peach, whom Masters got a heavy case on. Her name is Lois and she runs a tiny book-shop. Yr. talk about senility does not convince me.

Behold an amended version of the Methodist verses, with two additional stanzas, the contribution of a dean in the Episcopal cathedral here. Destroy the other draft.

About "Truth": haven't you the original book, got out by the "Bookfellows" in 1923? Or is it the adapted grove-play that you lack? Or both? Let me know.

That was an interesting article about the Crane kid.[36] If her sceptics knew anything about poetry they'd not have made the mistake of doubting her. She is merely unusually gifted and precocious. There's a young Yid here just now (not yet 16) who got out from N.Y. in 16 days, by "lifts" in automobiles, and packs around about two hundred poems, some of them good enough to bear Shelley's signature! Where he'll end God knows: my guess is a madhouse.

God guard you and Satan guide you!

Yours ever,

G. Sterling.

P.S.

I almost forgot to say that my bright young friend Cooksley, whom you said you'd be glad to see, writes that he's now ashamed to call, on acct. of a fool article in The American Parade, of which he's tenth asst. editor. I told him not to be a fool, but to see you. He wants you to mention his quarterly in the Mercury, preferably with a roast. But you'll find them too small game, I fancy. But Bert is a live wire in excelsis.

G. S.

[P.P.S.] Shall be on wagon till your arrival. I have to write light-opera libretto.

[288] [HLM to GS] [TLS, UCLA]

September 2nd [1926]

Dear George:—

I have neither version of "Truth". The Bookfellows fakers never sent me their edition in 1923.

Joe's place, I suspect, will be exactly to my taste. I am never quite comfortable in saloons on or above the ground level. I was taught the art in cellars, and they seem like home sweet home to me. I only hope there is a good pissoir, or at least plenty of space in the back-yard. My rifling is worn out, and I spread. But the girls will have nothing to complain of otherwise. I am bringing along a keg of Delayo.

Cooksley I have not yet seen. He called up my office in New York during the week, but I was out. Tell him not to bother about any roasts on me that he has printed. Such things come out at the rate of 20 a week, especially in the South and Middle West.

Just when I'll land in your great city I don't know, but I'll find out very soon. What a meeting it will be!

I have hay-fever, but prayer has reduced it to a triviality. It is scarcely worse this year than ordinary apoplexy or Bright's disease.

Yours,
Mencken

The Methodist strophes are now perfect! M

[289] [GS to HLM] [ALS, NYPL]

Sept. 1st, 1926.

Dear H. L.

I think this is a damned good poem. Mrs. Cobb is too shy or too indifferent to send out her own work, so I'm doing it for her.[37]

Robertson, my publisher, has just informed me that all the sheets of my unbound books (ten in all) have been destroyed by a fire at the binder's. Doubtless the act of a merciful Providence, and I'm not sorry, as I intended to junk over half of the poems anyhow.

Pardon me for writing so many letters to you. This one requires no reply.

I'm going to start that article about Pete M'Coy, the prize-fighter, this morning. It won't be (can't be) long.

God guard you, Satan guide you!

In the name of both,

G. Sterling.

[290] [GS to HLM] [ALS, NYPL]

Sept. 6th, 1926.

Dear H.L.

Here's the thing about Pete M'Coy—not too long, I hope, to bore you or your subscribers.

I'll get at the one on Stoddard soon. I have to pump Miss Cool-brith for a few anecdotes, first.

If you want some more copies of "Strange Waters," let me know.

Thirstily yours,

George S.

[291] [HLM to GS] [TLS, BAN]

[The American Mercury
730 FIFTH AVENUE
NEW YORK]

September 7
1 9 2 6

Dear George:

Somehow or other this poem does not lift me as it seems to lift you. It is not bad stuff but on the whole I don't like it enough to print it. My best thanks for the chance to see it.

I am engaged in the Herculean job of trying to arrange my work so that I may escape in October. My fear is that it will be late in the month before the thing becomes possible. This will bring me to the Coast, if I get that far, about the second week in November. I'll come in from the South and stop off in Los Angeles to look at the evangelists before going up to San Francisco.

Sincerely yours,

Mencken

[292] [HLM to GS] [TLS, BAN]
[The American Mercury
730 FIFTH AVENUE
NEW YORK]

September 10th [1926]

Dear George:—

Thanks very much for the M'Coy article. It is excellent stuff and goes into type at once. But aren't you in error in
referring to *Jack* Dempsey? Jack was no more than a beautiful
thought in God's mind in 1890.

It now seems likely that I'll start on my wanderings on October
13th. This will bring me to the Coast about November 5th.

Yours,
M

[293] [GS to HLM] [ALS, NYPL]

Sept. 15th, 1926.

Dear H. L.

I'm damn glad you can use the Pete M'Coy article! You
surprise me, though, by not remembering the original Jack Dempsey, the "nonpareil," the great middle-weight who was whipped
only by Fitzsimmons, if you except the time "the La Blanche
swing" landed on him. The present Jack Dempsey hadn't been
born, when M'Coy was still alive.[38]

I guess I forgot to mention something in my other late letter to
you. It's this: an attorney here has written a series of, let us call
them essays, in the form of letters to a woman, and in them he
has used many of the experiences that have come to him as a di-
vorce-lawyer. It makes (to me at least) a fascinating book, full of
wit, charm, and above all, wisdom as to sex. I wonder if you'd
mind reading the MS., and *if* it's as interesting to you as I expect
it to be, passing it on to Knopf with a good word for it. They saw
it once before, but Crofton, the author, has cut it down considerably, as well as excised some of the more risqué passages, and I've
a notion they'll want to use it, this time. It is hard for me to think
of their refusing so fine a MS.

It's great news that you'll really be here this autumn. As I've
said, I'm beginning to save sherry against the divine event.

Yours for all Methodists in Hell,

George Sterling.

[294] [GS to HLM] [ALS, NYPL]

Sept. 26th, 1926.

Dear H. L.

I've just spent ten days in Los Angeles, with the effect of making S.F. look better than ever. Yet the former city has much to interest one, and will be the biggest in the U.S., some day, when all Los Angeles county will be one vast town of about twelve million near-souls. Christ knows what the traffic-congestion will be then! It's bad enough now.

I have three sisters in L.A., and put in most of my time with them. Two have their own cars, and it was just as well, for the climate, except in winter, is too hot for walking. The daughter of one of them, a girl of seventeen, is now coast-champion at swimming—I think I've already told you that. It was interesting to watch her dash up and down the w. k. Pacific Ocean.

We went out to watch von Stroheim make a picture, one day.[39] I know him pretty well. He's a temperamental cuss, and swears at his "mob" prefusely. Wants to have my sister work for him, and she's just vain enough about her beauty to do so.

It said in one of the L.A. papers that you'd be Upton's guest when in the south. I hardly believe that, for it nearly *kills* him to see anyone take a drink. The girl (she's about 33) whom I had saved up for you in 1920 (only she escaped me somehow) is now living in L.A., and I think you'd find her agreeable and willing company. She's fairly intelligent, but not bookish. A big, passionate tigress. Let me know if I may not send you her 'phone number. Here it is anyhow: Westmore, 2331. Grace Cheney. Also a bright youth by name of M'Williams, taking a post-graduate course in law at the U.S.C., but connected with the legal department of the L.A. Times, is crazy to crowd drinks in you.[40] If you care to let him, notify me in time.

I'd like to know, also, how many days you can give us here, as I want to arrange for some dinners at friends' who have pre-war stuff. You won't be bored, for I'll not select any of the bourgeois. It would be fine to have Hergesheimer here too. I wonder if he's bringing his wife along.

Yes—a new girl is highly remedial. The trouble is that she doesn't stay "new" very long. By the way, I've just had a letter from a former sweetheart, now in Paris, asking if I won't let her have a letter acknowledging our adulteries. Only a lawyer and the Minister of Justice are to see it. I'm sending it on, with the assurance that I'd be proud to see it in all the newspapers. For she is a peach. Wants a divorce.

I went to a reception to our venerable poet-laureate, Ina Cool-brith, last night, for I admire the old girl immensely. She promises to send me some anecdotes for the article I want to write for you about Stoddard. I hope you'll send me proofs on the Pete M'Coy article, as I find a few errors, notably the use of the word "summer" when I mean winter.

I've let Jack Newbegin, the book-seller, know you're coming, and he's highly excited. Will collect only ancient beverages.

Here's a letter that may amuse you.

I made the trip to and from L.A. by automobile, with four women, all in the thirties. They were a jolly bunch. They nicknamed Pismo Beach "Urino Beach." Note some of the musical Spanish names on the enclosed road-card, and compare them with the American ones—Bradley, Orcutt! It is to weep. But the miners in the sierra did worse. One place was named "Woman's Crevice!"

I've gassed on long enough, so "may the Lord be with you, but inattentive!"

George.

[295] [GS to HLM] [ALS, NYPL]

Sunday evening.
[October 1926?]

Dear H. L.

This town is certainly on the qui vive for your coming, and I'm constantly besieged by persons that want to grasp the hand that doesn't care to grasp Coolidge's.

I'm writing to beg you not to give your first interview to the "Chronicle" men nor to anyone else but my little Hindoo friend Gobind Lal, who was one of the Hindoo conspirators here, during the war, and spent six months in jail for his connection therewith. He has lately been hit by an automobile, and is out in St. Luke's hospital, but is highly competent to interview you—a fine mind. I'm hoping to take you out there as soon as you arrive, and give him a chance at space rates—he needs the money. So let me know the train you're arriving on, and don't say too much to the other reporters.

The hooch is piling up, and an agreeable young woman hones for your passionate embrace.

Don't stay very long in the Angelic City.

As ever,
George.

[296] [GS to HLM] [ALS, NYPL]

Oct. 29th, 1926.

Dear H. L.

My friend in L.A., Carey M'Williams, sends me a clipping with the news that you're already there. I didn't expect that, for you thought you'd put in some time in Texas and Oklahoma and reach L.A. about the 2nd.

M'W. makes a piteous plea to see you, if only for a few minutes, so I'm writing him to drop in on you. He'll have some *good* hooch.

Am knocking around with Anita Loos and her husband at present. They'll be gone by Sunday. Please let me know by wire the day and hour your train will arrive in Frisco. Everyone here on the qui vive, and I'll have a hard job keeping the lion-hunters off your pelt.

Yours for larger and cheaper harems,

George.

M'Williams contemplates a Life of Bierce. Is a post-graduate law-student at present.

[297] [GS to HLM] [ALS, NYPL]

Nov. 3rd, 1926.

Dear H. L.

It's bad news to me that you're to stay in the south till H. gets screwed to a finish. I'm not sure of his powers, but it looks as though you'd not be left with very much time for San Francisco. I can only hope that he dates Clara Bow, who'll give him a swift finish, or Bebe Daniels, who started Dempsey on the downgrade.[41]

Mrs. Gouverneur Morris rang me up from her Monterey home a day or two ago and told me to be sure to bring you there for a visit—that she'd come up for us in her car. It's a 3½ hour trip.

It's a lovely region, and I'd like to have you see Pebble Beach and environs, which so old a globe-trotter as Somerset Maugham thinks the most beautiful locality he has ever seen, and where he wants to build and live some day. The Morrises are pretty "wet," but you'd not mind that. You could see Jeffers, his family and stone tower, too, at Carmel.

A couple of hen-clubs are phoning me, with the full intent of having you for a guest of honor—i.e., as heckle-bait. I'm telling them I'll let you know, but that they've not one chance in a thousand.

S.F. has gone wet by 3 to 1. Should have been 10 to 1.

In Christo,

Geo.

[298] [GS to HLM] [ALS, NYPL]

Nov. 8ᵗʰ, 1926.

Dear H. L.

Hergesheimer me no Hergesheimers! Some cinema cat has her claws in you, and I now fear your giving her your entire vacation and returning direct from L.A.

It will be all right by me, if it doesn't shorten your stay in this city. I'd hate to have you appear only to say you had to light out for Baltimore in two days. Spare the old town that! The newspapers are at me on the 'phone day and night, to find out just when you'll arrive. They'd make little less fuss over the Dear Queen. Also the Civil Liberties League and two or three hen-clubs are after you—and the local press-club.

I'm strong for going down to the Morrises for a day or so. That globe-trotter Maugham told Anita Loos that the Pebble Beach country is the most beautiful he's ever seen, and the only place where he intends to build his home! I knew it is supremely lovely, but hadn't much means of comparison.

I'm glad you detest L.A. I do myself, though I've had some good times there.

I note that our dear brother in Christ, Edgar Lee Masters, has again entered into the bonds of holy matrimony. Let us appoint a Day of Ribald Laughter when you arrive, and wire him congratulations and hopes for his future posterity.

Kiss the Kid passionately for me!

George.

The Examiner wants to steal you from the Chronicle—your weekly stuff.

[299] [GS to HLM] [ALS, NYPL]

Nov. 10ᵗʰ, 1926.

Dear H. L.

One might think you were Christ and Him crucified, from the fuss the local press is making about you. They have me on the 'phone day and night, each paper in dread that you'll come to town without their reporter being on the job. I tell them you'll be here Friday or Saturday, and I hope to Christ I'm right.

All the doctors in S.F. seem eager to see you, and proffer ancient vintages. Old Doc Robertson, whose book on Poe you didn't exactly go crazy about, wants you to come to his den and see his collection of Poe material and down his pre-Volstead beer. Can do, I hope. I'd rather have beer than anything except Berncastler Doktor. (Of course that spelt wrong.)

Here is a ballad I've just finished.[42] I'm sending it to you because I want quick action on it, and have a notion, anyhow, that it's the kind of verse you want for your great subversive monthly.

Have slept in the arms of sin all night, and feel a bit shaky this morning—6 A.M. The weather has been flawless for a month, but of course will begin to misbehave the minute you hit town. I have just done an introduction for Bierce's "In the Midst of Life," soon to be re-issued by the Modern Library (3000 words only.)[43] That animal Danziger has been mendacious about the old Titan in the last American Parade,[44] and I am paying him my compliments in print, lacking the chance to break a cane over his head, as Bierce did.

It will be damn wonderful to see you again, Hen. I've saved up my money twice, to go to N.Y. and see you, and both times when I was within $100. of the needed sum I went on a bat and blew it all in. I am ashamed that you have had to do the calling twice running, but so the vinous Fates have decreed.

Talofa!

George.

I see you finish as a high-priced comedian with the Mack Sennet Co.!

[300] [HLM to GS] [ALS, HUN]
[BOHEMIAN CLUB
SAN FRANCISCO]
Tuesday night [November 16, 1926]
Dear George:

I called twice and found you asleep both times. I surely hope it means that you are much better. I'll drop in again tomorrow. Lal is with me tonight.

Ys

M

[On envelope:]

Mr. Sterling

[Note under above:]

Found under Geo's door unopened.
Nov. 18 1926.

Undated Letters

[301] [GS to HLM] [ALS, NYPL]

Dear H. L.

Have motored 25 miles north of the Grove to visit old Fort Ross, once in the otter fur belt. An old Greek church here, long unused. The barracks are in ruins. Picked up a small kitten en route, miles from any house. Guess it fell from a car, as it's too small to walk far. Shall take it back to the Grove for a mascot. Named it Mussolini.

Broadway is nothing like this. Norris[1] sends you his best, as does

G. Sterling

[302] [GS to HLM] [ANS, NYPL]

No "Smart Set" here yet. Was it printed at all? I mean for December. If it was, for His sake save me a number!

Dreiser's dead if ever I see him.

G. S.

Appendix: Mencken on Sterling's Death

Good Life, Good Death, Says Mencken
Sterling Last of Free Artists

by H. L. Mencken

No artist ever kept his peculiar faith more resolutely than George Sterling. It was a sheer impossibility to dissuade him from the course he had marked out for himself. Through all the heat and fury of the jazz age he remained faithful to the classical tradition in poetry, and I am inclined to think the best of his work will long outlast the experiments he disdained. I say disdained, but the word is not quite accurate. He was extaordinarily hospitable to the work of all other poets, however much it differed in aim and manner from his own. He read it, studied it, and in many cases liked it. But he was never tempted to imitate it. His own work was always magnificently pure in form. There was often a voluptuous music in it, but there were never any metrical or ideational aberrations.

Sterling was one of the last of the free artists. Beethoven once said that they were the only happy men in the world. Certainly Sterling was happy. He had reduced his wants to a minimum, and could always meet them. He worked when the urge came upon him. He refused to do anything that he didn't want to do. Surrounded by pleasant friends and living comfortably in the most beautiful of American cities, he let the years slide by with scarcely a care. I think he enjoyed his celebrity, for it brought him agreeable contacts. But he never did anything to further it. He would not write to meet the current fashions. In the end, with age and illness upon him, he put an end to his life, quietly, simply and decently. It was, I think, a good life—and a good death.

I am glad I was here to see him before he died. He was in great pain when I called upon him at the Bohemian Club, but his mind was clear, and we had a brief and friendly palaver. I came away convinced that he was desperately ill. He showed every sign of

246

complete exhaustion. That was on Monday. On Tuesday morning I went to see him again, but found him sleeping. Tuesday night his door was locked, and the transom showed darkness within. I assumed that he was still asleep, and went away. No doubt he was already dead.

Such charming fellows make life more bearable among us. They stand against the idiotic strivings of a vain and preposterous age. The things they admire, in the arts as in life itself, are genuinely admirable. They know the high value of simplicity. They are without guile. The world would be happier if there were more of them.

[*San Francisco Chronicle,* November 18, 1926, p. 3; *San Francisco Examiner,* November 18, 1926, p. 8 (as "Poet's Death Ideal, Says H. L. Mencken in Tribute"); *Overland Monthly* 85, No. 12 (December 1927): 363 (as "Sterling"); separate publication (as *Sterling*) San Francisco: John Henry Nash, 1927.]

To John Cowper Powys [TLS, BAN]
[The American Mercury
730 FIFTH AVENUE
NEW YORK]

December 11
1926.

Dear Mr. Powys:

Poor Sterling's death is easily explained. He had been accumulating a stock of liquors against my coming and when I was delayed a week in Los Angeles he succumbed to it and got dreadfully drunk. In late years his successive drunks had brought on more and more appalling consequences. This time he was completely floored. When I got to San Francisco, five days after he had been put to bed, I found him unable to sit up and suffering dreadful pains. His doctor told me that he would undoubtedly recover. But with a series of parties started, some of them in the very club where he was lying, poor George fell into a mood of gloom, and on the second night after my arrival, he reached for the cyanide bottle. On the whole, he probably took the wisest course. He was 57 and for several years past he had found it a physical impossible [*sic*] to amuse himself in the ways he liked. A few drinks would make him drunk and once drunk he would be ill for weeks.

I am glad that I saw him before he died. On account of his depressing condition, our talk had to be short, but it was very pleasant. The town rumor was that he and I had quarreled, but this of course was nonsense. Charles G. Norris, Gouverneur Morris, Thomas Beer and various other old friends had gathered for the festivities. The first of the dinners was given by Norris in the Bohemian Club with George lying ill upstairs. It was, I am glad to say, a very wet party.

Sincerely,

H L Mencken

To Henry Dumont [TLS (copy), NYPL]

February 20, 1935.

Henry Dumont, Esq.,
244 Kearny St.,
San Francisco, California.

Dear Mr. Dumont:

I arrived in San Francisco on the morning of the day before George Sterling committed suicide. As soon as I had registered at the St. Francis Hotel I went to the Bohemian Club to see him. He was laid up there and suffering great pain. Needless to say, our meeting was amicable. Late that afternoon, in company with G. B. Lal, now science editor of all the Hearst papers, I returned to the club to see him again. We concluded that he was asleep and so Lal and I left. The next day while I was at lunch with Gouverneur Morris and his wife at the St. Francis, the Associated Press called up to say that George had been found dead. The chances are that he was already dead at the time Lal and I called on him the previous evening.

Morris and I went to the club, but the coroner was in charge of the room and we did not see the body. Morris and I naturally expected to go to the funeral, but when Jim Rolph, who was then mayor, announced that he was going to make a civic orgy out of it we decided to clear out. I went back to Los Angeles and Morris and his wife to Seattle. They sailed shortly afterward for the Far East.

There was absolutely no quarrel between George and me. He knew that I was coming to San Francisco and he had been accumulating a stock of wines and liquors against my arrival. I was delayed in Los Angeles by the fact that Joseph Hergesheimer, who was coming from the East to join me, was several days late. In the end Hergesheimer decided not to come to San Francisco with me. I was told by George's friends that while waiting for me he sampled some of his accumulated beverages and got tight. He had then reached such a stage that any excessive alcohol produced a violent attack of neuritis, especially in the arms. That was what he was suffering from when I saw him at the club, but he had then been in bed for some days and was, of course, perfectly sober.

While I was still in Los Angeles he called me up there and upbraided me gently for delaying my trip to San Francisco. All this, of course, was in perfectly good humor. Certainly we were on the best of terms when I visited him the day before his death. As I have said, he was in great pain, but nevertheless he received me very pleasantly and told me that he had arranged for a big party as soon as he could get out. The night before he died Charles G. Norris gave a dinner for me at the Bohemian Club. It was attended by probably fifteen men, mainly writers. George himself was to have been the principal guest, but his illness made it impossible for him to attend. I daresay that in his room upstairs he could hear the yelling of the other brethren.

My guess is that he committed suicide because he had found by bitter experience that it was no longer possible for him to live his old life. Every time he took a few drinks he came down with neuritis. Existence on the water-wagon would have been intolerable to so merry and charming a fellow.

Where I met him I don't recall clearly, but it was in New York. We had been in correspondence for years. Finally, he showed up in New York and we had a couple of pleasant sessions. At my suggestion, he wrote some prose articles for The American Mercury. They dealt, as I recall them, mainly with his own early days and were very beautifully done. Their success gave George the idea of writing his autobiography in full, but so far as I know he never actually did it.

The aforesaid G. B. Lal was one of George's closest friends. He may be reached at 1 University place, New York. Lal is an East Indian, who has had a really remarkable career in America.

Sincerely yours,
H. L. Mencken.

Notes

INTRODUCTON

1. H[arriet] M[onroe], "The Poetry of George Sterling," *Poetry* 7, No. 6 (March 1916): 310–11.
2. See *Dreiser-Mencken Letters,* ed. Thomas P. Riggio (Philadelphia: University of Pennsylvania Press, 1986; 2 vols.).
3. Carl R. Dolmetsch, *The Smart Set: A History and Anthology* (New York: Dial Press, 1966).
4. Dreiser to HLM (14 November 1920); HLM to Dreiser (20 November 1920); *Letters of H. L. Mencken,* ed. Guy J. Forgue (New York: Knopf, 1961), 208–9.
5. See Fred Hobson, *Mencken: A Life* (New York: Random House, 1994), 307–8.
6. *Faun on Olympus.* The manuscript is now at the Library of Congress.
7. HLM to Alfred A. Knopf (15 July 1931); *Letters of H. L. Mencken,* 332.
8. Richard Hughey is at work on another biography of this kind, which promises to be more rigorous and more sensitive to Sterling's poetic work than Walker's.

1914

1. It is not certain what poem is being referred to; possibly "The Slaying of the Witch" in *Munsey's* (January 1916); rpt. *CE* and *SP.* No such ballad appeared in *SS* at this time.

1916

1. Referring to HLM's review column in *SS.* A reader had suggested that HLM use his column to discuss more general aspects of literature rather than merely reviewing the publications of the month.
2. The reference is to a public protest led by HLM in response to the suppression of Theodore Dreiser's *The "Genius"* (1915) on the grounds of immorality and blasphemy.
3. The reference is to three fiction writers, Harry Leon Wilson (1867–1939), Jack London (1876–1916), and James Hopper (1876–1956), all friends of GS.
4. Presumably referring to "To Twilight" (*SS,* November 1915).
5. Brander Matthews (1852–1929), American critic who refused to sign the protest.

6. *The Man of Promise* (1916) by Willard Huntington Wright (1888–1939), a novel about a writer whose work is adversely affected by the women in his life.

1918

1. The references are to the essays in HLM's *A Book of Prefaces* (1917): "Joseph Conrad"; "Theodore Dreiser"; "James Huneker"; and "Puritanism as a Literary Force." There are several references to Bierce in the volume; GS probably alludes to the comment: "Plain realism, as in . . . the war stories of Ambrose Bierce, simply wearies us by its vacuity" (p. 146). James Gibbons Huneker (1857–1921) was a music critic, man of letters, and close friend of HLM.

2. A restaurant in New York (Sixth Avenue and 38th Street) frequented by writers and artists.

3. *Almayer's Folly* (1895) and *An Outcast of the Islands* (1896), the first two of Joseph Conrad's novels.

4. The references are to Rudyard Kipling's short stories "The Brushwood Boy" (1895), "Wireless" (1902), " 'They' " (1904), and " 'The Finest Story in the World' " (1891). GS's comment might have been impelled by HLM's remark in "Joseph Conrad" (*A Book of Prefaces*): "Kipling, with 'Kim' behind him, becomes a vociferous leader-writer of the *Daily Mail* school, whooping a pothouse patriotism, hurling hysterical objurgations at the foe" (p. 26).

5. John G. Neihardt (1881–1973), Nebraska poet and author of *Black Elk Speaks* (1932). He visited GS in late February and early March 1918.

6. John Masefield (1878–1967), who would become the poet laureate of England in 1930, visited San Francisco in March 1918. GS said of him: "He was desperately tired, much depressed by the war, and constantly telegraphing, so he was pretty gloomy company" (GS to John G. Neihardt, 11 April 1918; ms., NYPL).

7. Evidently "The Song of the Swineherds," an unpublished poem by GS (ms., Lilly Library, Indiana University).

8. John S. Sumner (1876–?), successor to Anthony Comstock (see n. 33) as head of the New York Society for the Suppression of Vice.

9. The poem was rejected; it appeared in *Century Magazine* (February 1919) and in *SM*.

10. Henry Milner Rideout (1877–1927), a popular writer of fiction.

11. Joseph Hergesheimer (1880–1954), fashionable novelist of the day and close friend of HLM.

12. Irvin S. Cobb (1876–1944), prolific and popular short story writer and humorist. HLM crucified him in the essay "The Heir of Mark Twain" in *Prejudices: First Series* (1919).

13. The *Saturday Evening Post* was published by the Curtis Publishing Co. of Philadelphia.

14. George Ade (1866–1944), American journalist and fabulist. HLM wrote favorably of him in the essay "George Ade" in *Prejudices: First Series*.

15. T. R. Smith, an editor of the *Century Magazine*. William Marion Reedy (1862–1920) was the editor of *Reedy's Mirror* and other newspapers and magazines.

16. "Moll" appeared in the short-lived magazine *Upton Sinclair's* (May–June 1918).

17. "Damaged goods" refers to previously published poems.

18. "Infidels" (*SS,* Aug. 1918).

19. Excerpts of sixty-five of these appeared in *The Letters of Ambrose Bierce* (1922), ed. Bertha Clark Pope. The rest remain unpublished.

20. Bierce would occasionally end his letters with "God be with you—but inattentive." See, e.g., Bierce to Herman Scheffauer, [July 1903] (ALS, BAN).

21. HLM, *Damn! A Book of Calumny* (1918).

22. Presumably a clipping relating to Prohibition.

23. "Ennui" (*SS,* September 1918) by Clark Ashton Smith (1893–1961), GS's pupil and disciple. The prose poem was reprinted in Smith's *Ebony and Crystal* (1922).

24. Presumably a reference to a suggested change in the sonnet "Infidels" (*SS,* August 1918). See further letter 12.

25. Ambrose Bierce. GS never wrote the booklet, but his article on Bierce, "The Shadow Maker," appeared in *AM* (September 1925).

26. " 'The White Logic,' " an unpublished poem (ms., SFPL). The title refers to a conception in Jack London's autobiographical novel about his alcoholism, *John Barleycorn* (1913), referring to the illusory insights derived from liquor.

27. Harriet Monroe (1860–1936), poet, critic, and founder-editor of the magazine *Poetry* (1912f.). She had accepted three poems by GS in 1912 but then rejected his later submissions. GS condemned the magazine for its radicalism of form and content.

28. "Ennui" (see n. 23). GS was convinced that Smith, who exhibited poor health throughout the 1910s, had tuberculosis; but Smith's condition was probably the result of nerves and poor diet.

29. James Gibbons Huneker (see n. 1).

30. Evidently a reference to HLM's article "Poetry and Other Vices" (*New York Evening Mail,* 1 April 1918). John N. Wheeler was the head of Wheeler Newspapers Features, the syndicate for which HLM wrote his newspaper column.

31. Lyman Abbott (1835–1922), Congregationalist minister, author, and editor of the *Outlook.*

32. The Bohemian Club put on an annual grove play in July or August, written by one of its members. GS wrote the plays for 1907 (*The Triumph of Bohemia*) and 1926 (*Truth*), and wrote the songs for the 1918 grove play by Richard M. Hotaling (*The Twilight of the Kings*). GS also acted in many of the grove plays. The earlier plays were collected in Porter Garnett, ed., *The Grove Plays of the Bohemian Club* (1918; 3 vols.).

33. The "lyric" is possibly "Dirge" (*SS,* November 1918), a song from *Lilith* (1919), a poetic drama begun as early as 1910. "Comstockians" is a reference to Anthony Comstock (1844–1915), founder of the New York Society for the Suppression of Vice.

34. Clark Ashton Smith, "Sepulture" (*SS,* October 1918).

35. Harry Leon Wilson and Booth Tarkington (1869–1946) collaborated on the play *The Gibson Upright* (1919).

36. Clark Ashton Smith, "Mirrors" (not published in *SS*); in Smith's *Ebony and Crystal.*

37. Mrs. Curtis Clark, daughter-in-law of William Andrews Clark (1839–1925), Senator from Montana (1901–07).

38. Orrick Johns (1887–1946), poet. The volume to which HLM refers is *Asphalt and Other Poems* (1917).

39. Josephus Daniels (1862–1948), Secretary of the Navy (1913–21).

40. The Lambs was a club founded in 1874 by figures in the theatre. It is now located at 3 West 51st Street.

41. Carrie Sterling had married GS in 1896; they divorced in 1913. She committed suicide on August 7, 1918.

42. GS's "girl" was Estelle Tuttle. Bliss Carman (1861–1929) was an American poet who gave a dinner in honor of Dreiser in New York.

43. See letter 22 (and n. 47).

44. "The Dryad" (*SS*, February 1919).

45. Leslie Nelson Jennings, California poet.

46. Wright returned to Los Angeles on account of his health; some years later he adopted the pseudonym S. S. Van Dine and began writing hugely successful detective stories. Several years earlier he had written an article—"Hotbed of Soulful Culture, Vortex of Erotic Erudition," *Los Angeles Times,* 22 May 1910—describing, and poking fun at, GS's literary circle at Carmel.

47. Perhaps a reference to Harrison Dowd, otherwise unknown. His poem "Hills" appeared in *SS,* June 1920.

48. HLM wrote for the *New York Evening Mail* (published by Edward A. Rumely) from 18 June 1917 to 8 July 1918.

49. Henry L. Stoddard, president and editor of the *New York Evening Mail.*

50. California painter Xavier Martinez (1869–1943). GS had written a poem to him, "To Xavier Martinez" (in *CE*).

51. George P. Brett (1858–1936), president of Macmillan (1890–1931).

52. HLM appears to refer to Odell Shepard's "L'Apres-Midi d'un Faune" (*SS,* November 1918).

53. "Presentiment" by May Greenwood (*SS,* February 1919).

54. William Lyon Phelps (1865–1943), American critic and professor at Yale. His *The Advance of English Poetry in the Twentieth Century* (1918) was reviewed by HLM in *SS,* January 1919. See further n. 71.

55. A reference to the American poets Ella Wheeler Wilcox (1850–1919), Hermann Hagedorn (1882–1964), Cale Young Rice (1872–1943), and Lizette Woodworth Reese (1856–1935). Rice was a friend of GS; Reese was a Baltimore poet with whom HLM was distantly acquainted and whose work he consistently promoted.

56. Presumably *The American Language* (1919).

57. HLM did not publish *Notes on Democracy* until 1926.

58. Vachel Lindsay (1879–1931), American poet.

59. Charles Hanson Towne (1877–1949), poet and journalist. He edited *SS* in 1904–8.

60. Charmian London (1871–1955). Some of London's love letters to her were published in her *The Book of Jack London* (1921).

61. *Our Hawaii* (1917).

62. The critics Francis Hackett (1883–1962) and Randolph Bourne (1886–1918).

63. Evidently an unpublished work entitled "One of the Family" (ms. non extant).

64. American poets Berton Braley (1882–1966) and Arthur Guiterman (1871–1943).

65. Paul Elmer More (1864–1937), American critic of whom HLM did not think highly.

66. John McFarland Kennedy, *Imperial America* (1914).

67. The short play "The Rabbit-Hutch" (*SS,* September 1919), a manifestly

irreligious allegory. GS did contribute to Max Eastman's magazine *The Liberator* in the early 1920s.

68. The letters and poems were written to Mary Craig Kimbrough, who later married novelist and social activist Upton Sinclair (1878–1968), with whom GS was also acquainted. After GS's death Sinclair published the sonnets as *Sonnets to Craig* (1928). The letters are at the Lilly Library, Indiana University.

69. "Two Met" (*SS*, April 1919); rpt. in *SM*.

70. The *SS* text reads: "Turned to your fragrance and consenting mouth." In *SM* GS changed the line to read "Turned to your fragrant and consenting mouth."

71. In his review of the Phelps book (see n. 54), HLM wrote: "Not a word about George Sterling. Not a word about Miss Reese" (*SS*, January 1919, p. 140).

72. GS refers to a sentence in HLM's review column in *SS*, January 1919: "Born two years before Huneker and exposed in youth to almost the same influences, he [Carl Van Vechten] reacted violently to the hair-raising *héliogabalisme* that was on tap in Paris during the '80's . . ." (139). The reference is to the Roman emperor Heliogabalus (more properly Elagabalus, r. 218–22), known in antiquity as a decadent voluptuary. See further letter 66.

1919

1. A joking reference to Edward W. Bok, editor of the *Ladies' Home Journal*.

2. Howard Willard Cook, who had written a treatise, *Our Poets of Today* (New York: Moffat, Yard & Co., 1918), that discussed GS.

3. William Stanley Braithwaite (1878–1962), editor of the annual *Anthology of Magazine Verse* (1913–29).

4. GS's poems on the war were collected in *The Binding of the Beast and Other War Verse* (1917).

5. Many years later HLM wrote a 20-part series of articles on the Johns Hopkins Hospital (*BES*, 6–28 July 1937).

6. May Greenwood, "Finality" (*SS*, May 1919).

7. A Mrs. Mitchell, otherwise unknown.

8. GS's "Altars of War" did not appear in the *Boston Evening Transcript* but in the *Bellman* (29 March 1919); it was reprinted in Braithwaite's anthology *Victory! Celebrated by Thirty-eight American Poets* (1919).

9. *Anthology of Magazine Verse for 1918* (1918). GS wrote a harsh letter to Braithwaite on the volume, and on Braithwaite's deficiencies as a critic, in a letter to Braithwaite dated 8 April 1919 (published in Dalton Gross's "George Sterling's Letters to William Stanley Braithwaite: The Poet versus the Editor," *American Book Collector* 24, No. 2 [November–December 1973]: 19–20).

10. Sam T. Jack (1852–?), the owner of a burlesque company that featured Creole performers.

11. HLM, "Prof. Veblen and the Cow" (*SS*, May 1919); rpt. as "Professor Veblen" in *Prejudices: First Series*.

12. Jack Johnson (1878–1946), an African American boxer and heavyweight champion (1908–15).

13. Mary Garden (1874–1967), American soprano of Scottish birth. Emma Alice Margaret (Margot) Tennant Asquith (1864–1945), British writer and wit; wife of former British prime minister Herbert Henry Asquith.

14. French-born Sarah Bernhardt (1844–1923), the most celebrated stage actress of her day.

15. Richard Le Gallienne (1866–1947), British poet who spent most of his life in the U.S. His poem "To a Boy on the Death of His Sweetheart" occupied an entire page in *SS,* April 1919.

16. Ruth Chatterton (1893–1961) was a well-known stage actress. GS wrote two sonnets on Chatterton, published as "The Masque of Dream" (*Ainslee's,* December 1919) and as "To Ruth Chatterton" in *SM.*

17. Apparently an essay by GS, unidentified and apparently unpublished.

18. "Here's How" (*Saturday Evening Post,* April 5, 1919), an essay supporting Prohibition.

19. HLM and GJN, *Pistols for Two* (1917) (as by "Owen James Hatteras").

20. Dr. Albert Abrams (1863–1924), a quack doctor in San Francisco whom GS long admired. See Miriam Allen de Ford, "Charlatan or Dupe: Albert Abrams," in her *They Were San Franciscans* (Caldwell, ID: Caxton Printers, 1941), 241–61.

21. The unpublished play "The Bluff" (ms., SFPL). The play deals with an artist who is having an affair with a banker's wife. When the banker confronts the artist in the latter's apartment, the artist pulls a gun on him, but later it is found to be loaded with blanks. The wife, irritated by this cowardly "bluff," repudiates the artist and returns to her banker husband.

22. [John] Henry Miller (1859–1926), English-born Canadian actor, director, and producer.

23. Albert Sidney Burleson (1863–1937), U.S. postmaster general (1913–21) who used wartime statutes to ban the mailing of publications critical of the government; George W. Perkins (1862–1920), financier who helped Theodore Roosevelt to found the Progressive party in 1912; Otto Herman Kahn (1867–1934), a prominent banker; for Josephus Daniels see n. 39 (1918).

24. James Gibbons Huneker, *Steeplejack* (1920). HLM reviewed it in the *Literary Review, New York Evening Post* (25 September 1920) and in *SS* (December 1920).

25. George Bronson-Howard, a contributor to *SS.*

26. Probably GS's "Three Voices" (*SS,* August 1919).

27. Dreiser, *Twelve Men* (1919), a series of biographical sketches.

28. A non-alcoholic malt produced by the Anheuser-Busch Company during Prohibition.

29. Joseph Ely O'Carroll, a writer for the *Los Angeles Times.* GS's letters to him have been published as "Some Letters of George Sterling," ed. John R. Dunbar, *California Historical Society Quarterly* 40 (1961): 137–55. No work of his appeared in *SS.*

30. A tropical South American plant whose roots were used as a medicine, usually to induce vomiting.

31. Aleister Crowley (1875–1947), British writer who practiced a variety of Satanic and occult rituals; he came to be known as "The Great Beast."

32. A reference to the line, "Grey dove, the moon is blue," in "Three Voices." The surviving ms. of the poem (at BAN) reads: ". . . the noon is blue."

33. An alcoholic liquor distilled from ti or taro roots.

34. *The Great Hunger* (1918), a novel by the Norwegian writer Johan Bojer; reviewed by HLM in *SS,* March 1919. Thyra Samter Winslow (1893–1961) was a frequent contributor to *SS.*

35. Richard Hayes Barry (1881–?), American novelist and historian; Owen Wister (1860–1938), American author of *The Virginian* (1902) and other novels.

36. William G. MacAdoo (1863–1941), secretary of the treasury (1913–19), and later a New York lawyer. Billie Burke (1886–1970), stage and screen actress in New York.

37. Thyra Samter Winslow, "City Folks" (*SS,* October 1919).

38. Possibly Witter Bynner (1881–1968), poet, playwright, and friend of GS.

39. In late July 1919 hundreds of white soldiers and sailors raided an African American quarter of Washington, D.C., on the belief that some black men had attacked white women. Five people (three white, two black) were killed and 70 were wounded. As rioting continued, Federal troops were called in to quell the disturbance, which subsided in a few days.

40. Sadakichi Hartmann (1869–1944), Japanese-born American playwright, poet, art critic, and friend of GS.

41. Probably GS's "Witch-Fire" (*SS,* December 1919).

42. California became a state on 9 September 1850.

43. HLM elaborates upon these ideas in *In Defense of Women* (1918; rev. 1922).

44. Steve Brodie (1861–?), a celebrated bridge-jumper and swimmer.

45. An unpublished poem by GS (ms., SFPL), also bearing the title "To a Sleeper."

46. A reference to GS's poem "Norman Boyer" (in *SM*). Boyer was a former editor of *SS* (see Introduction); he committed suicide in September 1914.

47. Yone Noguchi (1875–1947), Japanese poet, critic, and professor.

48. The novel is *Painted Veils* (1920), a story of the New York art world that had to be privately printed because of its racy and daring nature. For the autobiography see n. 24 above.

49. Most of Bierce's letters to GS are now at NYPL, with a few other letters in other libraries. GS refers to Bierce's statement to him: "I hope not to need any [literary executor], for if anybody ever publishes any of my letters without my specific assent . . . it will be in the face of a damning of all such rascality, which I mean to prepare against just that particular contingency" (Bierce to GS, 8 October 1907 [ms., NYPL]).

50. James Branch Cabell (1879–1958), *Beyond Life* (1919).

51. G. K. Chesterton (1874–1936), British essayist and novelist known for his paradoxical formulations.

52. GS in fact sent *Lilith* to Cabell and engaged in a sporadic correspondence with him; his letters to Cabell were published in *American Literature* 44 (1972): 146–53, and Cabell's letters to GS appeared in *The Letters of James Branch Cabell,* ed. Edward Wagenknecht (1975).

53. The phrase (meaning "Have mercy!") is found in Kipling's story "The Lost Legion," in *Many Inventions* (1893).

54. Cabell's *Jurgen* (1919) was in fact banned by the New York Society for the Suppression of Vice; but when the case finally came to trial in 1922, the judge recommended acquittal.

55. Robert Cortes Holliday, editor of the *Bookman.* He wrote about GS in the article "A Literary Lane" in his *Literary Lanes and Other Byways* (1925).

56. Hugh Walpole (1884–1941), British novelist.

57. George Moore (1852–1933), Anglo-Irish novelist who gained notoriety for his novel *A Modern Lover* (1883), his autobiography *Confessions of a Young Man* (1888), and other works.

58. *Heliogabalus: A Buffoonery in Three Acts* (1920) by HLM and George Jean Nathan.

59. The preceding two sentences have been crossed out in pencil, whether by GS or someone else is unclear.

60. Thyra Samter Winslow, "Aunt Ida"; L. M. Hussey, "Twilight of Love" (*SS*, December 1919).

61. Rupert Brooke (1887–1915), British poet who died in World War I.

1920

1. Robert Underwood Johnson (1853–1937), poet and secretary of the National Institute of Arts and Letters.

2. Henry van Dyke (1852–1933), writer, clergyman, and professor of English literature at Princeton.

3. GS refers to the following items in *SS*, February 1920: "The Last Love" by John C. Cavendish; "The Hope Chest" by L. M. Hussey; "Benediction" by F. Scott Fitzgerald; "The Guardian of Honor" by L. M. Hussey.

4. Apparently "The Iris Hills," a song from *Rosamund* (1920), also published separately in *SM* and *SP*. See also P. S. to letter 126.

5. Robert W. Chambers (1865–1933), popular novelist; Edward W. Townsend (1855–1942), author of *"Chimmie Fadden," Major Max and Other Stories* (1895), a volume of dialect stories.

6. George Horace Lorimer (1867–1937), author of inspirational books and an editor of the *Saturday Evening Post*. William Randolph Hearst (1863–1951), celebrated newspaper owner and publisher of many popular magazines, including *Cosmopolitan* and *Hearst's*.

7. "Some Ladies and Jurgen," a chapter from James Branch Cabell's *Jurgen*, ran in *SS* for July 1918.

8. Lord Dunsany (1878–1957), prolific Anglo-Irish novelist, short story writer, and playwright, now hailed as one of the pioneers of modern fantastic literature. HLM printed many stories and prose-poems by Dunsany in *SS*, beginning with "The Bureau d'Echange de Maux" (January 1915). Around 1916 Dunsany became tremendously popular in the U.S., and he was hailed with adulation during an American tour in 1919–20, when he became known as "America's favorite lord." HLM himself spoke of him glowingly in "The Cult of Dunsany" (*SS*, July 1917).

9. J. Jefferson Jones was the director of the New York office of the London-based publisher John Lane Co., who in 1916 refused to sell or advertise Theodore Dreiser's *The "Genius"* (1915) when it came under attack by John S. Sumner of the New York Society for the Suppression of Vice. See n. 2 (1916).

10. Sylvanus Stall (1847–1915), author of *The Social Peril* (1905), *What a Young Husband Ought to Know* (1907), and other works on sex education. He is mentioned in HLM's "The Blushful Mystery" in *Prejudices: First Series*.

11. The letter (dated 9 March 1920) survives at the Harry Ransom Humanities Research Center at the University of Texas.

12. "The Queen Forgets" (*SS*, June 1920).

13. A second revised and enlarged edition of *The American Language* appeared in 1921.

14. GS's mother, Mary Havens Sterling, died on 23 February 1920.

15. Maurice Maeterlinck (1862–1949), Belgian playwright. He visited San Francisco in March 1920.

16. Frank Crane (1861–1928), one of the most widely syndicated newspaper columnists of his day.

17. Guido Bruno (1884–1942), editor of several magazines and a crusader for artistic free speech.

18. *Pelléas et Mélisande* (1892), Maeterlinck's most celebrated poetic drama.

19. W. B. Yeats (1865–1939) visited San Francisco in the spring of 1920 as part of an extensive tour across the U.S. GS later wrote a preface to a limited edition of Yeats's *The Lake Isle of Innisfree* (San Francisco: John Henry Nash, 1924).

20. Rex Beach (1877–1949), a popular novelist and president of the Authors' League.

21. Canadian-born Margaret Anglin (1876–1958) was hailed as one of the finest actresses of her day. GS had written a poem to her, "To Margaret Anglin: In the Greek Tragedies" (in *CE*).

22. Clarkson Crane, "The House of Many Bottles" (*SS*, April 1920), a novelette set in the California coast range.

23. HLM, *A Book of Burlesques* (1916).

24. Robert Cortes Holliday. See n. 55 (1919).

25. William Jennings Bryan (1860–1925). The reference is to the Democratic National Convention, held in San Francisco in July 1920.

26. *Town Topics* was a San Francisco weekly that frequently mentioned GS and his activities.

27. "Mirage," *Nation,* 13 April 1921; in *SM*.

28. Benjamin De Casseres (1873–1945), "The Last Satire of a Famous Titan" (*SS*, June 1920), an article on Bierce.

29. Presumably an article by Arthur Brisbane (1864–1936), a widely published journalist who at this time was writing for the Hearst newspapers.

30. HLM, "Reflections on Poetry" (*SS*, June 1920): "Nor are two sonorous and extremely effective poetical plays to be forgotten: 'The Hollow Head of Mars,' by Herman Scheffauer (*Simpkin*), and 'Lilith,' by George Sterling (*Robertson*)" (144).

31. Herman George Scheffauer (1878–1927), *The Hollow Head of Mars: A Modern Masque in Four Phases* (1915). Scheffauer and GS were both early pupils of Bierce; Scheffauer's sentiments toward both GS and Bierce cooled noticeably when he observed that Bierce thought GS the better poet of the two.

32. Jane O'Roarke, a leading woman in a San Francisco stock company with whom HLM spent much time when in San Francisco.

33. John Owens, of the Washington bureau of the Baltimore Sunpapers and a close friend of HLM.

34. A daily regimen of prayer, work, and study for celibate Roman Catholics.

35. Irene Millier, otherwise unknown. See also letter 285.

36. Mrs. W. E. (Rosaliene) Travis, who wrote songs under the pseudonym Lawrence Zenda. She set several GS poems to music in the volume *Songs* (1916).

37. *Men versus the Man: A Correspondence between Rives La Monte, Socialist, and H. L. Mencken, Individualist* (1910).

38. Ernest A. Boyd (1887–1946), Irish critic and longtime associate of HLM (see *Life* 325–26).

39. GS's affectionate name for San Francisco. "The Cool, Grey City of Love" (*San Francisco Bulletin,* 11 December 1920; in *SM*) is one of his best-known poems.

40. Grace Cheney. See letter 294.

41. May Greenwood had three further poems in *SS:* "Nocturne" (February 1921), "Western Twilight" (March 1921), and "Finis" (November 1921).

42. The front of the postcard prints a picture of a group of swimmers on the shore of a river. GS refers to a splash of water in the river, presumably made by the swimmers.

43. Gobind Behari Lal, an Indian professor who wrote science articles for the *San Francisco Examiner*. He wrote a brief article on GS, "George Sterling's Bohemian Creed," *Overland Monthly* 85, No. 12 (December 1927): 369.

44. The reference is to *A Literary Critic* (1920), HLM's reprint of an anonymous article on him published in the *Christian Register* (24 June 1920).

45. Padraic Colum (1881–1972), Irish poet and playwright.

46. "The Little Farm," *Town Talk,* 25 March 1916; in *CE*. See also n. 4 (1919).

47. Houghton Mifflin did not publish any of Cale Young Rice's poetry volumes, most of which were published by The Century Co. GS had warned Rice in a letter dated July 8, 1916: "I'd urge it on my publishers, were I you, to insist a little less on my greatness . . . you don't need that sort of thing to such an excess, and I find that it has subjected you to considerable ridicule at the hands (or mouths) or your fellow poets" (ms., Western Kentucky University).

48. HLM, *In Defense of Women* (1918).

49. *Prejudices: Second Series* (1920).

50. Friedrich Wilhelm Nietzsche, *The Antichrist,* translated by HLM (1920).

51. "Meditations in E Minor," *New Republic* (8 September 1920).

52. See further n. 69.

53. The allusion is to Ella Wheeler Wilcox (see n. 55 [1918]), whose work was criticized for excessive sentimentality.

54. The *Appeal to Reason* was a radical magazine edited by Emanuel Haldeman-Julius. It was later titled the *Haldeman-Julius Weekly* and still later the *American Freeman.*

55. A reference to Warren Gamaliel Harding, who in fact won the presidential election of 1920.

56. Burton Rascoe and Vincent O'Sullivan, *H. L. Mencken* (1920).

57. "Tears," a celebrated sonnet by Lizette Woodworth Reese included in *A Wayside Lute* (1909), was frequently praised by HLM, as in his review column, "In Praise of a Poet" (*SS,* May 1910).

58. The reference is to John H. E. Partington, a San Francisco artist and friend of GS and Ambrose Bierce.

59. Amy Lowell (1856–1943), Imagist poet. *Can Grande's Castle* was published in 1918. HLM discussed her in "The New Poetry Movement" in *Prejudices: First Series.*

60. Harry Lafler, San Francisco businessman, poet, and longtime friend of GS.

61. James Branch Cabell, *The Cords of Vanity* (1909).

62. Richard Le Gallienne, *Junk-man and Other Poems* (1920).

63. *The Saint Francis Lobbyist* was a magazine published in 12 issues during the Democratic National Convention. These were later published in a single volume (San Francisco: Thomas J. Coleman, 1920).

64. Presumably GS's *Rosamund: A Dramatic Poem* (1920).

65. W. L. George (1882–1926), British novelist and essayist. HLM had high regard for his early novels, including *A Bed of Roses* (1911) and *The Making of an Englishman* (1914).

66. Nina Wilcox Putnam (1888–1962), novelist and wife of publisher Robert Putnam. W. Somerset Maugham (1874–1965), British author. *The Moon and Sixpence* appeared in 1919.

67. In October 1920 Harry Brolaski, former mayor of Redondo and a prominent Republican politician, was arrested for bootlegging. He was later convicted and sentenced to two years in prison.

68. An impure bicarbonate of potash used as an ingredient in baking-powders.

69. The poem in question was "Incarnation," published in *SS* (February 1921) under the "house" pseudonym "William Drayham." A manuscript of this poem is extant at BAN.

70. The references are to two essays in *Prejudices: Second Series:* "The National Letters" (on American literature and criticism) and "The Divine Afflatus" (on literary inspiration). GS is mentioned in the former.

71. *To a Girl Dancing,* published separately in 1921.

72. On 30 November 1920 two men were arrested in San Francisco as members of a gang who raped several women on Thanksgiving day. On 5 December three others suspected in the rape shot and killed three police officers in Santa Rosa who were attempting to apprehend them. The three were captured and placed in jail; later that evening a crowd of four thousand men stormed the jail in an attempt to lynch the suspects, but were restrained by the police. On 10 December a group of one hundred men broke into the Santa Rosa jail and lynched three of the suspects. The poem referred to by GS is "The Cool, Grey City of Love."

1921

1. The reference is to a scuffle in which GS was involved with W. E. Travis, husband of Rose Travis, GS's collaborator. Although the incident was written up in several San Francisco newspapers, GS appears to refer to an unsigned news article, "Poet Sterling, W. E. Travis in Fist Fight," *San Francisco Examiner* (27 December 1920): 1, 3, which speaks of GS's "eviction by force" from the Travis house. This clipping exists in HLM's papers (now at NYPL).

2. Marie Parmalee, with whom GS carried on an affair for some years. About a decade after Sterling's death, Parmalee was arrested on a charge of assault and battery for striking someone with a statue of the Venus de Milo, in which she had hidden GS's love letters to her. The letters fell out and were promptly published in the *Los Angeles Herald Express* (7–9 December 1937).

3. The nut of the areca palm was often wrapped in leaves of the betel tree and chewed.

4. "Conversations," an irregular column in *SS* from December 1920 to March 1923 that purported to record conversations between HLM and George Jean Nathan. The column for February 1921 placed the following words in Nathan's mouth: "And in the end you had to go to Chicago and half sweat to death, and then go to San Francisco and let George Sterling poison you with wood alcohol" (97).

5. GS's error for Noilly-Prat vermouth, a type of vermouth made in France.

6. Zona Gale (1874–1938), *Miss Lulu Bett* (1920), a best-selling novel about a single woman in a small town.

7. Sinclair Lewis, *Main Street* (1920).

8. Cf. Matt. 23:27: "Woe unto you, scribes and Pharisees, hypocrites! for ye are like unto whited sepulchres, which indeed appear beautiful outward, but are within full of dead men's bones, and of all uncleanness."

9. Evidently "The Three Gifts," an unpublished poem by GS (ms., BAN).

10. James Gibbons Huneker died on 9 February 1921.

11. For Mary Garden see n. 13 (1919). Huneker had written of her in *Bedouins* (1920).

12. Zoë Akins (1886–1958), poet and dramatist briefly acquainted with GS and HLM.

13. Christopher Morley (1890–1957) wrote in the column "The Literary Lobby" (as by "Kenelm Digby") in the *Literary Review, New York Evening Post* (9 April 1921): "We hear that *H. L. Mencken* has joined the glorious ranks of the married men" (16). HLM did not in fact marry until 1930, when he wed Sara Powell Haardt.

14. HLM, "Notes on Poetry" (*SS*, April 1921); rpt. with revisions in "The Poet and His Art" in *Prejudices: Third Series* (1922).

15. Herman Scheffauer, living in Germany, wrote such pamphlets as *The German Prison-House* (1919) and *Blood Money: Woodrow Wilson and the Nobel Peace Prize* (1921).

16. The references are to the boxers Jack Dempsey (1895–1983) and Georges Carpentier (1894–1973). They fought a heavyweight title bout in Jersey City, New Jersey, on 2 July 1921, won by Dempsey.

17. Evidently "The Secret Garden" (in *SM*).

18. Charles J. Finger, editor of the little magazine *All's Well*.

19. A slang term for wine, from its Greek derivation (*oinos*).

20. Frank Harris, "H. L. Mencken: Critic," *Pearson's Magazine* 46 (May 1921): 405–8.

21. GS, "Everest" (*SS*, November 1921).

22. Sinclair Lewis (1885–1951) stayed at Carmel for about a year in 1909–10 and was a tangential member of GS's Bohemian circle.

23. Bierce had a notorious and frequently expressed dislike of dogs.

24. The first poem is "Love and Time" (*SS*, September 1921). The other is unidentified.

25. HLM reviewed Phelps's *Essays on Modern Dramatists* in *BES* (23 April 1921).

26. S. K. Ratcliffe, "Mencken: An English Plaint," *New Republic* (13 April 1921): 191–92.

27. John Wooster Robertson, *Edgar A. Poe: A Study* (San Francisco: B. Brough, 1921), revised as *Edgar A. Poe: A Psychopathic Study* (1922).

28. In fact, HLM revised *The American Language* three times (1921, 1923, 1936) and also compiled two substantial supplements, published in 1945 and 1948 respectively.

29. The load line on the hull of British ships.

30. GS, *To a Girl Dancing* (1921), published by Edwin and Robert Grabhorn, specialty publishers in San Francisco.

31. GS has left a space after "2." The letter was clearly written subsequent to HLM's letter of June 20.

32. Edwin Arlington Robinson (1869–1935), American poet.

33. GS published 4 poems in the *Reviewer:* "The Last Island" (1 August 1921), "The Death of Circe" (October 1921), "The Lost Nymph" (December 1921), and "The Hidden Pool" (March 1922).

261

34. *Mary Rose* (1920), a drama by J. M. Barrie (1860–1937). Chatterton starred in the play, which premiered in New York on 22 December 1920.

35. Cf. Phil. 4:7: "And the peace of God, which passeth all understanding, shall keep your hearts and minds through Christ Jesus."

36. George R. Hyde, a San Francisco newspaper man and press agent.

37. Possibly "The Face of the Skies" (*SS*, September 1921).

38. Lillian Gish (1896–1993), American actress who later became briefly involved with GJN.

39. HLM, "The South Begins to Mutter" (*SS*, August 1921).

40. See n. 16. HLM covered the fight and wrote of it in "How Legends Are Made" (*BES*, 5 July 1921).

41. Ned Greenway, a California society leader.

42. GS apparently had many epigrams in *SS;* but, aside from the early column "Says George Sterling" (November 1914), most of them were apparently published individually and anonymously.

43. The unpublished play "The Folding-Bed" (ms., SFPL), in which a woman who finds a boarder in bed with her daughter kills them by folding them up in the bed and suffocating them.

44. John Exnicios, a Federal Prohibition agent for the San Francisco area.

45. In his correspondence, GS would address Theodore Dreiser as "Dear Megatherium" and the like, because of Dreiser's girth.

46. David O'Neil, author of *A Cabinet of Jade* (1917), a volume of verse, and coeditor of *Today's Poetry* (1923).

47. *SM.*

48. "The Thermometer of Man," a section of HLM's and GJN's column "Répétition Générale" (*SS*, September 1921).

49. See HLM, "From the Diary of a Reviewer" (*SS*, September 1921): "But nothing has ever been written in America to surpass 'Huckleberry Finn.' It is rather more than a mere book; it is almost a whole literature."

50. Possibly the separate publication of *The Cool, Grey City of Love* (San Francisco: A. M. Robertson, 1921).

51. HLM, "The Poet and His Art," *Prejudices: Third Series* (1922).

52. GS, "The Wiser Prophet" (*All's Well*, April–May 1923).

53. T. R. Smith, *Poetica Erotica* (1921–22). Smith in fact took all six of GS's poems, five of which were previously unpublished.

54. Smith had no poems in *Poetica Erotica.*

55. William Wordsworth, "Elegiac Stanzas Suggested by a Picture of Peele Castle" (1807), l. 15 ("on sea or land" in Wordsworth).

56. H. G. Aikman (pseud. of Harold Hunter Armstrong, 1884–?), *Zell* (1921); Floyd Dell (1887–1969), *Moon-Calf* (1920); Emanuel and Marcet Haldeman-Julius, *Dust* (1921). HLM reviewed all three novels: *Zell* in *BES,* 12 February 1921 and *SS,* March 1921; *Moon-Calf* in *SS,* February 1921 and March 1921; *Dust* in *SS,* July 1921.

57. Evidently "One Night," an unpublished poem (ms., EPFL).

58. HLM never edited Poe's essays.

59. A reference to the Washington Conference for the Limitation of Armament (12 November 1921–6 February 1922). HLM wrote several articles about it in *BES* (14 November 1921 to 16 January 1922).

60. "Schmidt" refers to T. R. Smith (see n. 53).

61. HLM, "The Next Round" (*BES*, 18 July 1921).

62. The phrase appears in Bierce's poem "Land of the Pilgrims' Pride" in *Collected Works* (1909–12), 4:80 ("by" for "of" in Bierce).

63. Possibly "Distance" (*SS*, January 1922).

64. Roscoe (Fatty) Arbuckle (1887–1933), American actor, was tried for manslaughter over the death of model Virginia Rappe at a party at his home in Beverly Hills on Labor Day 1921. The first trial ended in a hung jury. In 1922 Arbuckle was acquitted in a second trial, but hostile press reaction spelled the end of his acting career.

65. Alboin, in GS's poetic drama *Rosamund,* is the son of Audoin, King of the Lombards, who rapes Rosamund.

66. Possibly "Lost Sunsets" (*SS*, February 1922).

67. For the *Appeal to Reason* see n. 53 (1920). HLM did not write for it.

68. Arnold Genthe (1869–1942), a well-known photographer in California and longtime friend of GS. He wrote about GS in his autobiography, *As I Remember* (1936).

69. GS was mentioned in HLM and GJN's column "Répétition Générale" (*SS*, November 1921) in a satirical comment on the Ku Klux Klan: "Already, I understand, George Sterling has organized a corps in San Francisco and bought up several thousand second-hand hotel bed-pillows . . ." (35–36).

70. Clare Sheridan (1885–1970), British sculptor, travel writer, and novelist.

71. HLM did run two items by James Hopper in *SS:* the story "The Nonpareil" (May 1922) and the article "Swatting the Fly" (August 1922).

72. Apparently "Egon's Song" (from *Truth*), *Laughing Horse* No. 5 (1923): [29].

73. Charles Evans Hughes (1862–1948), Harding's secretary of state.

74. GS had engaged in a brief correspondence with Wells in 1904, after the publication of his "star poem," *The Testimony of the Suns.* He also wrote a poem, "To H. G. Wells" (in *Beyond the Breakers*).

75. HLM and GJN, ed., *The American Credo* (1920). The reference is to HLM's 100-page introduction to the volume.

76. Probably an unsigned article, "Would You Do Same Thing Again? Poet Sterling Would a Hunter Be," *San Francisco Examiner* (1 November 1921): 74, which quotes GS saying that if he had his life to live over he would be a hunter.

77. HLM, "The Cancer Problem" (*BES*, 31 October 1921).

78. Marshal Ferdinand Foch (1851–1929), supreme commander of Allied armies in France during World War I, visited San Francisco in December 1921 in the course of a two-month trip across the U.S.

79. GS, "The Gulls" (*Nation*, 22 March 1922).

80. *SM.*

81. Edward Joseph Hanna (1860–1944), archbishop of San Francisco.

82. *Ursula Trent* is a novel (1921) by W. L. George (see n. 65 [1920] and letter 178). It was reviewed by HLM in *SS*, January 1922.

83. William Caine, "The Three Kings" (*SS*, December 1921).

84. According to Betty Adler's conspectus of HLM's letters, *A Man of Letters* (1969), a letter of this date is in the library of Lehigh University; but librarians there maintain that they have no such letter.

85. Presumably expressed in the missing letter of 16 December 1921; HLM never mentioned the book in his review column in *SS*.

86. GS refers to his poems, "The Killdee" (*SS*, May 1922) and "The Wild Swan" (*SS*, April 1922).

1922

1. Ina Donna Coolbrith (1842–1928), the Poet Laureate of California.

2. GS refers to the California writers Bret Harte (1836–1902), Ambrose Bierce, Charles Warren Stoddard (1843–1909), and Joaquin Miller (1837–1913).

3. *The Letters of Ambrose Bierce* (1922), whose editor was listed as Bertha Clark Pope; the bulk of the volume consisted of Bierce's letters to GS.

4. In 1919, the Harris Prohibition Enforcement Law, a law sponsored by state senator M. B. Harris and delegating state resources to enforce the Volstead Act, was passed by the California legislature but was suspended pending a referendum in the 1920 election. The law was defeated in that election, but a similar bill, sponsored by assemblyman T. M. Wright, was passed by the legislature in 1921. In November 1922, the law was upheld in a state referendum.

5. Sherwood Anderson (1876–1941), *The Triumph of the Egg* (1921), a volume of short stories and poems. HLM reviewed the volume in *SS,* February 1922.

6. Mary MacLane (1881–1929), journalist and proponent of free love. She wrote two autobiographical works, *The Story of Mary MacLane* (1902) and *I, Mary MacLane* (1917), the latter of which was filmed as *The Men Who Have Made Love to Me* (1918), with MacLane playing herself.

7. "Ode to Shelley," *Scribner's Magazine* (July 1922). Written for the centennial of Shelley's death.

8. Wilton Lackaye (1862–1932), author of *Laconigrams* (1909), a volume of anecdotes about the stage.

9. Joseph Hergesheimer, *Cytherea* (1922).

10. On 25 March 1922, Harry Leon Wilson and the artist Theodore Criley fought a duel with fists in a glen near Carmel, the end result of a long-standing feud. Criley won the fight.

11. Apparently a reference to GS's "Things Worth While" (see letter 43).

12. For HLM's friend Paul de Kruif see *Life,* 275–82.

13. Norman Hapgood (1868–1937), historian and biographer.

14. James Hopper and E. E. Free began conducting a "Science of the Month" column in *Hearst's International* with the June 1922 issue.

15. Clark Ashton Smith, "Requiescat" (*SS,* August 1922).

16. An unpublished poem variously titled "The Trapping of Rung" (ms., BAN) and "The Trapping of Rhoom" (ms., SFPL).

17. Will H. Hays (1879–1954), postmaster-general (1921–22) who in 1922 was appointed president of the Motion Picture Producers and Distributors of America to oversee the moral tone of films, a move made to ward off threatened censorship of movies.

18. Possibly Ferdinand Hansen (1869–1927), *Democrats of France! An American Appeal,* ed. and tr. Theodore J. Ritter (Hamburg: Overseas Publishing Co., 1922).

19. Possibly "The Stranger at the Gate" (*SS,* September 1922).

20. Possibly "A Sceptic's Fate," an unpublished poem by GS found among HLM's effects (now at NYPL).

21. I.e., St. Anthony, an Egyptian monk of the 3rd and 4th centuries C.E. who reputedly founded Christian monasticism. His hallucinations of sexual temptations served as the basis of Gustave Flaubert's *La Tentation de Saint Antoine* (1874).

22. Nora May French (1881–1907), California poet. She committed suicide

while staying at GS's home in Carmel. A volume of her *Poems* (1910) appeared posthumously.

23. Frederick Clarke Prescott (1871–1957), *The Poetic Mind* (1922). GS's review has not been located.

24. Possibly "Sorcery" (*Snappy Stories*, 17 September 1922) or some other poem that was rejected.

25. Possibly "Song" (*SS*, October 1922).

26. Upton Sinclair was a fervent teetotaler. In *The Cup of Fury* (1956) he devotes several pages to GS's alcoholic excesses.

27. The reference is to GS removing his clothes and plucking lilies from the Chain of Lakes in Golden Gate Park for two women companions of Dreiser. See Robert H. Willson, "Ye Poet Leaps in Lake to Nip Lily for Lady," *San Francisco Examiner* (23 August 1922): 1–2.

28. Possibly "Venus Letalis" (*SS*, March 1923).

29. *Twenty-one Letters of Ambrose Bierce* [ed. Samuel Loveman] (1922). HLM reviewed this volume unfavorably in *SS*, January 1923; he briefly reviewed *The Letters of Ambrose Bierce* in *SS*, May 1923.

30. Albert M. Bender (1866–1941), San Francisco businessman, patron of several California writers, and longtime friend of GS.

31. Transcripts of 131 of Bierce's letters to Scheffauer are extant at BAN; the whereabouts of the originals of most of these are unknown.

32. Possibly GS's "After Sunset" (*SS*, April 1923).

33. A reference to such essays in *Prejudices: Third Series* as "On Being an American," "Star-Spangled Men," "The Nature of Liberty," and "Suite Américaine."

34. Possibly Dr. Joseph Colt Bloodgood, a Baltimore surgeon and longtime friend of HLM.

35. GS and Samuel Loveman (1887–1976) corresponded sporadically from 1909 to 1926. Loveman later became a close friend of both H. P. Lovecraft and Hart Crane. Some of his poetry is gathered in *The Hermaphrodite and Other Poems* (1936).

36. Anita Loos (1893–1981), American novelist and screenwriter. She became well acquainted with HLM in the 1920s.

37. Probably a review of the Prescott book (see n. 23).

1923

1. Genevieve Taggard (1894–1948), California poet and editor. She and GS coedited *Continent's End* (1925), an anthology of California poetry. GS's poem to her is "A Knee Is Bent" (*Liberator,* June 1923).

2. Probably "Suppose Nobody Cared," a poem included in *Suppose Nobody Cared* (1922), published by the Community Chest of San Francisco.

3. "The Black Hound Bays" (*Liberator,* Mar. 1923), a poem attacking George Horace Lorimer (see n. 6 [1920]).

4. HLM reviewed Lawrence's *Women in Love* in "Specimens of Current Fiction" (*SS*, February 1923).

5. Edgar Lee Masters (1868–1950), *The Spoon River Anthology* (1915).

6. "A Hymn to Americans" (ms., BAN).

7. Ben Hecht (1893–1964), American novelist, playwright, and journalist. He contributed frequently to *SS*. His novel *Fantazius Mallare* (1922) was seized

by the postal authorities and he, his publisher Pascal Covici, and the artist Wallace Smith were sued for sending "lewd, lascivious and obscene" literature through the mails. After a long delay Hecht grudgingly pleaded *nolo contendere* at a hearing on 4 February 1924 and was fined $1000.

8. "The Last of Sunset" (*SS,* June 1923).

9. The guest of honor at the American Academy of Arts and Letters function was Sir Frederic Kenyon (1863–1952), former president of the British Academy and chiefly known for his work on manuscripts of the Bible.

10. Carl Sandburg (1878–1967), American poet.

11. "Bah!," an unpublished poem by GS (ms., Lilly Library, Indiana University).

12. Ruth Suckow, "Other People's Ambitions"; Thyra Samter Winslow, "Ambition"; John V. Craven, Jr., "Monsieur Galespard and Mademoiselle Jeanne," a one-act play; Dashiell Hammett, "From the Memoirs of a Private Detective" (all in *SS,* March 1923).

13. "Pleasure and Pain," a pessimistic essay on humanity and the cosmos, influenced by Schopenhauer and Bierce. It was first published in *Resources for American Literary Study* 3 (Autumn 1973): 234–48 (ed. Joseph Slade).

14. In one ms. of "A Sceptic's Fate" (at HUN), each stanza concludes with the line: "Now Henry R. Macdougal is a ghost." In the ms. in HLM's papers (at NYPL), HLM's name has been substituted.

15. A reference to Sir Arthur Conan Doyle's late conversion to spiritualism following World War I.

16. Albert Philibert Franz, freiherr von Schrenck von Notzing (1862–1929), *Materialisationsphaenomene* (1914); translated as *Phenomena of Materialisation* (1920).

17. Stuart Edward White (1873–1946), American novelist who wrote several books on spiritualism.

18. A reference to an article attacking Abrams by A. Francis Morton, Jr., "The Latest Swindle: 'Psyching the Jack' Charlatan's New Game Prospers," in Henry Ford's weekly paper, the *Dearborn Independent* (Mar. 24, 1923).

19. George Hyde, "Scenes from the Life of an American Journalist" (*SS,* June 1923).

20. HLM reviewed Upton Sinclair's *The Goose-Step: A Study of American Education* (1923) in *SS,* May 1923.

21. Upton Sinclair, *Hell: A Verse Drama and Photo-play* (1923).

22. Theodore Dreiser, *Hey-Rub-a-Dub-Dub* (1919), an encapsulation of Dreiser's philosophy.

23. *Notes on Democracy* (1926), a book that had been conceived as early as 1910.

24. GS's *Truth: A Dramatic Poem* (1923) was published by the Bookfellows, a literary organization in Chicago.

25. Vincent Starrett (1886–1974), American journalist, critic, and fiction writer.

26. Hamlin Garland (1860–1940), American novelist and memoirist. He discusses GS in *Afternoon Neighbors* (1934).

27. The *Liberator* did not publish GS's "A Lumberjack Yearns."

28. HLM was organizing a committee to raise funds for a statue of Benedict Arnold for deposit in Westminster Abbey.

29. GS refers to the American poets Elinor Wylie (1885–1928), Edna St. Vincent Millay (1892–1950), Edwin Arlington Robinson, Maxwell Bodenheim (1893–1954), and Louis Untermeyer (1885–1977).

30. Rex Beach of the Authors' League had asked Dreiser to support a proposal (evidently originating with movie producer Adolph Zukor) to improve the quality of motion pictures, but Dreiser retorted with a public criticism of Beach and the League for failing to oppose the Clean Books Bill, a censorship measure that had recently come before the New York state legislature.

31. *SP.*

32. For Charles Evans Hughes see n. 73 (1921). For Otto Kahn see n. 23 (1919). Henry Morgenthau (1856–1946), realtor, lawyer, and U.S. ambassador to Turkey (1913–16). Oscar Straus (1850–1926), diplomat and U.S. secretary of commerce and labor (1906–9). Stephen S. Wise (1874–1949), prominent rabbi and Zionist leader. Horace B. Liveright (1886–1933), publisher. Louis Brandeis (1856–1941), lawyer and member of the Supreme Court (1916–41). Of course, these latter individuals are Jews, not Anglo-Saxons.

33. Alexander Marky, editor of *Pearson's Magazine.*

34. Presumably more epigrams.

35. In "Répétition Générale" (*SS,* July 1923) HLM and GJN announce as one of the "further planks in the platform of the editors of this magazine, candidates for the Presidency and Vice-Presidency of the United States": "They will appoint . . . George Sterling, of California, Secretary of War."

36. "To a Water-Fowl" (*SS,* October 1923), on the death of a water fowl. GS refers to a more famous funerary poem, *Thanatopsis* (1817) by William Cullen Bryant (1794–1878).

37. Evidently a reference to a poem by Allan Ross Macdougall, "My Father" (*SS,* May 1923), which GS had perhaps claimed was plagiarized.

38. HLM reviewed Maxwell Bodenheim's *Blackguard* in *SS,* June 1923.

39. The *Dial* (1880–1929) was a highbrow literary magazine published in Chicago.

40. An irreverent reference to the sudden death of President Warren G. Harding in San Francisco on Aug. 2, 1923, of an embolism. A few days earlier he had been reported as suffering from ptomaine poisoning.

41. A reference to John Gould Fletcher's unfavorable review of GS's *SP:* "Out Where the West Begins," *Freeman* No. 179 (Aug. 15, 1923): 548–49. GS's response was not published.

42. GS, "The Young Witch," *Century Magazine* (August 1923).

43. A reference to HLM's plans to begin *AM.*

44. John McCormack (1884–1945), Irish-born American tenor.

45. Harry Chandler, owner of the *Los Angeles Times* (1917–44).

46. Mary Miles Minter (1902–1984), American silent film actress. The actor and director William Desmond Taylor was shot and killed by an unknown assailant at his home in Hollywood on 2 February 1922. Both Minter and the actress Mabel Normand had visited Taylor on the day of his death. The case was never solved.

47. Eltinge F. Warner, publisher of *SS.*

48. Carl Van Vechten (1880–1964), American man of letters and a leading literary figure of the 1920s.

49. A fictitious cleric, the name being German for "heaven-raiser."

50. Fannie Hurst (1889–1968), American fiction writer, playwright, and screenwriter.

51. The clipping is from the *New York Times* (28 December 1923) and reports that Jane O'Roarke (now Mrs. James Jordan) was arrested for obtaining merchandise under false pretenses.

1924

1. Douglas Fairbanks (1883–1939) commissioned GS to write the "captions" or scene descriptions for *The Thief of Bagdad* (1924). Although GS wrote three hundred captions, only about twenty-five were used.

2. Mary Pickford (Gladys Mary Smith, 1893–1979), Canadian-born film actress, married Douglas Fairbanks in 1919.

3. Charles Chaplin (1889–1977), British-born actor and director.

4. Dreiser published four poems in the first issue of *AM* (January 1924).

5. Carleton Bierce. GS had been acquainted with Carleton and his father Albert (Bierce's older brother) since the 1890s.

6. Bierce did leave a will, in which he bequeathed all his literary property to his secretary-companion, Carrie Christiansen. Christiansen, who died by suicide in 1920, bequeathed this property to Bierce's daughter Helen.

7. Sherwood Anderson, "Caught" (*AM*, February 1924).

8. John McClure, "The Substance of Poetry" (*AM*, May 1924).

9. A reference to a section of HLM's and GJN's column "Clinical Notes" (*AM*, May 1924) titled "Sabbath Meditations."

10. Clark Ashton Smith wrote many epigrams for his local paper, the *Auburn Journal*. They have been collected in *The Devil's Notebook* (1990).

11. Upton Sinclair, *The Goslings: A Study of the American Schools* (1924). Reviewed by HLM in *AM*, April 1924.

12. Some of HLM's epigrams were collected in the section "The Old Subject" in *A Book of Burlesques* (rev. ed. 1920). See also "The Jazz Webster" (satirical definitions probably modeled upon Bierce's *Devil's Dictionary*) in the same volume.

13. The Republican National Convention nominated Calvin Coolidge for president on 12 June 1924.

14. The Democratic National Convention was held in New York (30 June–10 July).

15. Probably GS's boyhood friend Roosevelt Johnson.

16. Katherine (Fullerton) Gerould, "San Francisco Revisited" (*Harper's*, July 1924).

17. Robert M. LaFollette (1855–1925), governor of Wisconsin and Progressive party candidate for president in 1924.

18. GS did this on a number of occasions, most notably with a story published under Jack London's name, "The First Poet" (*Century Magazine*, June 1911), but written entirely by GS.

19. Evidently songs composed by Rosaleine Travis ("Lawrence Zenda"). The "Dirge from 'Lilith' " was included in the 2nd ed. of her *Songs* (1928), but also evidently published separately as sheet music.

20. Whit Burnett (1899–1973), journalist, editor, and short story writer.

21. Upton Sinclair, *Mammonart: An Essay in Economic Interpretation* (1925), evidently serialized in the *Haldeman-Julius Weekly*. One chapter ("The Eminent Tankard-Men") discusses GS and Bierce.

22. Jimmy Swinnerton (1875–1974) was a cartoonist, initially with Hearst's *San Francisco Examiner*, then later with the *New York Journal* and *American*. He illustrated many of Bierce's articles.

23. Edward Synnott O'Reilly (1880–?) wrote a memoir of his fighting days, *Roving and Fighting: Adventures under Four Flags* (1918), in which he briefly discussed having heard of Bierce being shot in Mexico by President Huerta's

soldiers in early 1914. An article by O'Reilly, "Well Oiled Institutions," appeared in *Liberty* for 20 September 1924, and was announced as the first of a series; but no more articles were published. The article does not mention Bierce.

24. Unidentified. No such poem appeared in *AM* at this time.

25. George Sylvester Viereck (1884–1962), German-born novelist, essayist, and editor. The two poetry booklets are *The Haunted House and Other Poems* (1924) and *The Three Sphinxes and Other Poems* (1924).

26. The incident was much discussed in the San Francisco papers; see "Poet and Girl Swim Unclad in Stow Lake," *San Francisco Examiner* (27 August 1924): 1, 3; "Poet's Back Aches After Night Swim for Lilies to Please 'Lady of Moment,'" *San Francisco Bulletin* (27 August 1924): 1–2; "Sterling in Hospital After Lake Swim," *San Francisco Examiner* (29 August 1924): 16.

27. Paul Jordan-Smith (1885–1971), American bookman. He wrote about Bierce in *On Strange Altars* (1924).

28. See *The Letters of Ambrose Bierce* (1922), pp. 200–204.

29. Countee Cullen (1903–1946), African American poet. His "The Shroud of Color" appeared in *AM,* November 1924.

1925

1. A reference to a recurring column in *AM* in which grotesque or ridiculous news reports from around the country were printed.

2. Sinclair Lewis, *Arrowsmith* (1925).

3. HLM, "Ambrose Bierce" (*Chicago Sunday Tribune,* 1 March 1925); rpt. in *Prejudices: Sixth Series* (1927).

4. GS, "The Shadow Maker" (*AM,* September 1925).

5. Raine Bennett, editor of *Bohemia* (1916–17), a short-lived San Francisco literary magazine in which GS's work appeared. Many years later Bennett wrote an article on GS, "Don Passé," *Literary Review* 15, No. 2 (Winter 1971–72): 133–47.

6. Idwal Jones, "San Francisco: An Elegy" (*AM,* August 1925). No book on San Francisco by Jones was published at this time.

7. Dayton, Tennessee, was of course the locale of the Scopes trial, about which HLM wrote numerous articles in *BES* that garnered him much celebrity and notoriety.

8. HLM, "Bryan," a celebrated and much-reprinted obituary in *BES,* 27 July 1925.

9. "Ballad of the Swabs" (*AM,* October 1925).

10. Willa Cather (1876–1947), *The Professor's House,* serialized in *Collier's* (6 June to 1 August 1925) and published in book form later in 1925. HLM reviewed it in *AM,* November 1925.

11. Anderson appears to allude to James Hopper as "the writer of football stories" in the "Epilogue" to his autobiographical work, *A Story Teller's Story* (1924).

12. "Ballad of the Grapes" (*Overland Monthly,* Oct. 1925).

13. Mrs. Ruth Guthrie Harding, "Mr. Boythorn-Bierce" (*Bookman,* August 1925).

14. With the November 1925 issue GS began a column of prose and verse miscellany in the *Overland Monthly* entitled "Rhymes and Reactions," maintaining it until his death.

15. A reference to Walter Neale (1873–1933), Bierce's former publisher. He attacked GS viciously in several chapters of his *Life of Ambrose Bierce* (1929). Gustav Adolphe Danziger (later de Castro) (1859–1959) was an associate of Bierce's who collaborated with him on *The Monk and the Hangman's Daughter* (1891). In their final meeting, Bierce broke a cane over Danziger's head.

16. [Unsigned], "Close-up of the Poet of the Sierras," *Literary Digest* (14 November 1925).

17. Rev. Dr. John Roach Straton (1875–1929), Baptist evangelist and author of *Fakes and Fancies of the Evolutionists* (1925) and other fundamentalist tracts.

18. B. Virginia Lee, editor of the *Overland Monthly*.

19. GS's titles for the article (*AM*, Feb. 1926) were "Moonshine and Memory" and "The Pleasure-Maker."

20. Friend William Richardson (1865–1943), governor of California (1923–27). GS wrote four sonnets on him that appeared in the *San Francisco Examiner* for 11, 14, 18, and 24 November 1925.

1926

1. See Stoddard's gay novel *For the Pleasure of His Company* (1903; rpt. San Francisco: Gay Sunshine Press, 1987).

2. HLM, "Dreams of Peace" (*BES*, 28 December 1925).

3. *Lilith* did come out in 1926, but the volume of selected poems never appeared.

4. Charles Warren Stoddard, *South Sea Idyls* (1873).

5. GS, "A First-Class Fighting Man" (*AM*, January 1927).

6. Apparently a reference to fables published in a short-lived San Francisco magazine, *Chic* (1893–94).

7. Some of Bierce's fables were published in *Fantastic Fables* (1899; rev. ed. in the 6th volume of his *Collected Works*). Bierce continued to publish fables until 1909. See now Bierce's *Collected Fables,* ed. S. T. Joshi (Columbus: Ohio State University Press, 2000).

8. Dreiser did indeed write an introduction to the Macmillan edition of *Lilith*.

9. Dreiser, *An American Tragedy* (1925).

10. "The Pathfinders" (*AM*, June 1926).

11. HLM reviewed *An American Tragedy* in *AM*, March 1926.

12. Gouverneur Morris (1876–1953), American short story writer and novelist. Pola Negri (1894–1987), Polish-born film actress.

13. Rudolph Valentino (1895–1926), Italian-born film actor. For HLM's obituary see "Valentino" (*BES,* 30 August 1926).

14. James D. Phelan (1861–1930), mayor of San Francisco (1897–1902) and senator from California (1915–21).

15. GS, "Grasshopper" (*New Masses,* May 1926), a satire in which people berate a "poor man" for appreciating natural beauty.

16. The reference is to a broadside issued by HLM relating to action taken by J. Frank Chase of the Boston Watch and Ward Society to ban the April 1926 issue of *AM* because it contained a story, "Hatrack" by Herbert Asbury, about a prostitute. See Richard J. Schrader, *H. L. Mencken: A Descriptive Bibliography* (Pittsburgh: University of Pittsburgh Press, 1998), 523.

17. HLM, review of Joseph Wheless's *Is It God's Word?* (*AM,* May 1926).

18. Herbert Parrish, "A New God for America" (*AM,* March 1926).

19. "Strange Waters," a poem on lesbianism, written in the style of Robinson Jeffers. It was published separately later in 1926.

20. Babette Deutsch, "The Plight of the Poet" (*AM,* May 1926).

21. Arthur Garfield Hays, a lawyer who helped to defend HLM in the "Hatrack" case.

22. Philip Goodman, a New York entrepreneur and longtime friend of HLM.

23. One of the books is *Notes on Democracy* (1926); the other is probably *Prejudices: Sixth Series* (1927).

24. HLM, "Books of Verse" (*AM,* June 1926).

25. Robinson Jeffers (1887–1962), American poet and a late associate of GS. GS's monograph, *Robinson Jeffers: The Man and the Artist* (1926), was published about this time.

26. Ben Hecht, *Count Bruga* (1926). In Hecht's own words, the novel is an "ironical history" of a mythical count, "full of murders [and] terse seduction."

27. *Truth* (1926), a revision of the dramatic poem of 1923.

28. An unidentified friend of S. Bert Cooksley (for whom see n. 31 below).

29. An invention by Gaylord Wilshire supposedly designed to cure neuritis, arthritis, and a variety of other ailments. GS described it as follows in his column "Rhymes and Reactions" (*Overland Monthly,* July 1926): "an appliance in the form of the inner tube of a tire, which, attached by a conducting wire to an electric light socket and placed around the body, immerses the patient in a field of magnetic flux, which magnetism permeates every cell and drop of blood."

30. Ms. formerly in the library of St. John's Seminary (Camarillo, CA), but subsequently sold; text now available only in Dalton Gross, "The Letters of George Sterling" (Ph.D. diss.: Southern Illinois University, 1968), 554–55.

31. S. Bert Cooksley, poet and associate of GS.

32. "The Seventh Veil" (*Nation,* 3 November 1926); "The Restoration" (*Overland Monthly,* January 1928).

33. Walter Adolphe Roberts, editor of the *American Parade.*

34. Apparently a reference to some verses, "Items for the Christian Witness," possibly written by GS or by Edgar Lee Masters. See further the reference to "the Methodist verses" in letter 287.

35. This sentence has been underscored in the ms., perhaps by HLM.

36. Nunnally Johnson, "Nathalia from Brooklyn" (*AM,* Sept. 1926), on Nathalia Crane (1913–?), a girl who had published two volumes of verse by the age of twelve, *The Janitor's Boy and Other Poems* (1924) and *Lava Lane and Other Poems* (1925).

37. Margaret Cobb, a Mendocino County schoolteacher and poet. Jack London used fragments of her poetry in *The Valley of the Moon* (1913).

38. John Kelly (1862–1895), an Irish-born American boxer who went by the name Jack Dempsey. In 1884 he became the first world middleweight champion, keeping his crown until 1891, when he was defeated by the British boxer Bob Fitzsimmons (1862–1917). He was no relation to the later Jack Dempsey (1895–1983).

39. Erich von Stroheim (1885–1957), Prussian-born actor and director. The film was probably *The Wedding March* (1927), a silent.

40. Carey McWilliams (1905–1980), author of the landmark *Ambrose Bierce: A Biography* (1929) and other biographical and historical works.

41. Clara Bow (1905–1965) and Bebe Daniels (1901–1971), American film actresses.

42. "Ballad of the Ghost-Arrow" (*AM*, February 1927).
43. Bierce, *In the Midst of Life* (New York: Modern Library, 1927).
44. Adolphe de Castro, "Ambrose Bierce as He Really Was" (*American Parade*, October 1926). De Castro later wrote a book-length memoir, *Portrait of Ambrose Bierce* (1929).

UNDATED

1. A reference to GS's friend Charlie Norris.

Bibliography

Selected Works by H. L. Mencken (to 1927)

Ventures into Verse. Baltimore: Marshall, Beck & Gordon, 1903.

George Bernard Shaw: His Plays. Boston: John W. Luce, 1905.

The Philosophy of Friedrich Nietzsche. Boston: John W. Luce, 1908.

A Doll's House by Henrik Ibsen (translated by HLM). Boston: John W. Luce, 1909.

Little Eyolf by Henrik Ibsen (translated by HLM). Boston: John W. Luce, 1909.

The Gist of Nietzsche (arranged by HLM). Boston: John W. Luce, 1910.

Man versus the Man: A Correspondence between Rives La Monte, Socialist, and H. L. Mencken, Individualist. New York: Henry Holt, 1910.

The Artist: A Drama without Words. Boston: John W. Luce, 1912.

Europe After 8:15 (with GJN and Willard Huntington Wright). New York: John Lane; Toronto: Bell & Cockburn, 1914.

The Smart Set: A Note to Authors. [n.p., 1915.]

A Book of Burlesques. New York: John Lane, 1916.

A Little Book in C Major. New York: John Lane, 1916.

A Book of Prefaces. New York: Alfred A. Knopf, 1917.

Pistols for Two (with GJN; as by "Owen Arthur James Hatteras"). New York: Alfred A. Knopf, 1917.

Damn! A Book of Calumny. New York: Philip Goodman, 1918.

In Defense of Women. New York: Philip Goodman, 1918. New York: Alfred A. Knopf, 1918, 1922.

The American Language. New York: Alfred A. Knopf, 1919, 1921 (2nd ed.), 1923 (3rd ed.).

Prejudices: First Series. New York: Alfred A. Knopf, 1919.

The American Credo (with GJN). New York: Alfred A. Knopf, 1920.

Prejudices: Second Series. New York: Alfred A. Knopf, 1920.

The Antichrist by Friedrich Nietzsche (translated by HLM). New York: Alfred A. Knopf, 1920.

Prejudices: Third Series. New York: Alfred A. Knopf, 1922.

Prejudices: Fourth Series. New York: Alfred A. Knopf, 1924.

Americana, 1925 (edited by HLM). New York: Alfred A. Knopf, 1925.

Notes on Democracy. New York: Alfred A. Knopf, 1926.

Prejudices: Fifth Series. New York: Alfred A. Knopf, 1926.

Americana, 1926 (edited by HLM). New York: Alfred A. Knopf, 1926.

James Branch Cabell. New York: Robert M. McBride, 1927.

Prejudices: Sixth Series. New York: Alfred A. Knopf, 1927.

Sterling. San Francisco: John Henry Nash, 1927.

My Life as Author and Editor. Ed. Jonathan Yardley. New York: Alfred A. Knopf, 1993.

SELECTED WORKS BY GEORGE STERLING

The Testimony of the Suns and Other Poems. San Francisco: W. E. Wood, 1903. San Francisco: A. M. Robertson, 1904, 1907.

A Wine of Wizardry and Other Poems. San Francisco: A. M. Robertson, 1909.

The House of Orchids and Other Poems. San Francisco: A. M. Robertson, 1911.

Beyond the Breakers and Other Poems. San Francisco: A. M. Robertson, 1914.

Yosemite: An Ode. San Francisco: A. M. Robertson, 1916.

The Caged Eagle and Other Poems. San Francisco: A. M. Robertson, 1916.

The Play of Everyman (translated by Sterling). San Francisco: A. M. Robertson, 1917.

Thirty-five Sonnets. San Francisco: Book Club of California, 1917.

The Binding of the Beast and Other War Verse. San Francisco: A. M. Robertson, 1917.

Lilith: A Dramatic Poem. San Francisco: A. M. Robertson, 1919. San Francisco: Book Club of California, 1920. New York: Macmillan, 1926 (preface by Theodore Dreiser).

Rosamund: A Dramatic Poem. San Francisco: A. M. Robertson, 1920.

The Cool, Grey City of Love (San Francisco). San Francisco: A. M. Robertson, 1921.

To a Girl Dancing. San Francisco: Printed by Edwin and Robert Grabhorn for Albert M. Bender, 1921.

Sails and Mirage and Other Poems. San Francisco: A. M. Robertson, 1921.

Selected Poems. New York: Henry Holt & Co., 1923.

Truth: A Dramatic Poem. Chicago: Bookfellows, 1923.

Robinson Jeffers: The Man and the Artist. New York: Boni & Liveright, 1926.

Truth: A Grove Play. San Francisco: Bohemian Club, 1926.

Strange Waters. [San Francisco: Privately printed, 1926.]

GEORGE STERLING IN THE *SMART SET**

"The Rack." 39, No. 4 (April 1913): 35–36.

"The Master Mariner." 40, No. 4 (August 1913): 8.

"In the Market Place." 41, No. 3 (November 1913): 56.

"The Last Monster." 41, No. 4 (December 1913): 130.

---

*All works in this and the following section are poems save where indicated.

"The Ballad of St. John of Nepomuk." 42, No. 1 (January 1914): 111–12.

"The Hunting of Dian." 42, No. 2 (February 1914): 8 (as "The Hunting of Astarte").

"Ballad of Two Seas." 42, No. 4 (April 1914): 33–34.

"'You Never Can Tell.' " 43, No. 1 (May 1914): 8.

"Says George Sterling" [epigrams]. 44, No. 4 (November 1914): 125.

"To Twilight." 47, No. 3 (November 1915): 238.

"Infidels." 55, No. 4 (August 1918): 386.

"Dirge" [from *Lilith*]. 56, No. 3 (November 1918): 262.

"The Dryad" [one-act play]. 58, No. 2 (February 1919): 81–86.

"Two Met." 58, No. 4 (April 1919): 95.

"Three Voices." 59, No. 4 (August 1919): 2.

"The Rabbit-Hutch" [one-act play]. 60, No. 1 (September 1919): 123–24.

"Witch-Fire." 60, No. 4 (December 1919): 2.

"The Queen Forgets." 62, No. 2 (June 1920): 64.

"Incarnation." 64, No. 2 (February 1921): 24 (as by "William Drayham").

"Love and Time." 66, No. 1 (September 1921): 4.

"The Face of the Skies." 66, No. 1 (September 1921): 130.

"Atthan Dances" [from *Truth*]. 66, No. 2 (October 1921): 87.

"Everest." 66, No. 3 (November 1921): 38.

"Distance." 67, No. 1 (January 1922): 2.

"Lost Sunsets." 67, No. 2 (February 1922): 90.

"The Wild Swan." 67, No. 4 (April 1922): 49.

"The Killdee." 68, No. 1 (May 1922): 60.

"The Twilight of the Grape." 68, No. 2 (June 1922): 56.

"The Stranger at the Gate." 69, No. 1 (September 1922): 120.

"Song." 69, No. 2 (October 1922): 2.

"Venus Letalis." 70, No. 3 (March 1923): 98.

"After Sunset." 70, No. 4 (April 1923): 54.

"The Last of Sunset." 71, No. 2 (June 1923): 5.

"The Immortal" [prose poem]. 72, No. 1 (September 1923): 9.

"To a Water-Fowl." 72, No. 2 (October 1923): 64.

GEORGE STERLING IN THE *AMERICAN MERCURY*

"The Shadow Maker" [essay]. 6, No. 1 (September 1925): 10–19.

"Ballad of the Swabs." 6, No. 2 (October 1925): 140–41.

"Joaquin Miller" [essay]. 7, No. 2 (February 1926): 220–29.

"The Pathfinders." 8, No. 2 (June 1926): 144–47.

"A First-Class Fighting Man" [essay]. 10, No. 1 (January 1927): 76–80.

"The Ballad of the Ghost-Arrow." 10, No. 2 (February 1927): 166–67.

Index